ADVANCE PRAISE FOR NONE OF THE ANSWERS

"If you know Dallas, you know Deep Ellum. But what you don't know are the stories of how it became a Dallas destination and how Jeff Swaney grew into the person who made it happen. This is a book full of stories that I watched and was part of. Read *None of the Answers* and enjoy."

—Mark Cuban, Businessman,
owner of NBA Dallas Mavericks,
and star of ABC's *Shark Tank*

"Prepare to be captivated by Jeff Swaney's thought-provoking and offbeat tales in *None of the Answers: Racing through Life in Reverse*. An enthralling blend of philosophy, humor, and entrepreneurial wisdom, this book beckons you to join the journey of embracing change and finding purpose in every season of life."

—Vince Poscente, New York
Times bestselling author of *The Age of Speed* and *The Earthquake*

"*None of the Answers* is a rich, textured page-turner, full of humor, wisdom, challenges, and adventure. So much adventure, it is hard to

believe that author Jeff Swaney survived all his exploits. This memoir has been one of the most exciting and rewarding projects I've been involved with during my twenty-five years in the writing coach business. If you're up for a crazy armchair ride that will surprise you, anger you, make you laugh, and ultimately trigger questions and answers about your own life, I urge you to read it."

—Linden Gross, Two-time national
bestselling ghostwriter and writing coach

"Are you ready for living life in reverse? It's been said that on a gravestone, the dash between the date being born and the year someone passes away is their life. In *None of The Answers*, Jeff Swaney stretches the dash of life and adds the flash, the brash, the cash, the bash, and even the crash—and then rinses and repeats. Tray tables up and seat belts on. Get ready for takeoff as this thrilling read will have you laughing, crying, and learning about life's answers on every page."

—Kent Billingsley, International
speaker and published author of *Entrepreneur To Millionaire: How to Build A Highly Profitable Fast Growth Company and Become Embarrassingly Rich Doing It*

"Anthony Bourdain meets the Dalai Lama. Jeff Swaney's chronicles take you on captivating escapades while sharing wisdom that can guide you to explore your future pursuits and live the life you have always imagined. By the time you finish this gripping book you will realize Swaney has a lot of the answers!"

—David Rosell, Wealth manager,
speaker, author of *Failure is Not an Option,*
Keep Climbing and *In The Know*

"Mr. Swaney has written a masterclass on entrepreneurism for those about to rock. It may read like a memoir, but that is because his life's book reads as one exciting challenge after another."

—Robert Workman, Bestselling author
of *Selling - The Most Dangerous Game: How*
To Be The #1 Sales Rep And Not Get Fired

"Masterful storytelling that has you laughing, crying, and rethinking life's priorities. Jeff puts himself on full display in a no holds barred expose that inadvertently challenges the reader to get out of the stands, onto the field, and take the ball. It is not often that you are entertained into becoming more. *Life in Reverse* could be the ride of your life—don't miss it!"

—Ed McLaughlin, CEO, Blue Sunsets
LLC and author of *The Purpose is Profit*

“A blend of entertaining stories, reflections, and a powerful reminder that positivity and belief in visions and teams can take you far, through the expected and unexpected.… Jeff’s book reminds us, life just isn’t a simple straight line! Hang on for a fun ride.”

—Sally Russell, First woman elected
as Mayor of Bend, Oregon 2018

“To say Jeff Swaney’s been there and done that would be akin to saying PT Barnum ran a puppet show for toddlers. Fluidity in thought, fearlessness in action, and universal warmth in care, are but shallow attempts to describe the DNA makeup of Jeff. Wisdom and experiences flow from Jeff in such a rapid and profound rate, most mere mortals would need a Neuralink brain chip just to store and process the stream of consciousness in real-time. Thank goodness he’s finally put all this into a book so everyone can easily access his life’s work and play. *None of the Answers: Racing through Life in Reverse* is THE textbook on learning from the hard knocks of life. Read and live it.”

—Victor Wong, Inventor,
Futurist, and Entrepreneur

"If you want to experience a roller-coaster ride through the varied, event-filled life of a fear less, full-on, risk-embracing force-of-nature, read this book."

—Lord John Birt, Former
Director General BBC

NONE OF THE ANSWERS

NONE OF THE ANSWERS

RACING THROUGH LIFE IN REVERSE

JEFF SWANEY

A POST HILL PRESS BOOK
ISBN: 979-8-88845-735-1
ISBN (eBook): 979-8-88845-736-8

None of the Answers:
Racing Through Life in Reverse

Cover design by Tim Karpinski
Cover composition by Cody Corcoran

DISCLAIMER
This book reflects the author's opinions and recollections of experiences over time. To respect privacy and anonymity, some names and characteristics of people and/or places have not been divulged or have been changed. Some events have been compressed, and facts and dialogue have been recreated and/or supplemented and are as remembered, subject to errors and omissions since memory is imperfect. The stories herein are truthful recollections of actual events in the author's life. They mean no harm to any person or agency, or to defame, invade privacy, or cause emotional distress. In many cases, candy-coating has been invoked and extraordinary grace has been practiced. Many stories that may be objectionable or unpalatable have been avoided. The intent of the book is to promote positive feelings, entertain, and provide lessons that can inspire.

Post Hill Press
New York • Nashville
posthillpress.com

Published in the United States of America
1 2 3 4 5 6 7 8 9 10

This book is dedicated to my children
Cozi and Ford Swaney. Just do your best.

CONTENTS

FOREWORD
BY RON HALL

A few years back, I almost spent a month in Portugal with Jeff Swaney, but he called it off as my wife Beth and I were packing. Seems like a lot of shit had blown up in Dallas, and he wasn't ready to talk about it. It was not like there are a bunch of Lee Harvey Oswalds hiding in his closet, but little did I know then that I was connecting with this guy at probably the most difficult point of his life. And difficult was something I could for sure relate to. Anyway, Beth and I had a dang good time in his prepaid, nonrefundable hotel suites coast to coast in Portugal. The dude has great taste—and a great story. We missed him there, but in time we became even better friends.

I don't stand in long lines, so it was after his roaringly successful Club Clearview that I met the genius behind the birth of Dallas's most remarkable, hip, night-life scene. Beth, my fiancée at the time—a six-foot redhead model who never had to stand in any lines—introduced us. And when he found out I was an international art dealer, he had some trippy Deep Ellum art he wanted me to see that was a crossbreed between Basquiat and Keith Haring. At that seminal moment, I realized Jeff was the Same Kind of Different as Me.

Like Jeff, I grew up too poor to even pay attention; also like Jeff, I've been lucky in life. My first book made it to number one on the *New York Times* bestseller list and stayed there for three and a half years. We even made it into a Hollywood movie starring Rene Zellweger, Greg Kinnear, Jon Voight, and Djimon Hounsou. Now, I'm excited and privileged to introduce you to an entertaining, rip-roaring, unforgettable ride around this globe penned by my good friend.

This gloriously fast-moving memoir is filled with a cast of characters, family, and friends, that shaped a life with a story—no, a lot of stories worth telling. I've probably read a hundred award-winning memoirs; and I'll be damned if my friend, Jeff Swaney, after much prodding, didn't just put a pen to his own life in what is destined to be a prize-winner every bit as good as the best. I've always known he had a brain faster than a first-generation Hewlett Packard computer, but I had no idea he could write this well.

Rags-to-riches stories like mine and Jeff's are as common as positive COVID tests for accident victims at hospitals during the pandemic. Jeff, or "Swaindog," a nickname he earned, could be likened to a modern-day Don Quixote, who used impractical dreams and nearly impossible means to achieve idealistic goals. For much of this adventure, he had no idea of where he was going; but with artistry and honesty, when he looked back, he was laughing his butt off at where he had been. It's like a rodeo bull rider that just marked eight seconds on a bull named Cowboy Killer. Wow, what a friggin' ride, cowboy! Congratulations.

Laughing my way through many chapters, I wondered who in the world influenced or mentored this crazy kid. Could it have been a carnival barker or show hawker for the circus that surely passed through his Detroit neighborhood every so often? Maybe it was his Catholic, tea-totaling mom or Baptist neighbors that put the fear of God in him, causing him to believe that alcohol and premarital sex were strictly forbidden, as both might lead to dancing. Maybe it was the mean streets that scared him straight and kept him out of jail…until it didn't—yup, he checked that off his list. Maybe it was the DNA of an honest, hardworking daddy and granddaddy. Maybe it was just plain luck.

According to newspaper reports in the '50s and '60s, Detroit sported a less than healthy environment. Absent Jeff's good luck, he could have ended up in an iron lung or tuberculosis asylum, having been birthed under clouds of poisoned air that spewed from giant white smokestacks resembling Cape Canaveral rocket pads on launch day. But there is a long list of famous people—you know them all—who survived childhood in Detroit, a city that sacrificed quality of life so the rest of America could ride in style, top down, on Route 66. Add the name Jeff Swaney, soon to be bestselling author, to that list.

None of the Answers is damn sure a memorable read. While it won't change the world, it is certain to entertain the hell out of you, and in the end make you wish you had dreamed bigger, tried harder, and had the balls and lived the life of Jeff Swaney. It will make you wish you were his friend and make you proud if you are.

CHAPTER 1

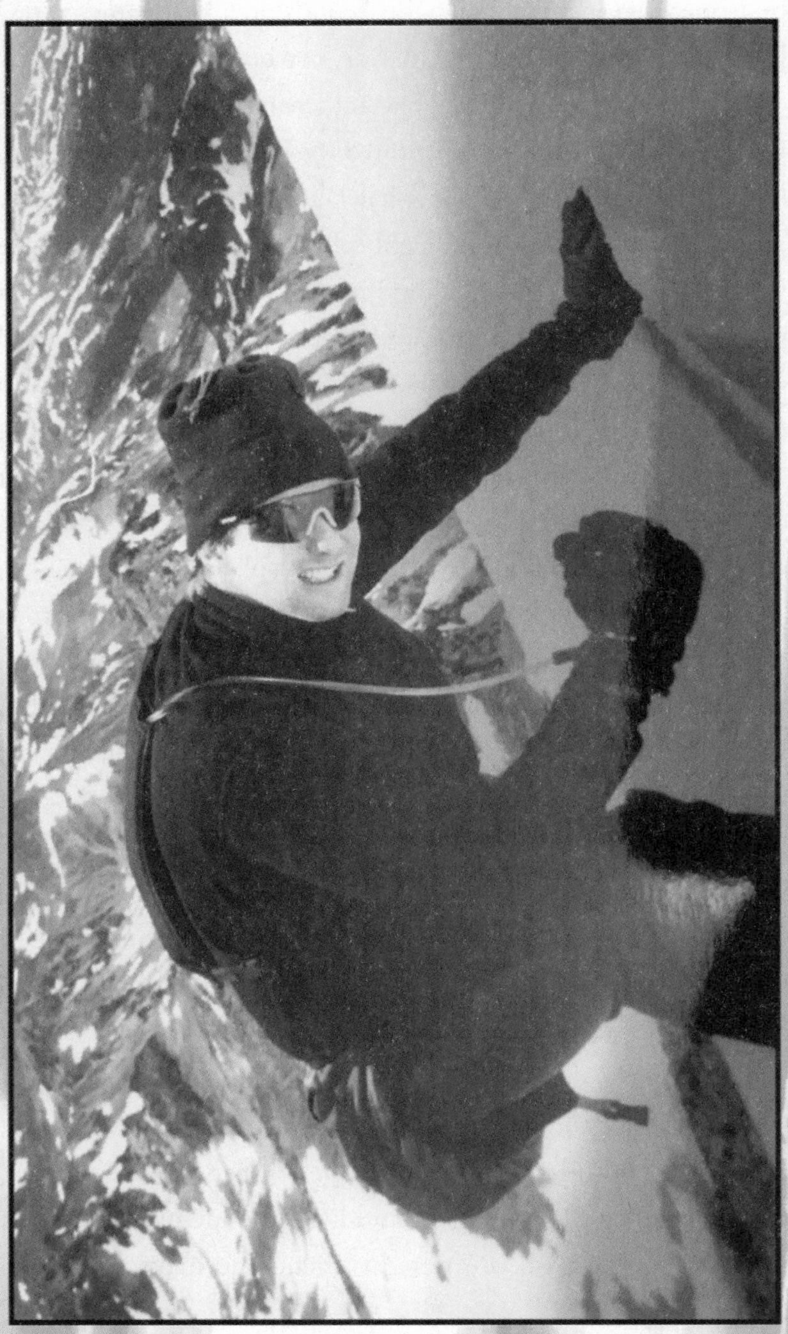

Spacebound - Free-climb summit of Mt. Harvard

CHAPTER 1

LIFE IN SPACE

I'm *flooooating…flooooating….*

One of my unearthly experiences on earth. In space.

An appropriate jumping-off place that will provide an introspective portal for a life.

On a multi-day summer backpacking trip thirty years ago with lifelong friends, in the highest-elevation wilderness in the continental United States—the Collegiate Peaks area of Colorado—I would be enveloped in an experience like none other. The area displayed remarkable beauty, showing off every color of the rainbow, and most notably surrounded by purple mountain majesties. I found myself singing "America the Beautiful" in my head while studying the bizarre dwarf Krummholz trees, each resembling a unique twisted creature from another planet. You would think that alone would be nirvana enough during that trip, but there would be much more to behold.

On our second day out—while witnessing a glorious, cloud-free, searing, burnt-orange sunset forming an umbrella over the mountains at our end-of-day camp—I finished one of many dehydrated dinners, along with the requisite chamomile tea, and took a deep breath. Summoned by nature to wander post supper, solo, to experience the wild's deep night, Petzl headlamp and light jacket on board, I sauntered out through the thin brush a few hundred yards off. With daylight nearly faded to nothingness, I noticed a layered rock pile, with makeshift steps leading to a tiny plateau sized for one intrepid soul.

Climbing up, scrambling about, and finally settling in, I lay face up to the heavens on that sunbaked, still-warm granite formation thirty feet above ground, where the entire universe was laid bare. Then the crystal-clear dark sky and a billion stars slowly swirling above came into focus. Stunning. *I am there—and everywhere*, I thought. *All at once.*

The sensation and reality of the whole of eight billion humans on earth behind my back and everything on and in our planet set in. I fancied myself in the front seat, the driver's seat, with nothing but the great out-there in view, captaining the earth ship sans seatbelt or instrumentation, with all its inhabitants in my rear-view mirror, hurtling through space at 67,000 miles per hour.

Whoa! It's real!

Breathing slowly, I'm there. Reaching. Feeling the edge of the expanding universe with my fingertips, my essence and pure energy in the interconnected cosmos entwined with a higher power. Stretching out impossibly beyond—to the farthest edges of the expansive bending infinite and wrapping my fingers around the flowing edge. Defying all knowledge of science and space and time. Complete. Centered. Calm. Utter perfection.

There lay all the answers.

That day had started out with breaking camp and setting out to bag two "fourteeners" that morning, as the fifty-four 14,000-plus-foot peaks in Colorado are called. In a group of type-A guys, everyone has his own plan, with all chiefs and no Indians. We backpacked annually and ended up separated during many multi-day trips, due to the stubborn nature of the guys—me being one of them. Many hair-raising experiences resulted.

This time, we had chatted about the route, which was unclear, absent any ground-in trail or signposts.

"Up this line over here, then over a bit—take the saddle, then crest to the top, piece of cake. Then back over to the south and bag the other peak," asserted one of the guys.

I disagreed. "Look at this line," I said as I surveyed the mountains before us. "Faster, probably just as wonky, but way doable. Let's go for that."

There was silence. Finding no takers, I decided this time to prove my theory solo.

"Well, I'm going to head up my way and meet you rascals at the top."

It did not pan out.

One thing most learn at a young age in the outdoors—and something I've taught my young kids—is that what is free-climbable going up is *much* more difficult coming down. And very high risk in steep scree sections at high altitude, with an unforgiving descent if you mess up. I put myself in this position. After cresting a few extremely difficult false summits, I found myself with no possible way to get up any further and going back down via the hard-fought foolhardy route up, the only option.

All systems halt. "Dang it, crap, rats!"

As a life adventurer, I'd previously experienced that uncomfortable mode, which would later be repeated many times. The heart rate rises, decision-making is clouded, and mild vertigo ensues. It is the onset of panic. Panic is the killer.

"Breathe, stay still, gather yourself, take your time, as long as it takes," I muttered. Shitsville.

After twenty minutes or more, I steeled myself to start the descent, with the realization that there was going to be a raw butt, some blood, and a lot of terrain crossed on all fours—even flat-out on the belly to self-arrest and avoid tumbling down to death or something close. Retracing my steps going down was impossible, hence now most of the footing was on scree that I'd somewhat avoided on the way up, which made for a lot of slipping and sliding.

Working my way down with that scree rock breaking away with regularity, tumbling, and crashing thousands of feet down, was really working the nerves. Stopping many times to gather myself and scout safe routes from such difficult angles would get vertigo bubbling up repeatedly and result in taking more and more time. After a couple of hours of this, fatigue developed, creating a little shakiness in the arms and legs. Luckily, a couple power bars that I'd packed and a Camelback full of water helped immensely. After countless hours, and some clawing and almost eating rock, I finally shimmied back down to a manageable zone and returned to base camp. There, my compadres, who had bagged both peaks with time to spare, greeted me with hugs, shared stories, and some matching wounds.

"There you are, old Swaindog! You look like hell! We missed you at the top!" one of them rang out.

"Yup, there's a dumbass born every day."

I have climbed many peaks—I think we all want to do that, to get to the top of the world—but when I came down from my failed attempt that day, I was humbled and unsatisfied.

Later, however, on that warm, flat rock, having no expectations, I found myself at the very top of it all. Higher than Everest. More rewarding than any summit. Life changing.

We strive for things that we may not attain and that may or may not meet our goals or feed our proverbial rat. Then, at times when we do not expect it—if we are aware, centered, and connected—we find ourselves at that magical place. The place we were yearning for. The lessons must be learned hands-on, like this one. And to get our collective footing in the big picture, we will need to go back to the starting point of our lives.

Back to the egg.

CHAPTER 2

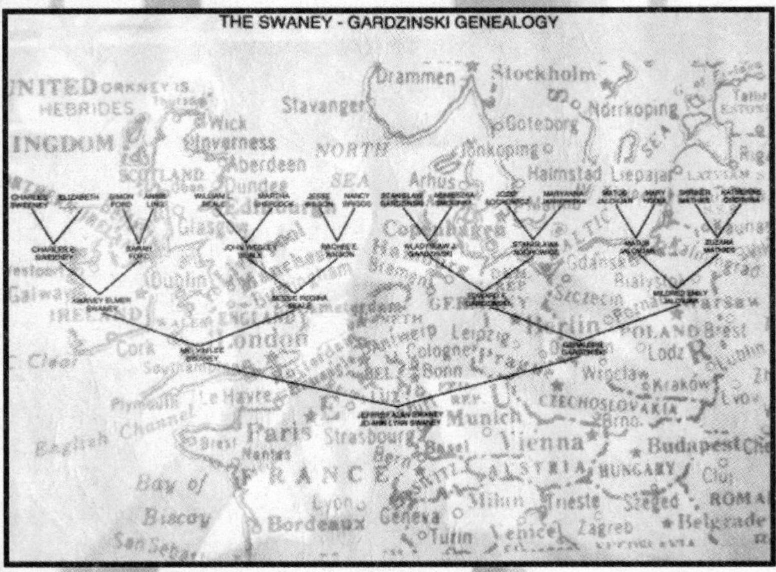

Geneology - Swaney family tree

Grandparents - Gallitzin, PA

CHAPTER 2

BACK TO THE EGG

My egg hatched in the fall of 1958 in Detroit, Michigan—a French fort born of the North American fur trade, turned industrial juggernaut. The City of Muscle, the Most Beautiful City in America, the Motor City, Motown, Rock City, Hockey Town, the Murder City. I was hurled bloody and screaming onto the scene, into a place loved and loathed, raw, and elemental. The town was quite possibly the center of the universe at that time and, if not, most certainly the center of mine. A modern-day anomaly that would crash and burn over the next fifty years, becoming a metropolis largely abandoned. From a prime peak pinnacle of worldly power and prestige, to a state of sad squalor. A byproduct of a fusion of protectionism, greed, the Peter Principle, racial injustice, and the grand deal-killer of them all—*fear*.

Thus was my starting position in the human rat race. Where was I and why, and what was all this to lead to? What purpose? Thus began my quest for all the answers.

The introspective life takes all data, factors, and various perspectives into account. Place of birth and lineage certainly are noteworthy. Not unlike the MC5, Alice Cooper, Madonna, Iggy Pop, Gilda Radner, Lily Tomlin, Tim Allen, Eminem, Ted Nugent, Mitch Albom, Kid Rock, and Jack White, both before and after me, the city's determined gritty energy emblazoned an indelible mark. I feel a kinship with this long list of famous and infamous Detroiters—we all got gifted a little special crazy gear ingrained from our relationships with that city. Diego Rivera's masterpiece mural exposé *Industry* at the Detroit Institute of Arts, the finest work of his career, saved by one hero Edsel Ford, further manifested the city's harsh, spunky spirit. These factors were the ingredients of my stew.

The mass immigrations of the industrial era beckoned the besieged Irish, Czech, and Pole blood that comprised my DNA. My paternal Irish grandfather's grinding out the coal miners' company store, whiskey-drenched life in the hills of nearby Pennsylvania, represented the fuel source for the monstrous machine that was Detroit. My mother's Polish-Czech, fire-and-brimstone Catholic parents pounded out a living in the hot, filthy, sweaty, suffocating factories of the city. A history of hand-to-mouth that, without much thought, you can smell and feel in the bones. Innate. These families of workers provided the wave of power that made America great. I was a product of this collision of cosmic forces, and this pedigree left me ashamed at times. I missed out on the royalty and silver spoon, but digesting

Detroit's detritus became a strength to be embraced and then relied on in life. Summarily, my background most certainly qualified me as an American.

An ancillary Detroit cultural influence of mine had to be *soul.* Barry Gordy's amalgamation of Marvin Gaye, Aretha Franklin, Diana Ross, and others, albeit procured in a contentious mode, certainly struck a chord. In a roundabout way, the accompanying racial flavor, which was at once the city's asset and Achilles's heel, made for an undeniable bubbling friction, feeding the *soul.*

Soul dictated that nobody and nothing in life is perfect, and that's the beauty. To spin the wheel again or get a choice between my road and what is behind Door Number Three, I'd without hesitation stay the course. Certainly, America in the baby-boomer, tail-fin-accessorized two-ton-autoed, myriad-miracle-gadgetized, cigarette-glued-in-the-mouth '50s was a great place to be born. Warts and all, love it or leave it. Look at the current world birthplace options.

I had a business partner in my day who eloquently regurgitated an oft-told story, brimming with his rural Texas sensibility, as we were talking about our lives—the good, bad, and the ugly—which we often did.

"Jeff," he recounted, "if you sat down with a group of folks and everyone put their bag of shit on the table and these bags were passed around, everyone would jump to retrieve their own bag back and run happily home to swim in it. Think about it, and trust me—that's the way it is."

Such was my case. This fundamental acceptance and love of ownership of your bag and the shit in it, whatever your metrics, is a certain requisite building block for survival, sanity, happiness, and joyful living. Don't spin the wheel and end up with a stinkier bag.

Going from that bag back to my egg: to conceive a me, there needed to be a joining of a sperm and that egg. In this case, it occurred when Mom and Dad met in the shipping-and-receiving department of downtown Detroit's J.L. Hudson Department Store, at that time the world's largest, except possibly for Macy's in New York. Mom, the unassuming post-Catholic-girls'-school clerk, connected with Dad, the laborer at the busy dock who was just back from a life-changing Trans-Pacific journey, courtesy of the Korean War. Love seemingly ensued after a brief dating stint, as Mom found herself hungover and half-naked one morning, after the first and possibly the only drink of her life—a Tom Collins—and after succumbing to Dad's charm in her small apartment. She repeatedly shared that story with me, never forgetting the maraschino cherry and the carnival-colored paper umbrella garnish. Now it was time to get married and join the baby boom. Everyone was doin' it! *Woohoo!*

Not like any of us really do, but they didn't have a clue. And who could blame them? Dad was the seventeenth of nineteen children born in unspeakable poverty in Appalachia—Gallitzin, Pennsylvania. And yes, the term that you might use to describe some folks in those parts could be *hillbilly*. Hillbilly not in the negative convention, but people of the hills, nonetheless. Sporting names such as Patsy, Cutzy, and Skoogie—all colorful characters. There was no *you guys* or *y'all* there in the hills. Folks were referred to (as my dad would call my sister and me) as *you-ins*, *yuzins*, and *you-nces*.

My father's dad, Harvey, was a coal miner and debtor to the town company store, as in the famous song "Sixteen Tons." His life consisted of the mine, drink, nookie, dinner, and a sound beating for any of his children who were bad that day at school, in town, or at the five hundred-square-foot home where they slept stacked like cordwood. All these activities are listed in no particular order. Then Harvey was up and at it again at dawn, back to visit with the captive coalmine canaries. As a sideline and hobby, supposedly being blessed with some ancient Celtic healing powers passed down through the generations, he laid his hands upon and healed some of the townspeople of their ills. The clientele was either all or primarily female, and hence the lore that he had fathered another fifty or more children around town, in addition to my dad's siblings at the cordwood repository. After a life of barefoot and pregnant, my dad's mother, Bessie, passed away after giving birth to the final two children. My guess would be that the coroner labeled it *exhaustion*. I would imagine that in her life she rarely caught the light of day and would not have recognized it if she had.

Coal powered the American machine, and the transport mechanism was the Iron Horse—the train. Boys love trains, and living in a small town that was a train destination, my dad was no exception. Home to the Gallitzin tunnels and one of the engineering marvels of that age, the World-Famous Horseshoe Curve, there was much to see and dream about in the world beyond. There had to be something better than the day-to-day life in Gallitzin—something far more glamorous. But you get what you get, so you turn those lemons into lemonade, your chicken shit into chicken salad. And so, the boys did.

"Well, some kids used to, on a dare, lay flat on the train tracks to let the trains go over top them and then pop up after the train finally passed," my dad shared with me.

"You had to make damn sure it wasn't a real long, slow one with a hundred cars or you could be down there a long while. I never did it; it was too crazy scary for me. Plus, I heard one time a kid got afraid partway through, panicked, and tried to get out. It was curtains for that boy."

He continued reminiscing.

"Sometimes we'd spend almost all day watching the trains go through the tunnels and watching the operations at the horseshoe curve. There wasn't much else to do in town in summer except swimming at the dam, where another kid met his maker.

"Oh, and another thing, Son, that we liked to do was hassle the stowaway bums that would jump off the boxcars in town, throwing rocks at them and having them chase us. They couldn't catch us or find our hiding places. No one wanted them in our town—too much trouble. One of them, name of Goombates, we were told, was a one-armed rascal who never left even with as much hell as we gave him. He was a scraggly, toothless, tattered hobo, and he became our town bum, I guess. We didn't know where he lived, we would just always see him walking along the tracks looking for cigarette butts to smoke. I always wondered if Goombates, like that kid who panicked under the train, lost his arm that way. We never talked to him. Ya knows, Jeff, I don't know if he could even talk."

Dad survived his early home environment, such as it was, running unbridled with the other town boys, hither and yon. He went somewhat unscathed under Harvey's reign, due to luck, a happy demeanor, the protection afforded him by the older children, and making himself scarce.

I could see the brilliance in my father that never got a chance to blossom—in his speech, doodling, and moments of reflection. Those moments hit infrequently, as he worked tirelessly in my youth at a cement factory turning out burial vaults, patio stones, and birdbaths. Unrealized potential locked out by a lack of parental direction, or parenting at all for that matter, and that key education piece, never availed or pursued. Or perhaps all was impacted by PTS inflicted by the Korean War and the memories he could barely talk about.

Dad did relate some stories of the war to me. He had kept a miniature parachute that the enemy would fire in multiples into the American camp. The inscription, in broken English, read:

> *You boys can't win war. Truman know. Even you beat us you having beat 500 million Chinese. Save your life boy—go home. Or die here.*

There was an incident where Dad's sergeant was killed, and he had to lead men in combat retreat during which many fell. He also witnessed a comrade jumping on a hand grenade, which would save Dad's life and the lives of others in his troop. The horrors of war.

The father-son relationship is a special and challenging one in life—sort of a friendly war—and takes a lot of energy to get right, as anything does, and to harvest reward. I experienced a very minimal connection with this man in my early years, as he seemed not exactly present. This was due to several factors, including his long workdays, the fact he never had a role model in the relationship with his own father, and that my mom nudged him out, elbowing hard in the nest throughout my early years. But all this would change later.

Mom's initial life ambition was the nunnery. This was her passion, something she regretted not pursuing. As a beleaguered stepchild, she found a connection in the themes of suffering and penance so germane to the Catholic ideal of the day, and comfort in the hope that there had to be something better in the end. This life was blessedly short, and for your pain and steadfastness, eternal life in heaven was the prize. Earn in. An age-old doctrine perfected in Medieval Europe to yoke the masses here on earth, a program thankfully now being humanized to some degree by the venerable Pope Francis. Some religions profess an afterlife, and some don't. However, I could never understand that desiring and even seeking pain and suffering in life could be helpful in the next one.

Mom attended Felician Academy in Detroit, an all-girls school of the Franciscan order a la the humble St. Francis of Assisi. Replete with a fully integrated Christian everything, including an orphanage, it provided her the structure and thus the courage to deal with her Cinderella duties of raising her entitled stepsiblings and being the family housekeeper. She swallowed the doctrine and responsibilities whole.

She purportedly never had a birthday celebration until I tricked her into one on her seventieth. Her first ever. Daughter of a cold, abject, resolutely impossible, stubborn mother, Mom had a surprisingly silly and sarcastic sense of humor. Her biological father, who had left early on in his wanderings, was reportedly found dead in a boxcar along the railway in Chicago. Upon getting word of this, my grandmother instructed the messenger to report back, "Just keep the body."

Hence, I had no real grandparents to share love with since I never met my father's parents, nor my mother's biological father. Instead, I was burdened with my cold maternal grandmother, who had been civilized to a degree by my mother's stepdad—the man had been no saint but had mellowed with age.

The neglect my mom suffered in her childhood, most details too ugly to put in print, made her tough, that's for sure. She also developed a nurturing, loving, forgiving, and tolerant side, which in fact boiled over into what could be described as overprotective and codependent. I didn't understand all this until many years later, since they never taught psychology in school, even though it should be a core subject for all of us starting in kindergarten.

Luckily, how we are raised does not necessarily dictate how we live or how we raise our children.

I work hard these days as a single dad for my young children, focusing on love, something I never heard from my parents, not even once. I temper the helicoptering, submitting to the rollercoaster. White-knuckle grip some days. Learning from your childhood experiences to not repeat any toxic hand-me-downs, and breaking the cycle on those, can lead to a tad of parenting success. Doing the best that you can in that noble quest to grow those children from their eggs. Knowing yourself better is a good place to start.

CHAPTER 3

The Swaneys - 1963

Choir - St. Pauls 1972

CHAPTER 3

SPROUTING IN AMERICA

Taking stock of one's youth requires deep digging—bare-bones brutal honesty, pull-your-pants-down full-monty fun, resulting revelations, and ofttimes pain. You'll find a lot there in the figurative playground of those formative and post-formative years to challenge your overall mindset—confusing and conflicting messages, along with truths, lies, and utter bullshit to wade through. In a world no longer predominantly tribal—and especially in the good ol' U.S. of A., a hodgepodge of group interactions takes the place of the age-old humanoid paths—in school, church, neighborhoods, family, and extended family glumps. All these groups are inherited, not chosen—as if you'd know how to choose—and they then comprise and define your young world, all subject to change in an instant. Through that jumble, ultimately our neuro-nets get wired. You start becoming you. Whoever that may be.

It's almost as if I innately inherited this chaotic beginning—a challenging, high-energy tyke who at age eight, I was told, drove my mom nearly nuts for an entire year, causing her to break out in hives. I vividly recall the proclamation she repeated when at the frayed end of her rope.

"Jumpin' Jesus, jumpin' Christ! Jeffrey Alan, I hope that when you grow up you have a kid just like you! I really do!"

Many times, when my son gets out of bounds, I'll point up to the heavens. "Well thanks, Mom—hope you're enjoying the party up there!"

She had a vision for a better life for my younger sister and me—a parental mantra and an American anthem. Start point, after a stint in public school from kindergarten through second grade that did not go well, was agreeing to a church and church-based school that could temper my demeanor. Since Dad was a quasi-Methodist and Mom a devout Catholic, a reasonable and surprising compromise seemed to be Lutheran—aka *Catholic lite*—and the bonus was the Lutheran school and church were close to home and affordable. Buddhism, Islam, Judaism, Taoism, Hinduism, or any of the other hundreds of religions on the planet weren't on the board. In that era and socioeconomic strata, you were directed to your belief system without a vote and blessed to have that connection with spirituality. A window to all of the answers.

In my little world, organized sports were forsaken for the focus of spending an inordinate amount of time after school on religious study. There was, however, opportunity in the neighborhood for boyhood wildness in the streets. These activities included street football, played at full speed between the sidewalks and using parked cars as blockers, fort-building and burning, outdoor basketball, and wiffle ball, Frisbee slinging, boot ice hockey in our makeshift rinks with hard checking to knock guys silly, snowball and ice-ball bombings of each other as well as house windows and passing cars, and battling with and capturing kids from adjoining neighborhood streets for mild ritual torture and beatings. We elevated the tortures in time to include sacrificing kids to our friend's mutt of a male dog, aptly named Bingo. Bingo was a particularly horny animal and was fond of gathering fallen laundry, dirt piles, or whatever he could climb on top of to bring himself to orgasmic bliss. Once we could get a kid down and bring Bingo around to get on top of him, the kid would have to curl up and succumb to Bingo's humping, lest he be bitten and scratched up badly. Once Bingo had his way, he would joyously trot off, leaving the kid balling and us giggling our asses off. *Bingo!*

With all that went on in the hood, I broke quite a few of my bones, suffered at least a couple of concussions—one of which was life-threatening—and lost a front tooth in all the fun.

Since my mom traded the nunnery to raise two kids, she was determined for at least me to realize her past dream of having a career in the church. The most punishing part of this process was the nightly requirement to begin the exact and flawless memorization of Martin Luther's small catechism. This book included the Ten Commandments, and all three versions of the Christian creed, deemed to be important: the Apostles's, the Athanasian, and the Nicene Creeds, along with Luther's complete explanations of all. Mom dug deep in the pocketbook to get me the onion-skin version with pages so pleasing to the touch, clocking at about a zillion words. It took months to memorize. Sitting any eight-to-ten-year-old boy still that long was ridiculous, as was expecting anyone to memorize that much material. Add the fact that I certainly had the ADHD and/or OCD thang going on, and could hardly read at that point, made it near impossible. This was years before the alphabet-soup-acronym-analysis-fest of the now, whereby diagnosis and medication can be the requirement for *spirited* kids. The memorization task was pure torture—the worst imaginable since the Spanish Inquisition. But somehow, I did it, and in the process developed a near-perfect photographic memory skill that was just crazy amazing. Thankfully, I never had to take the next step to the large catechism, to which Luther had directed parents thusly:

> "After you have taught them this Small Catechism, then take up the Large Catechism and give them also richer and fuller knowledge."

No thank you, Martin. That was enough.

When it came to the monumental time for the requisite recital, I was the first and only one in class to raise my hand. I promptly stood up ready to regurgitate the entire repertoire. As I made my way to the front of the class, I could feel the other kids fidgeting.

"Alright, Jeffrey, you are the first, and thank you. Let us start with the Apostles' Creed with Luther's explanations, and we can move from there."

I cleared my throat and looked out to the class, giggling at the beginning nervously as a couple of my mates twisted their faces at me in harassment. To avoid further interruption, I focused on a fire extinguisher at the back of the room as I spilled it all out.

"I believe in God, the Father Almighty, maker of heaven and earth. And in Jesus Christ, His only Son our Lord, who was conceived by the Holy Spirit, born of the Virgin Mar....

After bellowing out the entire book, which took over twenty minutes, the teacher found there were no other takers. None of the students could even recite one of the creeds correctly, which was bittersweet. The reward was my anointment as head altar boy status, and the honor of having my name as such in the inaugural program of the much-anticipated, newly built church then under construction. After that first standing-room-only church service, I even got to slide that program into the church cornerstone and help trawl the mortar around it, to seal it for eternity. At that, I had felt my commitments to my mom, God in all his manifestations and forms, and the Church had been satisfied, and I did not seek, want, or willingly acquiesce to further accolades or responsibilities in that arena. I still had and have my beliefs, but my lifetime plenary indulgence had been bought and the ticket punched. Amen.

Through all my struggles in school, I am glad I wasn't studied or medicated. Alternatively, I was subjected to hog-tying, paddling with a dazzling array of paddle styles, painful neck gripping, my nose being cranked down on a chalkboard spot for hours, forced soap chewing, and writing hundreds of times, "I will not ____________ in class ever again." All to help me with my logorrhea and squirminess. Superstar altar-boy status did not spare me my punishments. In today's world, all the teachers' practices there would probably result in their being terminated or jailed. Discipline has certainly taken new directions, one of many radical societal pendulum swings crisply evident.

The kids at the Lutheran school where I completed my elementary education were a diverse lot, and their company was a mixed blessing. Many were sent there from Detroit to escape the violence, disarray, and mania of their neighborhoods and their broken school systems. Subsequently a lot of "bad kids" were enrolled at the school. As a quasi-chameleon, I related to all the mini-groups that were forming. The emergence of jocks, freaks, geeks, and hoodlums was happening, and I kept connected with each clique and loved it all. Admittedly, I found special allure in those Detroit kids with a handle on the gangland lingo and mannerisms of their underworld. Allowing them to steal answers on tests with slumping shoulders and hand signals earned me the privilege, stimulation, and excitement of being in their "club."

There were, however, some costs associated with the variety of students imported. Experiencing the chaos when one of the school kids—a sixth-grader—shot his father dead and had to be talked down from the church's bell tower, where he was holed up with his still-smoking gun, was an eye-opener for us all. Another student—one of my best friend's sisters—met her end by throwing herself in front of a train during school recess, fifty yards away from and in clear view of the playground, which was particularly shocking. This event turned the school on its ear and, after witnessing something so disquieting, students were brought in during the next weeks to talk with counselors. In all this, we learned that life would go on and that most kids were incredibly resilient. I would revisit that fact later in life.

A school project around that sixth-grade level that incorporated writing, painting, and the creation of a book struck a chord. Mine became a masterpiece essay on individualism, through a character named Herbie. I explored Herbie's differences and how unique they made this human. It was introspection at a young age, developing confidence, comfort, and happiness in an onliest, uncommon, and special skin. The perspective found to view life from oneself, in the third person, and seeing Herbie's life as an adventure to be embraced, was a landmark event. I had stumbled upon the realization—without knowing that I even had—that randomness and the quantum-physics life in an ever-expanding universe of dynamic range were to be consumed, shared, and celebrated. Herbie and I were different animals than the rest of the pack. Way different. And it was good! Getting some footing via some early, rudimentary form of self-actualization, through producing the Herbie storybook, was huge, as the unintentional absence of self-esteem and encouragement from home required delving within.

Outside the home, the extended family proved quite a circus. To some degree, that's what all families are—a microcosm of worldly disorder. Right? Dad's family—at least the aunts, uncles, and cousins we visited—were a fun-loving bunch. My dad's older brother and best friend, Uncle Sonny, born fittingly on Valentine's Day, was the favorite. An Irish Pennsylvanian version of Yogi Berra sans the pedigree and fame, he sported the same rounded face, short hair, large grin, and gravelly voice as the baseball legend. The Swaney cousins' visits did not happen as often as I would've liked but were always something to look forward to—even when semi-annually my uncle would administer the Swaney boys—myself and Cousin Michael—his ultrashort, scraping version of the summer buzz cut.

"Just hold that cue ball of a head still, Jeffers, and I'll be done in a jiffy," Uncle Sonny would warn with his Gallitzin twang.

And indeed, a few minutes later, with a couple of small bloody patches on the scalps and our bushel of collective hair in wads on the home's basement floor, it was over. We were bald. It was no wonder that, quite possibly as a subconscious rebellion, both my cousin and I wore our hair uber-long in college, something that we did not have as kids.

While visiting with the various cousins, the parents playing pinochle and drinking Mogen David wine, or other cheap varieties, we kids would sneak around the houses, getting into minor mischief, and on a couple of occasions nervously and rapidly shuffling through the drawers in the parents' bedrooms looking for anything forbidden. Once we unearthed parental underwear, which we ceremoniously put over our heads and laughed uproariously to the point of abdominal pain and tears. The topper of the diggings was the bonanza discovery of a dirty magazine, which we had never seen before and was quite the page-turner. Other indoor activities included making prank phone calls from one of the cousin's house phones in the basement, wrestling and dogpiling with up to five kids and crushing the one on the bottom, and playing the age-old games of Twister, Candyland, Operation, Battleship, and others.

Outside, there was playing in the sandboxes—always awesome—and just tearing things apart, de-legging insects, dissecting earthworms, and for our insect karma kickback, getting ravaged by ants. Bottle-hunting for the two-cent deposits that could be taken to the party store and exchanged for candy or baseball cards was a joy. Felt like a proper childhood.

Mom's family visits were a horse of a different, non-Crayola color. The runs to Grandma's house were a dreaded, dutiful, biweekly requirement, typically a Sunday afternoon affair, where we would go after church services dressed in our Sunday best. The fact that my mom was the stepdaughter, and treated as such in the most disgraceful manner, and that her family loathed my father—and that I was his son and the only grandson, a usually happy yappy kid—had us boys set up to suffer. The proverbial table had been set, I found out years later, the afternoon after my parents were wed. The grandparents held a small reception in the basement of their small Detroit home at the requisite home bar—a Polish family tradition, it seemed. Boilermakers and *zimne piwo* (Polish for "cold beer"). Early on that afternoon, Uncle Sonny slipped a bit on one of the shaky barstools, was declared drunk, and within fifteen minutes thrown out. My dad's brother and best friend hadn't even had a drink.

My mom and dad would make the thirty-minute trip to Grandma's Detroit home, toting Sis and I in the backseat, sans seatbelts, in the mint-green 1962 Mercury Comet, with the windows rolled up tight and them both chain-smoking 'til we siblings turned a weirder shade of green than the car.

"Mom, Dad, we feel sick from the smoke, I think I'm going to throw up. Please do something!" I pleaded.

"That is nonsense, Jeffrey. All the smoke is up here. You're having a pipe dream. And don't you two roll down those windows; it's too damn cold out!"

Oxygen was at a premium!

We'd gather on those unpleasant Sundays, the grandparents there in attendance with my mom's brother, the unusual Uncle

Frank, and his sister, Diane, a single mom to Cousin Sandy, and listen to them rattle on for hours on a variety of topics. The storyline was always the same—praise for Sandy, verbally abusive innuendo doled out to me and my family, and consistently outrageous, inflamed rants from the lot of them. All the while my grandmother's ferocious Pomeranian was poised to protect her from us all, which resulted in, from my memory, never having a hug or body contact with her in my lifetime. The dog barked, foamed at the mouth, and rubbed its rear end against the walls, which made for an interesting series of stains around the sitting room. This all formed the backdrop for my uncle's fulminations, which took top bluster awards.

Frank, Diane, and Sandy were all marginally educated at best and were giants, well over six feet tall. Frank, a momma's boy, veteran potato-peeler of post-WWII Germany's occupation, and auto factory worker in his parents' footsteps—as well as, I believe, a virgin to his grave—was a particularly odd-looking duck. In line with the rest of them, I couldn't help but draw visual similarities with the popular TV series of the day—*The Addams Family*. Tall and gawky with poor hygiene, dress, and a bulbous, purple, veiny nose supporting his Coke-bottle-lensed glasses, he would spout his wisdom of the world.

"I'm telling ya and I know! All the Jews and Blacks (liberal use of these words in that house was standard procedure) should be killed. Students in college"—he then glared at me—"should be put on the front lines in the Army. That's where they'll learn something!"

That was his plan for a new war that needed to be started tomorrow—wherever it was and for whatever reason. He had all the answers. Lovely. Shocking. It certainly cured me of any bigotry, instantly and for life. Whew! And if the verbal bombast wasn't enough, there was more in store. Obsessed with coins, he would show off his collections of bushels of them in the basement there at the house. It was madness. He and the rest of the family knew my parents were struggling horribly financially, and yet it seemed to bring them all great satisfaction to see us look on, at what looked to me like the total sum of all earthly treasure imaginable, in drooling amazement and wanting. He even went so far as to glue a jillion pennies to completely cover the walls and ceiling of the basement of his home, which took years to accomplish. I'm not sure that's ever been done before. He had us over for the unveiling. Ever since, I've had on-and-off bizarre dreams, aberrated snippets of the coin-overload witnessed.

Near the end of some of the visits, an immense, plastic, two-foot-long toy hypodermic needle would be produced to chase me with in the backyard. My terror always had them all giggling with joy.

"Look, Jeffrey, it won't hurt, it's just plastic," they'd say as they howled in delight.

I am still squeamish about needles to this day and regularly pass out when getting my blood drawn.

"Just to let you know, I probably need to get the draw lying down here today," I'd notify the nurse at the annual blood draw for my physical. "I've almost fallen out of the chair and gone boom boom on occasion."

A swimming lesson at one of Grandma's friend's backyard pools consisted of tossing me in the pool and watching me sink to the bottom 'til my dad jumped in and pulled me out. He wasn't happy about my forced and ill-advised swim lesson, and the car ride home was less than cheerful.

As I got on to my early teen years, the grandparent visits became less common, excepting the tradition of the dinner at our house for Thanksgiving, which I had to suffer into my forties. Even though my dad had passed away in my thirty-fifth year and the grandparents years before that, Mom beseeched me to attend the dinners and let her siblings rattle. The fact that my birthday was that same week, and occasionally that same day, made for a gift I could live without. Still, in deference to her and against my brazen will, I had to sit quietly and suffer that family of hers. Not sure if holding my tongue in acquiescence to my mom and my sister's wishes was the right thing to do, but I did.

I'd fly into Detroit, visit old college friends, and attend the local Thanksgiving Day parade with them, and then ofttimes watch the hapless Detroit Lions football team lose yet another Thanksgiving Day game. My friends' companionship and the trips downtown were my treats and the sole antidote to having to go back to the house and gag my way through that family Thanksgiving dinner. One year there was so much chaos and disrespect there that I decided to break with tradition and never to return for a holiday.

I thought it was over with Mom's family, but Uncle Frank wasn't done with me yet. My sister sent me a copy of his will after his passing, wherein my mom and sister were slighted to the benefit of Cousin Sandy. I'll never forget Uncle Frank's first and most important wish. I think it was repeated twice in different wording in the document, which my sister believes Cousin Sandy drafted and had him sign on his deathbed.

"I specifically leave nothing to Jeffrey Swaney, for reasons personal to me."

Mercifully, those years of ridicule were now a case closed with forgiveness. The same could not be said of the rest of my adolescent trials.

My pubescent life was that of probably many a blue-collar, suburban high school kid. Bumbling my way through, as most kids do, catching the educational tail end of a once-lauded college prep school that slowly degraded into a vocational program and eventual closure. I chameleoned myself through those years to a largely net-positive result—sweating, slithering, grinding, and sometimes even gliding my way in the classrooms and social waters of what for all of us is a challenging and ofttimes rewarding voyage.

There was, however, the mega road hump of freshman year, when I somehow landed in the remedial English program with Miss McGann. The kids there were having an impossible time trudging through the *See Spot Run* books that I clearly mastered. But as always, I had a hard time staying tuned in. Miss McGann singled me out, and by some magic spell, working with me a bit after hours on my reading, she inexplicably unlocked aptitude. I went from a one to a ten in a month. Maybe part of it was that she was the most attractive teacher at the school, with super-short skirts and the practiced prance that accompanied those, which annoyed the staff while making her the apple of every teenage boy's eye. Whatever it was with her—she was pure amazing.

"Jeff, I don't think you belong here, and I don't know why you are here, but I'm going to transfer you on, even though I will miss you. Please stay in touch; you're a great kid."

"Well thanks, Miss McGann—for everything."

I was instantly transferred to Miss Hildebrand's advanced class—playing catch-up on the novel they were finishing up, *The Learning Tree*. Devoured it. Then raced ahead, reading over twenty books that semester, of which only three were required. I had become the Wang Lung of Pearl Buck's novel *The Good Earth*, with my cerebral rags-to-riches, newfound wealth-of-mind expansion. Miss Hildebrand stayed after class with me on occasion to discuss the Vonnegut, Huxley, and other nutball authors' books she fed to me as she ratcheted up the lunacy. A relatively mild-mannered and quiet lady of conservative dress, a beehive hairdo, and buttoned-down aura, her interest in the way-out authors suggested she had a wild side, maybe more so than Miss McGann. I was now on a path to a previously foreign universe, and my appetite for adventure in life was supercharged.

Teachers must be the most overwhelmed, underpaid, under-appreciated, and invaluable saints on the planet. I'd often felt the need to reach out and thank all those who took a special interest in me, but shamefully have never made that time. Thanks to all of them—Riley, Stout, Rameriz, Pittman, Krenzke, Wiebush, Montgomery, Parks, and the many others on the ride. Thinking about those souls who made a humongous difference is an ethereal exercise. These days I'm getting the second go-round with teachers as a single dad with young kids. They all know how much I appreciate them and the impact they're having on my son and daughter.

Ponging along through the high school maze, I fancied myself an observer, and it paid dividends in spades. As I did in Lutheran school, loosely aligning with sports jocks, band jocks, freaks, and bookworms (or "brains" as they were referred to in those times) helped develop a pillar of my ingrained self as an accessible and accepted high schooler. I cannot recall another student there that was so aligned yet not party to the concept of clique or group-think. I was that Herbie guy discovered years before—a one-of-a-kind.

In my family, school was one thing, but there had to be work. The work part of the equation on weekends and after school was never a dread for me. I must have started at seven years old shoveling snow, pulling weeds, scraping rotted wood, raking leaves, washing, waxing, and detailing cars, painting, delivering newspapers, gathering dog poop, and any other crappy jobs that I did at home or for spare change in the neighborhood. At age ten I sold candles, magazines, cookies, or whatever, door to door—for the church and myself—exploiting every opportunity. I was always in second or third place in the contests behind the auto-worker executives' kids, whose parents pressed all their underlings at the companies to purchase the random items at work, or else. Cheaters. I found accomplishment and release in these endeavors—work ethic personified.

Since my family and their friends had no money, I had to go to more affluent parts of my neighborhood to make my sales. The church-school sales gig benefited me with free magazines and learning the routes to houses where moneyed and kind people lived, which I revisited in the winter for my snow-shoveling work. I excelled and built a year-round client base back when the Midwest had reliable snow to shovel through winter, and sustainable backyard ice rinks to play on pre-global warming. I loved the winter months. My older neighborhood shoveling partner and I would set out early in the morning on weekends or immediately after school and kick ass, on a good weekend pocketing up to thirty dollars each per bustling ten-hour day. My dad would freak when I carefully pulled out all the dough, which was securely stashed in my inside jacket hiding place. He would take his cut, then it was time for a shower, some hot chocolate, a snack, and watching football flat on my back in the family living room. I had no fear of rejection—I had seen and heard it all and unknowingly become a successful salesman at a tender age.

As I approached fifteen years old, my dad was always asking around to find me a steady-paying gig. He made it clear that he had nothing for me and that it was my responsibility to make it on my own. The first job in which I secured an actual paycheck was illegally at fifteen years of age. I rode my Stingray bicycle three miles, rain or shine, to a sketchy part of town on a nine-mile road at the I-75 interstate exit, to earn my $1.35/hour at the bottom of the fast-food burger totem pole. I was treated like the dog I was every week, but it was worth it for that skimpy paycheck. I questioned authority once, when I was asked to quickly bus and clean tables during rush time with the same rags I'd been cleaning the poopy bathroom with, but learned to stay out of the politics when I was summarily berated and nearly had my head taken off.

"Just do as you're told here, Jeff—we are all super-busy and don't have time for your silly details. Do your job if you want to keep it."

I went on with the unappetizing task. Eventually, there was an upgrade as I got my driver's license and a position at the local dry cleaners. I did every perceivable chore that no one else would do there, including janitor, handyman, and the exciting task of emptying all the incoming clothes pockets. I remember finding everything from $1,200 (which I dutifully returned and got a fifty dollar tip) to vomit and feces, as nursing homes in the area were among our biggest customers. Yuck.

The work environment introduced me to Jewish life, as two brothers of that persuasion owned the business, employing their elderly father, who must have been ninety, as a tailor. The father spoke infrequently, but never to me and never in English, a cultural eye-opener. Being from my myopic, all-white, Melba-toast hood and school, this was foreign to me. I'd seen every walk of life at my previous burger gig but never spent much time with anyone there.

Dad said, "Listen to those Jewish guys—they are smart and know how to make money."

An interesting directive. I learned a little Yiddish that has served me well over the years, as well as other bits and pieces, language, and slang. I also was introduced to aspects of a belief system different from my Lutheran upbringing, that was appreciated.

I worked hard there and would always report back to the onsite office to do more chores.

"I dunno what to tell you, Jeff. Just go do something, *anything*, even if it's wrong. Can't have you sitting here with us in the office," the boisterous brother, Harry, would say.

Money to me was a primal bare necessity, and experiencing the stress my parents went through in their hand-to-mouth existence, and the occasional tumult it wrought in the home, solidified the need. Not an end-all goal, but a simple standard staple and a means to an end.

I vividly recall the sleazy, bright-orange, polyester, leisure-suited, door-to-door Prudential insurance salesman who, when I was fourteen, fast-talked my parents into a rip-off insurance policy they couldn't afford. Over my parents hushing of me, I challenged him.

"Well sir, I'm looking at the math on this, and if we don't have a death real soon, it looks like the payback long term will be pitiful. Even the death benefit of the cheaper plan is paltry."

It was about to ruin his closing.

"Now kid, I'm sure you don't understand the complexity and the importance here of this security for your family," he said as he rolled his eyes. "You think you are bulletproof, but nobody is. You can't live your life as a nickel-'n'-dime millionaire or you will end up in the poorhouse, buddy."

My parents ordered me out of the room while they signed up. Years later when I was in college, they had to cash out for peanuts when they desperately needed money, and I, struggling myself, couldn't yet help them. They did ask my opinion more often after that. The experience verified to me once again my ability to discern truth from bullshit and really served as motivation to get to a place of self-reliance and financial stability.

I wasn't always that smart as a youth.

In teen years, of course, I got exposed to smoking, drinking, girls, and cars. Smoking was cured early as my buddies and I hit the jackpot, getting someone to buy us a carton of stinkerettes. We were so excited, we dashed behind the store into the alley and wildly began to chain-smoke them, getting so sick we barely wobbled home. I summarily dry-heaved all afternoon and night—a Clockwork-Orange therapy. Seems I forgot my experience in the car with my parents years before.

Beer, like wine, was a gift from God, as Ben Franklin noted, and I think everyone in the school used fake Arkansas drivers' licenses a kid was selling in school (we were in Michigan). These were accepted as valid at a few party stores near the high school that gladly up-charged us all for the privilege of the illegal buys.

The girls loved me and I loved them, but dared not love on them. My take was love and lovin' was special and, per my Christian training, designed for marriage; hence I secured my sacred virginity for later, which became college. I survived several mutually embarrassing efforts of a few experienced girls' aggressiveness in trying to turn me to the dark side.

High school wound down, and graduation was an unceremonious affair. I still have the photo of me barely being able to keep my grad cap on over my bushy bushel of wiry hair, in front of my matchbox of a home with the paint peeling off, and just Sis, Mom, and Dad in attendance, and a Hallmark card in hand.

Everyone worth their salt had some kind of plans after school. Mom suggested I start a career at the local hardware store, where she had landed me an interview. No thanks—had bigger plans and was hedging my options. Applying and being accepted at both the University of Michigan and Michigan State University, with partial scholarship and grant money, was big, and I knew I had to cash in. As Dad had prophesized, there was no future there for me in Royal Oak. I had to work hard that summer after school to have a good start and a few bucks in my pocket at the

U, even though I was working every angle and more to avoid having to be enslaved.

A real passion and mad desire was to bike across the country in the 1976 Bikecentennial USA, celebrating the big two-hundredth anniversary of our great country. Wanted that bad. My biking buddy and best neighborhood bud, Mark, who came from a family of athletes, had it all planned out for us. He had been a savior who taught me the joy of running, basketball, and my true love, bicycling on my freedom machine—my Schwinn Varsity eighty-pound, ten-speed bike.

My love for cycling would be tested early on. At fifteen years of age, we loaded up those Schwinns and rode some three hundred miles, up to northern Michigan to camp on the lake beaches—the farthest I had ever been from my home. On the way home, I got hit by a drunk driver's truck that sideswiped me and missed killing me by an inch. The guy, reeking of liquor, stopped briefly to see if I was okay, then quickly sped off, surely relieved to see me in one piece and praising the Lord for his escape. My mates and I hammered the machine into rideable shape with a large rock, pounding away at the steel rim that had been practically pretzeled, so we could continue with the oblong wheel, *bump-de-bump* along the way. That Schwinn Varsity, a colossus by today's standards, performed well in the collision. Off we went, me a little bloody but not broken, fortunately, even without the bike helmet that no one wore back then.

Somehow, I survived the five years we'd been riding together. My bike, like books, was another miracle gateway to a world of adventure, and I rode it regularly and with a passion, rain or shine. The Bikecentennial would be the big kahuna, which was planned along with him, and I even had painfully ponied up the non-refundable fee, knowing all the while that it was probably less.

As the time drew nearer to make this epic, historic ride—versus get to work and save a few nickels to put some clothes on my back for college—it was painful to finally pull the trigger with my friend and tell him I was electing to stay behind and work. This left him mightily pissed and betrayed, but he rolled on and sent me postcards from the road.

If I had to do that over, I would've gone on the ride and sorted out poverty on the return. Certainly never missed following my heart after that experience—and never will. That was the lesson I leveraged from that day on, and post-college would double down to make up for my mistake. Take chances. Advance your opportunity. Live your dreams.

CHAPTER 4

Michigan State University

Upon the Nomination of the Faculty of the

College of Engineering

has conferred upon

Jeffrey Alan Swaney

the Degree of

Bachelor of Science

Given under the Seal of the University at East Lansing in the State of Michigan on this twentieth day of March, in the year Nineteen Hundred and Eighty - One.

MSU Diploma

College Madness

First view of Rockies

CHAPTER 4
RISING ABOVE

We morph into the beings we are via our doses of 75 percent DNA and 25 percent environmental influences, according to the Minnesota Identical Twins study done umpteen years ago. What that may tell us is that the holy grail of proper, promising parenting or failure cannot determine an individual's outcome, but it can tip the scales. It is a relief to conclude that there is an against-the-odds possibility to ruin a "good kid" or salvage a "bad kid." Some lucky changes in environment and the influence of earthly angels can help get you off the bubble—and in my case, that happened.

Post-high school, I was destined to be an in-state Michigan college rat (freebies for a poor boy). By good fortune and an insanely high SAT score, I was accepted at both Michigan State University (MSU) and the University of Michigan (U of M). I opted for Moo U—the perceived easier route. U of M felt too Ivy League and would demand performance, which invoked a fear of failure, as there was little support from family for the choice to even attend college at all.

So, in the fall of 1976, the parents begrudgingly drove the ninety-minute haul to East Lansing, Michigan for the drop-off at MSU, their only visit 'til my graduation four-and-a-half years later.

"You're not college material," Dad explained on the drive.

"You should've taken the job at the hardware store in Royal Oak," Mother lamented. "It was a good job. College is going to be the ruination of creation for you. You're not going to make it."

Upon our arrival, we met the new computer-selected roommate—Tony—one of sixty-five thousand students there that year. Tony was drunk. Not only that, he had some serious hygiene issues that he basked in. He said "Hi," and the parents wished us luck and then disappeared within five minutes.

The duffel bag and mini backpack hit the floor with a smack, next to the beat-up foot locker Tony lived out of. As if the sound was the bang of a starting gun for tongue-wagging, Tony began orating his life story after offering up whiskey from his signature flask.

"It's good stuff," he slurred.

I accepted against my better judgment.

"I'm from Buffalo, New York. My dad is a horrible guy. And I'm a genius—I'm a math whiz, dude, just try me. I got a *full ride* here." He continued, staccato, scratching his gruffy, zitty chin intermittently to gather his next thought. "Don't ever touch me or touch my stuff. I need to warn you, I have a switchblade. Also, one final thing. You see that glass over there on the shelf? Don't touch it. It's mine."

Meandering over and peering into the glass, I couldn't quite figure out what was in it. I would find out later that he collected finger and toenails along with scabs and other unidentified ingredients in there marinating in a stew of his saliva.

"Okaaaaaaay..."

I submitted the roommate change request the next day, which would take two semesters to complete. God bless him.

We were now inmates of the sprawling and loathed Brody Complex on the far west side of the enormous 5,200-acre campus, in Armstrong Hall unit #326, on a floor nicknamed The Chickenpits, in a twenty-by-ten, asbestos-tiled, bunk-bedded, peg-boarded room, with a primitive, campus-wide, radiant-steam-heat system and massive, athlete's-foot-laden group showers. It seemed like a thousand miles from classrooms, as well as any life I'd imagined here at the enormous MSU campus.

A yuppie, hippie, wild man was set loose, clothing consisting of a pair of jeans, shorts, a few T-shirts, a jacket, shoes, hat, scarf, and boots, and about seven pair of "Wilbert," cement-factory uniforms adorned with the name patch "Mel." These were my Dad Melvin's (hence "Mel") extras that he had saved for me, as they were too worn out for the factory in which he worked. The uniform had me labeled as Mel—outrageous, infamous, and mostly loved.

Freshman year was a blur of failing miserably, dropping from dean's list to dopes' list academically while succumbing to beer, booze, and babes in a titanic way. I remember going to classes only on occasion and blowing off midterm exams since I knew nothing of the material.

That year in the Brody complex, barely separated from a zillion co-eds, the sports were drinking and bong-hitting contests (kegs were stored in the community showers and kept cold 24/7), as well as panty raids of the adjacent girls' dorms, where there were contests on how many unoccupied panties you could grab on the run—then gathering outside that dorm in the courtyard with a full, gross moon display of sixty dudes hollering and smacking their naked bottoms. Insane. Streaking, unmentionable pranks worse than any hazing I've ever heard of, coordinated two-hundred-plus person primal screams conducted in the middle of the night, NoDoz nausea, vomiting and overdoses from maniacal test cramming, and antics resulting in near and actual deaths.

The administration took a hard look years later at all the craziness and vices relating to drinking, drugs, and the like, most all made illegal now. The many privileges didn't die easily, as evidenced by the reaction in the '90s when booze and beer were finally banned from the MSU campus. Live footage on the national news showed rioting, overturned and burning police cruisers, and the calling out of the National Guard, while enacting curfews to quell the student response.

I scooted through just in time to live the good party life there before the draconian measures and still survive my freshman year, while also dodging the epidemic mass-shooting madness nationwide at schools that shocked MSU in 2023.

Tired of being penniless the first year, over the summer break it was time to take on numerous bottom-of-the-barrel jobs, working practically around the clock to scrounge up cash. One of the most egregious was a good-paying job in downtown Detroit at an ancient parts factory. The Budd Wheel Company conjured up images from an American classic novel on Mrs. Hildebrand's playlist—Upton Sinclair's *The Jungle*. I can still smell and taste on the tongue the hundred-year-old greasy steam that comprised the air in the stiflingly hot, rattling building. Towering ceilings caked with baked, filthy batter three to five inches thick, and surrounded with broken windows that over some fifty years had become opaque from lack of cleaning, made for pigeon roosts looming above. Underfoot, cracked cement floors with the aggregate materials exposed beneath a thick sheen of oily grime made walking there a bit hazardous, akin to navigating black ice, requiring the perfect boot and moving cautiously as a penguin. Additionally, it helped to beware of the deeply worn grooves in the floor, ground in by workers who had lived and died there decades before.

When the place was running at full bore, the building shook and throbbed with the startup and pounding of the 1930s mechanical monsters. Breathers in the breakroom were short-lived, and I would sit in there like a zombie until the bell rang to crank it all up again. As an ethnic minority—a long-haired, fair-skinned, definitively white pretty boy—amongst some rough characters, keeping one's head down and shutting the mouth was the MO.

"I think you need a talking to, boy," one of the guys said as he grabbed me by the arm and spun me around.

"Oh, yes," I babbled.

"You know, I see you out there and man, you are not cutting it. No one wants to be on the same line with you, you are too f.*&%ing slow and are a pain in all our asses. And don't be squealing this crap to the boss man here, that's gonna get you in deeper shit with the guys. Don't be a pansy-ass!"

"Well, okay, I'll pick it up then. All cool here."

"One more thing," he bellowed. "If you can't make it here, you can't make it in life. Hear me—I know! Got it?"

"Gotcha."

Holy crap, I said to myself. *This is hell.*

I think I made it there about a month before exiting in spectacular fashion. On a particularly simmering summer day, a day that would be cut short, I was working a line producing wheels for buses. The wheels weighed about sixty pounds each and had to be lifted and mounted on a valve press machine. The scalding, just-pressed steaming wheels would roll down the line to be saddled on the machine, the operator then pushing two large red softball-sized buttons on both sides of the press, to ensure a hand didn't end up in the mix. This caused a metal mega-anvil to drop down with tremendous force and punch a valve hole in the thick steel wheel, then to be taken off and rolled down the line as the next wheel would arrive in a blink to be mounted. Rapid-fire non-stop, with a production quota for the day at over two hundred wheels. If the crew on that line could speed up production, they'd get longer breaks in the afternoon. That's what the guys were always chasing. No matter what. Homemade devices the men would craft allowed you to cheat the machine and somehow only have one hand on one button, but you risked losing a hand or arm.

The guys upstream were pushing hard that day, possibly to kill me. The heat was unbearable and with the noise and earplugs you couldn't hear anyone, and they couldn't hear you—in essence, you were just part of the machinery. Everyone on the line had an industrial-sized fan blowing on them to keep from melting in the heat, and if that went out you were in big trouble. In the meantime, the wheels were coming at me at the fastest pace I'd ever encountered. Even as a human octopus, focused and bustin' butt, keeping up proved impossible.

As I lost pace, the wheels started backing up. First one ("Well hell, that's only one"), and then a full-on cascade started falling off the line and bouncing everywhere, like boulders in a landslide. It was like an *I Love Lucy* episode from the '50s, with me dodging, waving, hollering, and finally jumping around yelping for help in a panic. One of the wheels bounced and hit, cutting my fan cord, which sparked a Star Wars laser-style blast and halted the lifeline that was the fan. It was curtains. *Boom.* With the fan out, the temperature soaring, and the blood pressure at redline levels in of couple minutes, I passed out to the floor. I avoided being fatally crushed by the bouncing wheels, as someone shut down the line when they determined the valve press guy was AWOL.

I woke up in the break room to smelling salts and the foreman telling me my mom was on the way to pick me up. I saw the guys come in for the break laughing their asses off at me. I was going home, not to return. Wasn't gonna make it there, you were right buddy, but I was going to make it in life.

The Budd Wheel was the hardest job ever and *not the answer.* Dirty Jobs. Even my step-grandfather, who toiled in the factories his whole life, told my mom, "That place is a hellhole, I've heard, worst factory in Detroit—I couldn't work there."

There were more other crazy gigs, not as life-threatening, but close. After the Budd fiasco, working for Michigan Bell

Telephone, back when rotary phones in use were screwed to walls in homes. Three other neatly clad college summer workers and I met in a downtown warehouse on a sunny Saturday at seven a.m. to receive our marching orders, along with official Bell helmets, beat-up twenty-five-year-old Bell Tel vans assigned and equipped with a collection of mismatched tools. We were slated for phone-out duty in the bowels of the downtown Detroit residential areas, a landscape of burned-out buildings, vacant lots piled with mounds of stinking trash, car and truck tires, drug paraphernalia, stray animals—some running in packs—feces, and the like, among the few remaining, marginally habitable, scattered homes and apartments. It was apparent to me that we were just another fresh crew in a rotation of workers who couldn't cut the mustard.

"Welcome, guys," said our boss, a man cut of commander-grade military, conjuring images of *Full Metal Jacket*, *Saving Private Ryan*, and *Platoon* characters.

"Your job is to retrieve the telephones from these locations noted in the paperwork I've supplied, so they're returned to the company. You will each work a geographic area on your own, as you see in your paper files on the clipboards, with the current Mapsco books provided to get you to those destinations. You will see the addresses and the account histories in there, some having been delinquent and without phone service for over ten years. It matters not the condition of the units; we just want to get 'em back in somewhat recognizable form and close out these accounts. Use the pry bar, claw hammers, cutters, or whatever, and get them out. Then mark down where you retrieved them from and any comments you have. Questions?"

We all looked at each other, shaking our heads. It seemed a ridiculous quest, but a good-paying gig.

"Okay, get on with it, and thank you—see you back at five o'clock."

These were some of the most pitiful residences in the USA at the time. A *National Geographic* article on Detroit observed that the inner city had gone back to the wilds, featuring photos of trees growing through old buildings. Raccoons, skunks, and other once-dominant animals had now taken back the area after a two-hundred-year hiatus, comingling with feral dog packs. I stopped at some vacant houses early on and heard critters scatter as I crawled through broken-out windows and doors and past shockingly beautiful marble stairs, wrought-iron work, and exotic wooden paneling, to recover a couple phones. Of course, most of the time any brass, copper, or other useful, detachable metal, along with the phones in these homes, had been pilfered long ago.

Dreaming of what those houses might have looked like intact in the past opulence of this fallen city, I headed to my next stop, a sketchy-looking apartment building that was going to be an adventure, for sure. Mothers, completely topless, sat on the weed-choked lawn out front, nursing their babies, while the resident toddlers ran around wildly in this makeshift playground, strewn with Mad Dog 20/20 and Thunderbird bottles, along with a mishmash of other litter. Was I in the USA or Uganda?

I went up to the second floor on a staggeringly humid day that was probably well over one hundred degrees and knocked on an apartment door. A man in his twenties, sweating profusely in a ragged T-shirt, opened it and invited me in. As I entered cautiously, a few dirty, threadbare couches loaded with guys covered in blankets and shaking in the heat came into view. Junkie central. I could practically smell the heroin. I mean, for real.

"It's good man…they finally sent someone to fix this f&*(^ing phone," he rejoiced.

"Well…that's not exactly why I'm here, sir.…You see, they sent me an order to pick up the phone," I explained, sheepishly pointing to my clipboard paperwork.

When he went into an f-bomb tirade, I just put my hands up.

"Well, give me those papers!" he demanded.

I promptly handed him his work order, which he promptly and violently shredded.

"Dude, it's cool, all cool. I'll tell them it's all good."

I was outta there.

At a home a few blocks away, an elderly woman answered the door of one of only two homes left standing in a war zone of a city block that at one time had held about fifty structures. She could speak no English. I surmised that she was Polish, based on long Sundays at the grandparents' home, the sounds unmistakable. Pointing to the Bell emblem on my helmet and breaking into an unrehearsed pantomime show a la Chaplin, raising the wire cutters gently snipping in the air, I indicated it was time for phone removal. The work order indicated the phone service had been turned off five years before.

In despair, she motioned me into the house, which was dirty, cluttered, and unfit for living, and then out into the backyard where she pointed to a man that must have been her husband. He was walking in a circle on the perimeter of the backyard and had worn a path through the rocks and weeds literally a foot deep, which must have taken him years to accomplish. I looked at him, a pitiful soul, then back at her. She broke down in tears, whereupon I instinctively hugged her and shed a tear of my own.

"Okay, okay," I said.

Walking back into the house, she showed me the phone on the wall, and I explained somehow it was hers now, showing her the work order and tearing it up, and giving it to her, indicating that it was going to be just fine. She thanked me profusely, rattling, crying, and clasping her hands together so tightly to thank God for a phone that would never again be useful.

My first day was nearly over. Feeling that I was dreadfully behind schedule, I focused on vacant houses on the way back to the warehouse, amassing a grand total of twelve phones. Thinking I'd be fired for sure for that paltry sum, not to mention two shredded and lost work orders, I made my way back to headquarters, where the rest of our group had assembled. When we all offered up the phones, the boss looked over the booty—twelve of mine and ten that the three other workers had retrieved between them.

"Good work, all of you. See you tomorrow at nine a.m. Except you, Sweeney (mispronouncing my name); we need to talk."

"Yessir," I said obediently.

"Look, son, that is too many phones for one day! Don't take any chances out there, okay? It's not that important. It's a jungle out there, so don't push your luck; I want you back safe.... You're excused."

"Yessir, see you tomorrow, sir."

So now I knew how the game was going to be played. I've always been very good at games, from board games to the games of life, so once I understood the rules, I rolled up my sleeves. Step one was showing up to work the next day in the rattiest clothes I had and going unshaven. I noticed the other two workers (there were only two more now, one having quit after a day) had dressed down as well. This was a safer look and would help when traveling the world solo, post-college. Look like a bum and people will leave you alone. Flash a smile when you want to connect—that pierces all veils in every culture and in every circumstance—and don't look the devils in the eye.

Having to gather fewer phones per the new mandate now allowed me the luxury of what was needed most. More sleep. Since I was also working the local delivery service for the neighborhood Chicken Shack, I was always exhausted, sometimes confusing deliveries and getting the boss pissed. Although between the two jobs I was up to eighty hours a week, now I could work more chicken deliveries later at night and sleep a good part of the day downtown in the Bell van. Perfect. I was able to save up enough money from the gigs to start my sophomore year of school.

Coming of age that second year, I escaped the freshman madhouse dorms for the cool, old, funky, hippy-dippy enclave in the center of campus, which felt like winning the lottery. The new roommate by random selection once again was a short, brilliant, beady-eyed, uber-long-haired real genius named Joe. Son of some Yale University professors, he was an expert on all things ethereal, including everything that fell into the experimental category on campus. We partied like '60s rock stars—an era we reclaimed—when Joe wasn't sitting in the entry lobby of the dorm with his legs behind his neck yogi style, as a line of people waited to get his advice on life.

I knew Joe was just a special human being and wasn't sure if he even was one. We had a cosmic connection that quickly led to a close friendship as well as a business venture. Although pot, which is legal most everywhere these days (and in which I have no interest) was widely used, it came with a five-dollar fine if you got caught smoking it in the city or on campus. With my drive and Joe's be-here-now aura, we made a great team. Our pot deliveries paid better than the slimy, grimy, brutal dishwashing job in the dorm cafeteria, which I thankfully quit. The social aspects were also rewarding, allowing me to hang out with a very diverse crowd, mostly of the privileged and genius sort, morphing into Mr. Party Central with my chameleon-like personality and love of people. We never got busted, but some of our friends did.

Despite losing touch with high school and old neighborhood friends as I moved on to college, I made it a point to stay in contact with Mike from the old hood, one of my besties who seemed to always be in some kind of trouble. Always in and out of jail, he ended up in prison many years later in Fort Worth, Texas, where I visited him, which was the experience of a lifetime, swallowed down in one afternoon.

The pen was a high-security facility, and visitors had to be thoroughly checked out, frisked, and studied, and then a limited number of them at a time would enter a holding tank surrounded by two massive, ten-by-ten-foot, mechanically operated metal gates. The one gate would roll open and allow the "guests" in, then slam shut. After a fifteen-minute period standing in there, they'd finally be cleared to enter the prison under escort.

I chatted with the prison guard while I was in there.

"This is quite an operation here. How many folks come on any particular day? More on holidays or fewer?"

"You would do best to keep your mouth shut," he snapped.

"Okay."

A red light flashed above. The gate was about to open.

"Alright, y'all carry on. Except you," he said pointing at me. "You will stay right there where you are."

Waiting through the next cycle, mouth shut as recommended, I was finally allowed through the gate and eventually escorted to an inmate lunchroom to meet Mike.

"Jeff, I can't believe you're here! No one has come to visit me in almost a year," he proclaimed.

"I can see why they haven't."

Mike was studying me while I talked. "Can I have those sunglasses, dude?" he asked. "And the watch?"

"Why on earth do you want those? They are cheapies."

"Dude, I need them. I owe some guys here—the guards. They're helping me out and money isn't worth shit here. A couple months ago, two guys got in my cell and clobbered me with a sock full of metal balls. Somehow it was deemed my fault, and I had to do two weeks in the hole. Solitary, man—the worst dark pit. Bro, I seriously almost lost my shit in there. I don't think I could survive it again," he whispered agonizingly.

I put the glasses and the watch on the table and slid them over his way. In a minute, he raised his hand up. A guy came by and he backhanded him the watch in a clandestine fashion as the inmate walked by. Gone. A minute later he raised his hand again and another resident swung by and plucked the sunglasses, then disappeared.

"That's how it works in here, Jeff, it's freaking nuts. Oh, and thanks."

I knew I never wanted to be in there and would not make it. Mike was a big six-foot-two-inch guy, tough, strong, and scrappy, and I was a five-foot-ten-inch wimp by comparison. Thankfully, he got out several years later and disappeared to surf in Baja, Mexico, where I suppose he is today.

Another reconnect on the home front during that sophomore year, a noteworthy occurrence but not a shocking one, was Dad's filing for divorce from my mom. I was at home one weekend with the parents to visit for their twenty-fifth wedding anniversary, and my dad had timed it perfectly to have the papers served for his divorce while I was there. That morning, I answered the knock on the door from the living room couch, sleeping off the hangover earned partying hard with my remaining Royal Oak friends the night before.

"Hey Mom, there's a guy here for you."

Mom was in tears. Dad wasn't there but I was, just as I was always there for her 'til her dying day, with regular visits and the horribly missed Sunday phone calls. But with the way things were going for them, one really couldn't blame him. He knew I'd be there to comfort my mother, and he had been unhappy for years. It was surprising they had made it that long. I felt relief for both, not the despair that one perhaps was supposed to feel. Thankfully, it was civil, as they still were going to live under the same roof due to their financial lot in life, which provided the opportunity to still bicker about the strength of the morning's coffee brew. It was a life-changing event for me, albeit a cakewalk compared to the torturous, two-year-long divorce—with two young children in the mix, and accompanying tailing years of grief—I would suffer years later, after my own filing.

I was grateful to return to school for my junior year. A few newfound, amazing friends and I moved off campus, ending up in a rental house that we practically turned into a nightclub once a month with our giant parties, hosting well over five hundred people. It ruined the quiet residential neighborhood, turning that into a student slum almost overnight, with people always stopping by to visit, play basketball out front, or just party and hang out 24/7. Backyard bonfires some nights would have flames rising thirty feet and melting the old phone wires on the poles. All-night parties serving drunken and stoned guests, disguised mayonnaise-enhanced cat food with chips in giant bowls licked clean, toilets overflowing, and people pooping and peeing all over the neighborhood, together with activities such as writing on the walls and wooden cabinets with handfuls of permanent markers made available—it was a riotous scene. And then finally almost burning down the house one night in an encore party—where we broke down all the furniture and threw it into a fireplace that got overloaded, catching the wall on fire—resulted in leaving the house and grounds in ruins, with little hope of getting our security deposit back.

With a party invite to the house being the gold standard, I became the dealmaker extraordinaire at that time, trading test answers in the core courses for party favors and anything else nontoxic. The phone rang off the hook. As one of my college roomies noted, it was an inevitable precursor to a career that, just five years later, would put my team on the international club-mongers' hipster, must-see map, where underground worldwide fame awaited.

Had I realized what was coming, I might not have worried so much about my grade point average, which after my first two years was a dismal 2.38. Just as bad, my ratio of completed coursework projected me to be there for five years, not four. It was a mess. Time to fix that. Knowing from experience what it was like to do manual labor provided motivation. So, somehow, amidst the partyrama atmosphere, the quest was set in motion to perform at or near the 4.0 mark, so I'd end up with at least a 3.0 GPA, the minimum for most companies doing college interviews. The whole point here was to get a good job and go out and conquer the world while paying off the student loans that, back then, were not to be forgiven. Right?

I had tested out and been directed by the high school college counselors (due to math prowess and blue-collar upbringing, I'm guessing) to engineering school. Wasn't so sure about that selection, but engineers are nearly guaranteed jobs on graduation with good pay, so you do it.

It was time to learn Rule #1—TANSTAAFL, written up on the chalkboard in one of the intro classes first semester back in freshman year.

"Alright, students. Welcome to engineering school at MSU. Let's get started, shall we?" the balding professor said, pointing to the chalkboard as he peered over the top of his bifocals.

A hundred heads stared at the acronym, with no takers.

"Can't any of you Einsteins even take a wild guess? We clearly have a lot of work to do!" he exclaimed emphatically.

"TANSTAAFL—There Ain't No Such Thing As a Free Lunch. That's the fundamental premise of your engineering education here, so remember it if you don't remember anything else!"

I understood, since to me it was a truism already experienced. Engineering and its guiding tenets explained the world. Math, chemistry, and physics—$a^2+b^2=c^2$, f=ma, and the big enchilada, $e=mc^2$, with calculus wedged somewhere in between. I could not grasp calculus for the longest time (something high schoolers know nowadays), and then somehow it finally clicked. Brilliance! It was like, "Wow, how the hell did that guy come up with that?"

Calculus was hatched by a couple minds—the lauded Isaac Newton and Gottfried Leibniz—independently of each other, their discovery creating the foundation for our space age. The learning experience sometimes has you battering walls, and then when you are about to give up, there is a revelation. Such is life. Never give up. And in this engineer's world, there was always more to learn—Diffy Qs, thermodynamics, and leaping to quantum physics. It just kept coming....

The engineering disciplines give a base in logic and building blocks in what was and is the physical world—as well as a tad of philosophy. There's a point where science and spirituality meld, and that fusion point was always of particular interest. Felt it. But, foremost, before getting too carried away, engineers were charged with fixing things for mankind, and this commitment was to be never-ending, tasked forever and again to discover the panaceas to man's flubbering, only to get to the next level of greater complexity and fix it again. A virtual factory, that just unknowingly ratchets up the problem levels in a continuous do loop. More food, more energy, more of everything supporting spiraling overpopulation of the planet. Continuing industrialization, overcrowding, nuclear proliferation, global warming, budding Star Wars, AI growing madly, and the rest. The lemmings march on. But there is hope.

Where it all came together for me was in reading Einstein and his brilliant philosophy, virtually unknown to most and manifest in his famous quote:

"Imagination is more important than knowledge."

Resonating, it made me rethink my direction at the university.

I loathed the engineering classes and that crowd, and had to escape the nerds, and dreaded the culmination of graduating into a miserable existence as an engineer, which I was not passionate about and was unsuited for. Blessed and cursed with many skills and a master of none, I was an artist trapped in a businessman's body, and I knew no matter what, I had to make a nickel from all this. A philosophy degree would leave me penniless and back at the hardware store, as my mom had planned.

As I explored options, my salvation came via a newly minted engineering and marketing program, where I could delve into creative marketing, including grad-level classes, and wrap up some engineering courses. The corporate world was starved for these types, which they begged the schools to create, who could understand technical products and knew marketing tactics. Couple that with people skills, and you were golden. Finally, the avenue to appreciate unpleasant-at-times engineering coursework that helped ground and provide order, efficient study, land problem-solving methodologies for the mega-challenges yet to come in life—yet another salvation. TANSTAAFL.

With finding a purpose for a diploma, and newfound excitement and direction, the table was reset. Now it was about finding a bit more money, lessening chances to spend it, and building some resume pieces. After searching high and low, I determined that the next options for the summer between junior and senior years included going to North Carolina for ROTC's Platoon Leadership class or an internship in Montana with Conoco, a Houston-based oil and gas company. The ROTC thing included basic training in North Carolina, which probably would've been a bonus for me to get my ass whipped into shape but promised to be brutal. Detroit boy was going to take the desk job.

What we find in life is that whatever we have the least expectations for can really bowl us over with blessings, when we hang it out there. I packed up my rickety Oldsmobile Cutlass after school that early summer and headed out to Billings, Montana—a dusty oil, cattle, and ag town that was not the most beautiful spot in the state. Far from it, but not far from the mountains and grandeur of Glacier Park, the Tetons, and Yellowstone.

Settling into that desk job, there were options for field work that the local management didn't relish. I volunteered for part of the job that involved having folks renew their leases for mineral rights on their properties, which ended up being quite an adventure. Since many of the properties were far out in marginally civilized no-man's land, I wound up meeting many an interesting character and hermit out there.

On one such mission, I was confused as to a location of a particular homestead in the middle of BFE, which encompassed a vast acreage and was obviously a huge moneymaker. Out there in northern, central, and eastern Montana at that time, homes and ranches were many miles apart, requiring full gas tanks with beef jerky and water caches on board. There was no GPS use then, only frequently inaccurate maps and the requisite paperwork to be completed.

Lost in a town with maybe three buildings, I spied a saloon with a few pickups parked out front, and desperate for help, since this was such a large and important tract, I popped in to see if I could be afforded assistance. I stepped through the double doors of a spaghetti western, in a run-down, funky hole-in-the-wall harboring a few scraggly, leather-faced characters, and bellied up to the dilapidated, warped, wormy bar top with a toothless bartender providing service. It was 10 a.m.

"Well, c'mon in and grab a seat up here, stranger," he yammered. "You're not from around here, are ya?"

"No sir, I'm in from Billings, and I was wondering if you gentlemen could help me out?"

"Well, come sit down up here and get you a drink and we'll talk, young'un," he offered. "What'll you have?"

I looked at the others at the bar who had stopped their conversations and were fixated on me. "I'll have what they're having."

"One whiskey coming up," he chirped, pouring about four ounces into a glass. "What are all those papers you have there, and what're you looking for?"

I laid out the map on the bar and explained my task, showing them the location of the homestead.

One of the old drunks perused the map, then stabbed his finger at a point on the map. "Hot damn, that's the old crazy cat lady's place!" he blurted out. "She's as crazy as a shithouse rat and practically an animal. If she sees you, she's liable to jump your young bones. I imagine she's not had any for a while. I wouldn't go there if I was you, ya whippersnapper."

"Well, I'd appreciate it if you showed me the way."

As we drank, they drew side maps to augment mine, which explained the route to the cat lady's house. After settling with the bartender and bidding them a good day, I set out with one helluva buzz on. *Yeehaw!*

Over rough road, I was out in front of the cat lady's house in twenty minutes. Like an abandoned homestead from a Western landscape painting hanging cockeyed on a wall, it looked uninhabitable. I gathered myself to go up to the door, approached, knocked, and waited in trepidation. Eventually, the door creaked open.

It was the cat lady. She kept the door ajar and I could see, hear, and smell what seemed over a hundred cats jumping about in the background. On stimulus overload, my senses focused on the putrid smell wafting through the doorway, likely from years of cat excrement mingled with whatever else was in there. Barely looking at her face, I showed her the papers, explaining in my pantomime style the signature required—an *X*, since I assumed she was illiterate. When I handed her a pen, a wrinkled, discolored, claw-like appendage slipped through a thin coat donned even in the dead of summer, as if kin to the Grim Reaper himself. The claw shook as the pen made a shaky *X* mark in the spot pointed out. Then she bowed her head with a smile and closed the door. Walking back to the car in amazement at how simple the process had been compared to encounters in downtown

Detroit in that previous year's summer job with the phone company, I had to pinch myself.... This was *Montaaaanaaaa.*

There were many other experiences during that summer's work, but none compared in intensity, beauty, and impact to my first visit to Montana and the majestic Rocky Mountains. That was the pearl in the oyster of lackluster summer jobs.

During my first trip out of the town, the nearly expired, landau-roofed, blue and white Oldsmobile chugged its rattling hulk up the famous Beartooth Highway to the mountain pass far from gritty Billings, Montana. At the ripe age of twenty-one, this then-not-well-traveled city boy had never seen a mountain range in person. Awestruck by one of the finest mountain highways in the world, I got out of the car (which I wanted to abandon) numerous times, reveling and vibrating in the grandeur of the Beartooth Pass at 10,948 feet above sea level. Muir and Thoreau—two early literary heroes—came to life in Panavision, and I experienced pure nature like never before, but would many times again: a natural world to escape to, which would serve me well for the rest of my life, providing solace always—especially in difficult times.

Being surrounded and engulfed in nature is our ultimate therapy. And that day, going over that pass, truly seemed to mark the beginning of a thirty-five-year run where blessings poured out and it seemed I could do no wrong.

After that first experience with the serenity of the wilds, I would never spend another summer weekend in Billings. Getting out of there as soon as possible on every weekend and holiday, and heading to the Rocky Mountains, Glacier Park, Yellowstone, and the Grand Tetons, was priceless. Especially since in the late '70s there were no tourist hordes like the present day.

Encounters with moose, bison, bears, and other wildlife were thrilling, and occasionally adrenaline-producing. Underestimating an angry female moose was nearly fatal. This was not your Bullwinkle cartoon moose! A Detroit boy had to learn on his own, as the newspapers always played down the maulings to avoid scaring off tourists.

As that summer wound down, I had been transformed by my experiences in nature in ways that would prove permanent and perfect. I returned to college to finish my senior year that fall. Feeling like such a complete, consecrated soul after my experiences out West, coupled with my newfound success in school, my battery of incredible friends, financial stability, and good health, I was savoring all that life had to offer. Admittedly getting excited about the prospects, the ego swelled and I wore it. After many years of self-doubt, that felt dang good.

Unfortunately, I proceeded to get overly excited—self-absorbed, haughty, and growing to become overbearing and intolerable without being aware of it. Surrounded by privileged friends by virtue of my wit, gift of gab, and willingness to put everything out there, I looked back at my family with disdain and felt ready to disown them. Why did I not ever have the privileges of others? It wasn't fair! And that ugly thought began another transition for me at the tender age of twenty-two, in the ups and downs of this worldly existence.

The wake-up call for me was provided by one of my housemates, my namesake, Jeff, who had a wild side but was definitely well-grounded and focused. I remember him tapping me on the shoulder one evening. "Hey Jeff, I want to catch up with you on some things if you have some time."

"Sure, Jeff, let's do that. What's on your mind?"

"Let's get together tonight."

And so, we did. He invited me into his room and sat me down. I felt like I was a pupil about to be schooled.

"Jeff, you know that people really love you and care about you and you're a really great guy," he said in his typically calm, benevolent manner. "But I've noticed some things that I can't help but share with you, and I'd like to be candid about it."

"Sure, bro, fire away what's up my man we just haven't chatted in a while."

"Well, I've just noticed you've changed a lot, and honestly not for the better. Frankly, I've just seen your ego getting out of control and people are talking about it and talking about you poorly and I hate seeing that. I wanted to share that with you and I think you might take it to heart."

I was floored—speechless. I had so much respect for this guy and I knew he was right. I was defenseless.

"Okay…well…is that it?"

"Basically, yes. I love you and I just want the best for all of us."

I chewed on that for probably about a week, and I must say it was a life-changer. I promptly dialed everything way down. It was a good lesson to learn at that age and never forget. Self-esteem has not been an issue for a long time, but the skill of managing the self is a lifelong journey for us all.

Having digested that, it was time to focus on getting in position to be employable. I kept my nose to the grindstone for most of that last year in college, as well as the extra semester for the makeup of my disastrous first two years. My efforts came down to the wire. Upon getting final test results and corresponding report card, I discovered that I had missed the boat landing at 2.9998 final GPA, which wasn't going to cut the mustard. After a minor moment of melancholy followed by some diehard noodling, I determined that there might be opportunities in two of the classes to improve my GPA. The engineering class held the best bet for improvement. It was time to dig in.

I got in contact with the professor and requested that my final exam be returned to me. Once received, I went about strategizing on how to improve the score and push my overall grade point to a 3.005. Never ever ever give up.

The graded test showed about ten incorrect answers, but seven of those could potentially be successfully be argued. I only needed two more correct answers to get to the goal line and turn the tide. After setting a time with the professor, whose name I can't recall now, we sat down together in his office to discuss the exam.

"Thank you so much for making the time to go over the test with me," I said in a most polite manner.

"No problem, Jeff. I rarely do this but always like it when a student comes in to discuss these things."

"Well, I have about seven of the answers I'd like to review with you and explain my rationale."

"Fire way young man, I'm all ears."

For the next thirty or more minutes we went over the seven questions. He shot down my arguments at each turn. "I see what you're saying but it's incorrect, Jeff," he'd say. Or, "No, your calculation's off. Here's the correct route."

In the end, I had lost all seven arguments and felt somewhat dejected but had to remedy the situation. Ultra-Energizer-Bunny, super student had to get the fix.

"Well, let me show you some calculations that are germane and the primary reason I asked for your time today."

I shared the calculation for my grade point and how this test score would impact my employment prospects in a huge way. In short, I begged. Analytical as he was, he checked my GPA calculations meticulously, and finding them correct, leaned back and scratched his head. There was a moment of silence—seemed like an eternity—and I kept my cool. *Shut up!* I thought to myself. Knowing when to shut up is a gift.

"Well, let's go back and look at some of those questions again and revisit your arguments."

He focused on two which he decided to give me credit for, which made for the needed bonanza. That was the first successful, pivotal negotiation of a sprouting business career. Putting together all my life lessons to that point in synthesis to a great result, with logic, candor, honesty, and humility—not book smarts, politicking, or deceit—had won the day.

Beating the odds—the failure my mother predicted, albeit ignorantly and with good intentions, and which I nearly subconsciously bought into as a lemming—put me on the launch pad!

But I wasn't quite ready for the corporate world yet. I had other far-flung ideas, hatched in early high-school reading and college summer trips that had whetted the appetite for some far more sweeping and distant travels. I had started pre-planning those to some extent that year, together with a friend for the ages—Craig, the Rock, who would accompany me on some of

CHAPTER 5

Surviving Hong Kong

Stunned - Ryoanji: Kyoto, Japan

Hungry yet Free - Kauai 1981

CHAPTER 5

WE'RE EXPANDING

We've all often been asked by others, or ourselves in our introspection, to identify and explore that seminal moment in life. That one biggie that defined, redirected, changed, or saved us. In my case, there seem to have been so many, a constant steady staccato diet of them. Each seemed to amplify and set the stage for the next altogether attenuating and amazing visceral blast. Mostly good. Some not so. This is our personal evolution.

Post college, time to be flung out by slingshot onto the world stage, starved for stimuli and wanting to eat the world in giant-size bites, playing subconscious warp-speed catch-up. As much as had been learned in college, with confidence peaked, it was time to risk that once again, pushing way outside of any comfort zone. Break down to build up stronger. No pain, no gain. Like the seemingly self-destructive artist driven from deep inside, who must paint even though there is no food on the table, I could not hold back on perceptibly reckless undertakings.

So at twenty-two, it was time to tackle the world solo with just a backpack, minimal clothes, a World Airlines 'round-the-world air ticket, a prepaid Eurail pass, a passport, and a pittance in foreign currency, together with $850 in American Express travelers checks stored in a money belt for security. Going as far as all that would take me, along with a pocket address book of names and numbers, no experience, and no guide. Damn the torpedoes!

It was the moment to tell the parents, who were divorced but still living in the same house, of the plan. Returning to their small suburban home, the only one I'd ever known, to lay it out was surreal. Both the hood and the house—a square, squat, white, aluminum-sided cracker box with red shutters and one immense maple tree in the front yard that dwarfed the place—seemed tinier each visit, feeling like a Barbie's, world scale. Walking into the back door, looking at the worn carpeting, cracked kitchen tiles, and faux paneling in the adjacent dining room that forever eliminated the need for re-painting, harkened blue-collar, Midwest, salt-of-the-earth living.

I plopped onto a beige, plastic-cushioned chair with a seat-back sporting some nondescript flowery designs. The rickety six-chair set surrounding the matching cheap faux-wood and brass-trimmed dining table with the crooked extender leaf and wobbly worn legs would be my launch point. Over the years, this was where we took our meals, I toiled many nights on my catechism and homework, and the family business, as they called it, was discussed. I was not sure I'd ever see it all again.

As my parents made their way into the room, I proudly announced, "Mom, Dad, I'm going to do it—heading out to see the world."

After that bike crash in my youth and the early college years of near disaster, Mom was not thrilled. "What, really? I know you want to go to Hawaii—why not go there and bum around for a couple months then come back and get a job?"

"Yes, I'm going to do that *and* everything else. I've planned it out. Sorta. I'll get a job or do some side hustles along the way and again on my return to make money. I've got a top education as an engineer with a 3.0 GPA. It'll be no problem when I want to join the workforce."

"Well, then how long are you going for and where to?"

"Around the world, wherever the wind takes me. I must. I'll call often and send postcards. Probably a year or more, since there's a lot to see."

"Jumpin' Jesus, jumpin' Christ! That is just crazy," she exclaimed.

Now Dad chimed in.

"I understand that we really have nothing here for you, so just be safe and call your mother."

He wasn't as concerned about my welfare as Mom was. As a teen, he had volunteered to be shipped off to Korea over a stormy Pacific Ocean to fight a war he knew nothing about. He realized there was a time for a boy to strike out into the world to face the unknown, which was part of becoming a man.

"Before you leave, there's a little story to share with you," he added.

"There was a dad and his son. The son was ready to head out on his own on a fantastic adventure. The dad hugged him and wished him well. It had been a few months and the dad had not heard from his son. When he finally received a letter from the young man, he opened it to find this greeting. 'No mun, no fun, your son.' The dad pondered this obvious request for money, then he wrote back. When the son got the letter, he opened it gleefully, anticipating a wad of cash. Instead, he read, 'Too bad, too sad, your dad.'

"So that is what I got for you, Jeff," he concluded. "I hope to see you out in California, like we talked about, when you get back from Asia and Hawaii to get the Plymouth Valiant from my sister in Palm Desert and drive back to Michigan. Don't leave me stranded there in the summer; it's too damn hot!"

The plan was that I'd return from the Orient and Hawaii and connect with him in California, where he was going to stay for six to nine months, and then drive back to Detroit in a gifted fifteen-year-old, hundred-thousand-plus-mile car that he coveted. I knew that it was going to be a big moment for us, being captive in that beater for days. Despite a sense of trepidation, I was looking forward to it, as I had many questions for him about his life and his answers, and felt the need to get closer to the man who had been distant as a father. It was going to be integral to personal growth and an adventure unto itself.

So, armed with this loose-knit plan, tepid parental blessings, and imparted wisdom, the stage was set for an epic world tour for this novice. Backpacking and a certain type of hobo living in minimalism on the bottom tier of the food chain would serve me well for the challenges ahead in life. We don't know pleasure without experiencing pain, and at the level of my planned subsistence, there was going to be plenty of discomfort. The bonus is we find the greatest joy in life is achieved when there are no expectations, and *kablam!* There you have a taste of nirvana.

For a couple of reasons, I decided to start off solo in Asia—China, and specifically in Hong Kong.

> Reason #1: During college studies, I'd connected with Eastern thought, feeling that Lao Tzu, Confucius, Buddha, and the gang may have cornered many of the answers that might come into view.
>
> Reason #2: This was to be an adventure as my entree to the globe, not as a lemming in a line of American students doing the European capitals tour with their parents' credit cards.
>
> Reason # 3: My dear friend in Japan, whom I longed to see, would be in Asia midtrip, which provided an anchor for me.

I bypassed early stops in Anchorage, Taipei, and other ports of call, to initially hit it hard in China. The rest of the world travels would then be a piece of cake, I figured. Yearning for the blast—*The Harder Path* as my friend Lord John Birt titled his bestselling book—I may have been spot-on with my vision.

Working that meager budget to fly circuitously over thirty-five hours, with multiple stops in the World Airways antiquated 747 jet—packed with budget travelers and refugees rolling in and out at each stop, whose body odors combined with the plane's, resulting in a thick stench that couldn't be escaped—was a B movie. On we bounced in the unrecognizably worn and broken threadbare seats, with the screwed and duct-taped-shut overhead bins, to Hong Kong, this city of absolute chaos where stinking poverty and ostentatious wealth juxtaposed and slammed within millimeters of each other like nowhere else on the planet.

Disembarking there—going for full intensity right at the start, even though I'd never traveled outside the United States before that point in life—would certainly exceed any expectations. Be it known this was China in 1981. Living on the ultra-budget side of the Hong Kong equation, feeling I could slice a penny into a hundred pieces to get by, was going to be onerous.

When I checked in at the youth hostel I had charted out in a nightmarish, jet-lagged delirium, I found that it was in the dark basement of a skyscraper, with no windows, stuffed with about fifty three-tier rickety bunk beds and fluttering buzzing incandescent lights. It looked like a setting for a *Terminator* movie, which was not welcoming. Feeling no desire to hang out there, I paid up for my five nights, getting a key and the rules, then hit the streets to escape and attempt to gain equilibrium. Staying awake until nightfall was essential to get the biological clock synced up and to be exhausted enough to sleep in that pit of a hostel. I went through the motions with no recall of what was experienced on day one, living life as a zombie.

After two days of wandering somewhat aimlessly as an errant pinball in the city, and returning for nary a wink of sleep, bunked in that filthy dark room smelling of feces and urine to burn the hair out of your nostrils, tossing and turning in damp and dirty sheets with heroin addicts moaning and groaning though the night from missing their fix, I decided it was time to change the game or lose my shit completely.

Sleep deprivation had taken over and I wasn't sure if I'd had a bath in three or four days. Becoming so desensitized, so used to the pungent smells of all things unkempt and unhuman on the plane stuffed with refugees, and in the rat hole of the youth hostel, my sense of smell had been stunted by the brain, for self-preservation. I do recall various times in my travels when folks had described me as "ripe," but for now from a relative perspective as a street urchin, everything was a-okay, hygiene-wise.

One might think, "Well, you are miserable and at risk and have $850 in your pocket—go find a decent hotel rather than the two-dollar-a-night hostel, you fool!" But being committed to a yearlong adventure wouldn't accommodate such luxury; the mandatory toughing it out required abject stubbornness. This intense discipline and frugality would continue for my entire worldly walkabout, with much learned in the dregs. I found a back alley of food stalls near the hostel where I took meals of egg concoctions, BBQed pigeons, soups, squid, and some other unrecognizable foods, along with homemade candies, dried meats, sea creatures, and seaweeds to stuff in the backpack. The patrons here were impoverished, grunting, and slurping the grub that sold for pennies.

I decided to catch the ferry out to Victoria Peak on Hong Kong Island, now the location of the most expensive homes in the world, for some fresh air. Broken down, scared, and fried beyond words, I was desperate for divine intervention. *Never felt so alone.* There wasn't a soul to connect with, no friendly faces, and it seemed as if even God had forsaken me. Of course, my international travel social skills to aid in connecting hadn't been forged yet, and in that present molasses, it was hard knocks. Spending a couple weeks in China before going to Japan, I seemed to be running out of time to get my bearings in this populous city and appreciate it. Prayers swirled in my head.

I made my way on foot out to the docks where the ferries were moored along with age-old Chinese junks, humongous nondescript freighters, and all manner of floating contraptions. It was time to burn the twenty-five-cent fare on the ferry. This brisk morning, even in my muted condition, I was overcome with the diesel fumes at the boarding plank, the belching thick blue-and-white clouds of smoke, oily to the tongue and lungs, piercing my brain's protective sensory shield. The water at the dock was littered with trash of every sort—plastic bags, food scraps, dead birds, and items defying ID, all in a swirling rainbow-colored petrol glaze atop the water. I rumbled over the metal walk—*clang, boom, whoop*—onto the ferry, one that probably should have been decommissioned, with its time-worn deck, whitish walls with light blue railings, all weathered, rusted, and stained. Making a beeline for the bow to trade the fumes for fresh air, I gazed out onto the busy strait as the boat gurgled and lurched away from the dock. It was off to the island.

A slight breeze in the hair helped settle me down a bit and lift spirits. About the time I was capturing a modicum of peace, I felt a presence behind me, something very creepy, cold, and eerie. Slowly turning, I faced a short, dark-skinned man of mixed race, with a deep, jagged scar from ear to ear. Someone had done a wicked number on him, ala the Joker of Batman fame.

"Boy, I was going to slit your throat," he said in a gravelly voice and unrecognizable accent. "You look so fresh! You are a lucky punk that something told me not to kill you. So, you will live today. I've been following you all day. You are in danger here, you silly boy. It is time to go home while you can."

In my depleted condition I was a wreck, but to him must've looked like filet mignon wrapped in a bow. I groped for a response.

"Well, thank you," I said, showing no emotion whatsoever, not having the energy to shit my pants.

Then—*poof*—he vanished. I had arrived at Hong Kong Island.

I barely remember the visit there except for an old photo from the Peak I took, treasured ever since. I spent the day exploring thoroughly, harboring my intense and hard-to-grasp personal struggle that had somewhat eased. Then it was back to the hostel, the only home I knew and would afford in Hong Kong.

After a return to Kowloon and another marginal night of sleep in the dungeon, I was about to truly fall apart. It was like a bad acid trip without the acid, feeling out of sorts with senses altered and bizarre sensations—tingling, hot, cold, and jittery feelings in random-order rotations, with objects seeming closer and then farther away at times for instances without cause. The feelings of stress, helplessness, and being radically out of my element were overwhelming. I clutched my hands together with all my might praying for relief, deathly afraid and thousands of miles from anything I knew. Things were not as foreseen. I fought back the urge to call home and scare my poor parents. *Why did I come here?*

There is an answer for the why, found in ever-present, underlying reasons for time and place. Cosmic swirling energy—you catch waves, go through portals, momentarily it seems. Surreal vibes, out-of-body reveals, communion with singularities, and one-in-a-trillion chance occurrences are part of the symphony that defines our path if we are tuned in. I imagine that most all our daily lives incorporate some albeit unrecognizable smidgens of this, and it is all part of the plan. Miraculous and inexplicable things are meant to be, and as additives, reoccurring dreams and premonitions can be clues concerning future events.

In that vein, what happened next would be one of two mystical revelations that I'd never experienced prior and have never since revisited. Encounters conjuring unique energies, both instances occurring on this, my virgin Orient adventure. Again, things that are meant to be.

As I stumbled out of the hostel at the break of dawn in a new level of delirium, surrender was imminent. The brief respite on the ferry bow and explorations the previous day, excepting the dark soul's interruption, signaled there was hope of getting the wheels back on. I just needed a longer and sustained interlude that was coming.

Wobbling to a local park and finding a mud puddle under a drinking fountain, I began smearing the slurry on my backpack, boots, and clothing. As Scarface had orated to me, looking like a newborn fawn with a bright blue backpack, the price tag practically dangling off it, and crisp new hiking boots—damn, it screamed, "Hi, I'm fresh meat…come eat me!"

Now, remembering the benefits of doing the phone removals in downtown Detroit that one summer, it was going to be about looking very grubby. Follow the same formula—get dirty. Why hadn't I learned from my experience?

We don't always get a second chance to learn the same lesson. If you look like you aren't worth a dime, people won't bother you, and as a student traveler you get a hall pass—and a second bite at the apple.

After ceremoniously mud bathing, somewhat relieved, I had received my much-needed second baptism. Directly next to the fountain and mud pit, there was a park bench. I took a couple slogging steps and popped aboard, my backpack securely gripped in place with both arms through the straps, holding tight to that lifeline. I was baptized but still torn up, wrapped in insecurity, suffering radical sleep deprivation, and on the verge of passing out. Who could imagine what my body chemistry looked like at that moment?

Starting at about 7 a.m., as I was transfixed and staring into space, nonstop tears flowed a river ride on a Magical Mystery Tour. All day, people walked by, waved at me, talked to me, and beckoned others over to observe this statue of a traveler. I barely noticed. I was as unresponsive as an insect in a spider's web under paralysis from its venom—powerless to move or even twitch. With those natural body chemicals gone haywire under the stress, there was no turning back. Everything progressed like a low-budget short film rolling by in slow-mo. It went on and on without notion of time or place.

Twelve hours or more later, I recall a brilliant dazzling orange ball of sun sliding down below the horizon. This unscripted mass purging, unprecedented in scale, had provided a desperately needed total emotional core dump and release, with the mind and body jettisoning everything eating at me, just in the nick of time. I rose refreshed, clear, and new, my clothing soaked in the tears; years of anything unpleasant and memories of such, along with any self-doubt I'd instigated and all worries, seemed to have been wiped clean. It was a life-changing metamorphosis.

Coming to grips with the physical world and recognizing the dehydration caused by the nonstop tears, along with a gnawing hunger, I rambled off to take in my dinner feast of pigeons and accouterments in this amazing city. When I exchanged smiles with a group of workers in the familiar alley, they waved me over to dine with them, then splurged and bought us all beers. The celebration was on as we laughed together, not understanding a single thing that was said.

I had accomplished my stated objective of opting for the harder path to steel myself, albeit painfully, and having survived the gauntlet, was ready with newfound energy to take on the world once more.

A quick visit to the Portuguese colony-turned-gambling-mecca of Macau, and then a 180-degree cultural flash on a journey to Canton, China, had me on the move again. In Canton, I may have seen two white people and felt like a modern-day Marco Polo as throngs of Chinese followed me everywhere, wanting to touch me and talk to me.

After that toe dip in China, I arrived in Japan to visit my friend there and spend a month exploring. Like my kids would tell me forty years later, "We loved the traveling with you, Dad, but the best part is always our friends along the way." Indeed, I was hoping to find peace in Japan. In this fascinating country, I would reap the rewards of that muddy yet fiery purging in Hong Kong.

I was fortunate to have as my emissary Kenya, an American-educated Japanese student of stellar character, who I had become "pen pals" with after meeting him at a mutual friend's New Jersey wedding. Looking back over sixty years, I must say he has been the most influential person in my life, having a manner both worldly and otherworldly about him. We seemed to feed off each other's differences and mutual addiction to adventure.

In every conversation, Kenya played the perfect listener, engaged and then carefully electing whether to respond or not. Not to say he wasn't bright as anyone for lacking a response—quite the contrary—he always had a timely anecdote for any situation. Listening and withholding immediate response was not my forte, and it would take forty more years for that to sink in after much study, including my first Al-Anon exposure in my fifties. He had a tongue-in-cheek humor and just exemplified the measured fine art of human communication, dispensing impeccable wisdom at the critical moment.

"Hmmmmm," he'd respond often, nodding politely. This, when he wasn't asked a question, or the comment was anything from ridiculous to complex. He had learned the art of patience, as a teen guiding worldwide for Japanese tourists with Japan Airlines. And man, did he have it.

On arrival, Ken, as I called him, met me at Narita Airport, and we jumped on the packed high-speed train into Tokyo. I was in for another high-intensity, mind-melting culture shock. I barely comprehended what was going on around me. So many bodies moving at such a pace and so much nonstop stimulation totally and completely blew me away.

I kept close to Ken as we rolled into Tokyo and his apartment, which must have been two hundred square feet in total. Once I acclimated, I had an incredible adventure. The restaurants with the glorious Japanese food in even the smallest dives, the bizarre bars featuring everything from S&M shows to punk rock disco, the museums, the legendary stores, the markets, the music, the lights, the people, the swarms—I will never forget. But there was way more. I was living in emoji-land before Americans even had a clue. While the Japanese adopted many of our traditions and consumerism, in the '70s and '80s they took ours to another level, resulting in Americans now incorporating the Japanese versions. A fascinating cross-cultural melding has been the consequence.

Ken asked me if I'd like to visit his brother, mother, and father on the Izu peninsula during Children's Week, a national tradition that celebrates family, children's personalities, and happiness. Bingo.

"But it would probably bore you," he quipped, "You can have my apartment to yourself, and with all the girls and fun here in Tokyo, you'd probably prefer to stay here, and I completely understand."

"No, no!" I cried out. "I'd love to visit there; it would be an honor."

I was about to have one of the finest, most satisfying cultural encounters of my young life, and not only that, but more importantly, begin to understand where this guy was coming from by meeting his accomplished, interesting, warm, and inviting family. I must say I would wind up a bit envious of how well-rooted they were, although envy is a sin to be eschewed. My visit with them would set the table for being hosted by friends around the world and me, in turn, hosting them and their families over the years. Family is everything, and where there was somewhat of a lack in my family ties, I've made friends a family of choice—a never-ending life quest and mantra.

We arrived in the Yamamoto family's village, worlds away from the hustle and bustle of Tokyo. Where in Tokyo commercialism ruled, here Shinto traditions set the pace. Walking the narrow-packed dirt streets towards the home, I noticed various art hangings, mostly of vibrant, feather-light paper or plastic-made koi—a staple of celebrations—adorning the simple stone facades. It was fantastic and dreamlike, with the art bursting in colorful movement at the slightest breeze, as if in a virtual 3-D art museum.

My memories of the visit almost forty years ago to that modest home remain distinct. Buzzing with love and energy, we dined on exotic local foods in their home atop tatami mats. The food was exquisite and, though I prided myself on my knowledge of the country's cuisine, most was unrecognizable.

"What are these?" I asked Ken, pointing to some small, dried fishes. "And this fabulous vegetable medley that your mom is serving? Delicious!"

He didn't have a clue, so he asked her in Japanese. Adorned in traditional Japanese fashion, she went through a series of explanations in almost mime-like dances from Kabuki theatre, which I followed with glee. Then she stopped and, looking at me while smiling ear to ear, waited for Ken to translate.

"She said these are some vegetables we grow and some that are gathered on the mountainside. Most of them they don't have names for."

"And the fishes, what species are they?"

"Just tiny fishes they catch in the nets. Whatever they can get that day."

His mom looked at me to see if I got the message. I rubbed my stomach and licked my lips in delight, then made a small bow. She was pleased.

As dinner rolled on, we drank sake to excess with Ken's highly animated, Renaissance man of a father, who was a fisherman, mason, carpenter, farmer, philosopher, you name it. He was an emblem of strength—lean, sinewy, with a leathery glowing skin shaped by the elements of land and sea, and an expert storyteller despite the language-barrier-imposed limitations.

We got so intoxicated with his father jumping about, waving his arms around, talking a thousand miles an hour to me in Japanese, and Ken trying to keep up in the translation that, in a beautiful scene, we all just broke down laughing uncontrollably from the belly for about ten minutes. A fabulous night ended as we all slept well and comfortably on the futons placed on the wooden flooring.

The next day, Ken invited me to his elementary school, where he visited teachers and communed with the kids as part of Children's Week. The school was incorporated into a Japanese garden, a tranquil place for learning. In impromptu fashion, I became a special guest—an American student to speak English with them, which all Japanese students of that time coveted and their families paid tidy sums for. I had received many unsolicited offers in Tokyo and recall considering moving there after my travels to do just that and be paid handsomely. To their delight, I deftly answered their questions about things like Mickey Mouse and cannabis, which fascinated them. As they saw me as one who had many of the answers, I returned to the school several more days to "teach" the kids and hang out, as well as enjoy the surroundings alone. So sweet.

After the visit to Izu, I was chomping at the bit for Kyoto, the ancient capital and epicenter of Japanese culture, and setting for books, stories, and art. Once there, I would experience the next cataclysmic tsunami jolt to my being, at the world-famous Ryoanji Temple.

The standards of the youth hostels and ryokans (traditional inns) in Japan eclipsed in quality the pit in Hong Kong. The clean, orderly hostel in Kyoto had a communal table for breakfast, perfect for chatting up fellow world trekkers. Searching for answers wrapped in the mysteries of Kyoto, I was going to stay for at least ten days and would meet travelers from many nations. One fellow was a reserved and kind Swiss traveler—my opposite—with whom I struck up a conversation as we perused some worn-out travel books from the hostel's collection. We quickly determined that we had a similar bucket list.

I had visited some other worthy sites in town, but after much reading on the subject was holding back on the lauded Ryoanji visit. I was waiting for the perfect day in time and space. Finally, taking various aspects into account, I felt this was going to be that day. At the communal table, I studied the last document I could find on the topic—a tattered French booklet on Ryoanji.

"Ryoanji—a special place, right?" the Swiss man began as he noticed me ogling the pamphlet.

"Yes, I've been pondering it, and today is the day. Perhaps we can go together now to beat the crowds."

"It is a highlight to me, something I've looked forward to for years. I am fascinated by the lore. I'm planning to spend the day there."

Having read tales of other visitors' mind-bending and out-of-body experiences there, we departed the youth hostel that sunny morning with high expectations of what we would behold at the sacred place. Quietly walking through the ancient capital, we contained our excitement regarding what lay ahead.

On arrival at opening time, we acknowledged without words that we would stroll the surrounding gardens independently, then tackle the fabled central rock garden last. I moved at a snail's pace, absorbing every detail in the gardens, the ponds, the torii gate, each individual rock, plants, and even insects, in solemn preparation for the prize that awaited.

The moment was to come as we entered the main Zen Garden. The plan involved arriving with a clear mind and open spirit, carefully working at finding angles and perspectives that would lock me into catching a wave of the supernatural. Except for an occasional glance, I was careful to not get in my new-found friend's or others' way. Not being able to get connected, I got creative, choosing certain yoga-esque poses and utilizing different breathing techniques to facilitate an encounter with another world.

I spent a couple of hours patiently wrestling with the garden for a breakthrough, focusing on different rocks in the Zen display, and on the various renowned interpretations. Renditions involved anything from a mother tiger and her cubs fording water, to describing it as a model of the universe or a description of infinity. My efforts were for naught. After exhausting the current energies, I needed a break and reconvened with my intrepid friend.

"I'm not getting anything here, Jeff."

"Me neither—it's cool but isn't really happening in the way I'd envisioned."

We had both concluded that it was just not meant to be. Quite possibly we had worked too hard and thwarted any possibility of a revelation. We headed despondently for the exit around the side of the structure that guarded the Rock Garden. Suddenly, we both froze in place as the Magical Mystery Tour Part Two unfolded.

We were looking out at a simple circular disc with a trickle of water going through a bamboo shoot as is seen in many Japanese gardens. At its face, it was pretty much an afterthought, an arraignment common as carrots.

Somehow, however, it captivated and locked us in. We both stood transfixed for what seemed like hours but might've been thirty to sixty minutes as tears rolled down both of our faces and soaked our shirts, much as they had with me in Hong Kong, but tears now of a different ilk. Once again, people passed us, probably asking if we were okay, but we did not respond at all. Then at the exact same time, we looked at each other, then back at the fountain, and nodded quietly. These two travelers who really did not know each other had accessed an energy, a portal, and a life lesson together. I found out later that this little place was called the Garden of Contentment, which made perfect sense after the struggle we had at the Zen Garden minutes earlier. *Wham-oo!*

My mother saw me as a malcontented soul and was right. She had suffered a Cinderella childhood without the ball, and had come to a point where she was content in her life.

I always asked her, "How can you be happy not traveling, not doing this, or not doing that?"

"Jeff, I am content. I hope someday you will be and pray you will settle yourself someday."

This was a lesson for me that I'd had to go back to many times in life, but quite frankly had not integrated. Understanding the message of the garden of contentment—"Be here now," living one moment and day at a time, and finding joy in the simple things in life—resonated. Keeping realistic expectations or none, to avoid disappointment, and accepting gifts in life that are free for the taking, are keys to serenity and happiness.

After the Orient's culture shock and bodily reshuffling—in a good way—the next stop was the Hawaiian Islands. Compared to where I had been thus far, the islands would be a vacation, as they were relatively unspoiled and livable in those early '80s.

Conquering all the islands in the chain without much of a pre-plan would take a couple months or so. I would suck it all in, reveling in the glory of nature in the rainforests, reefs, waterfalls, sacred places, canyons, and beaches.

Honolulu was the stop for World Airways from Japan, so I began in that zoo. They call the USA the world's melting pot, and Honolulu is the epicenter of the melt. I was accustomed to uber-stimulation now, so I took the city in stride—again on the bottom layer of society, where I saw myself as a humble yet educated beggar, melding with locals and seeing the underbelly. Riding below the glitz of the resort-bound tourists, you learn a hell of a lot, not just about ancient culture, which I devoured at every opportunity and outpost, but about the current vibe. As an add-on to my immersion, I read Michener's monster historical novel *Hawaii* while there, which provided context.

With the absence of affordable options, the YMCA—Young Men's Christian Association—downtown would be my home for a week. The Y was more than a bit sketchy, a rundown den of degenerates and thieves at that time, hardly evoking Christian living, and exuding a definitively aggressive homosexual bent. Not being bigoted, this did not bother me too much even though I was straight, since I was experienced at deflecting interested parties. Various prostitutes, petty drug dealers, and other unsavory characters hung out there and outside of the building—where an even lower grade of human hustled the patrons continually.

Coming home after a luxury night of imbibing at a beachfront dive bar, I was hit on by a stunningly beautiful creature. In my softened state, she—or perhaps he—convinced me to join in on a walk along a full moonlit Waikiki beach, where they then solicited me in the shin-deep water of the Pacific. As a twenty-two-year-old man-boy with the associated hormones, offers such as this were tempting and with the right person, the setting was heaven on earth.

I was taken by the aura of this soul, the perfect engaging face of a golden Thai doll, their movements, and their rhythmic enchanting voice all adding to the allure. However, in a snap, it came clear this person was *kathoey*—a transgender person—and this one likely a prostitute and possibly a thief. Self-control, a life skill, kicked in. I attempted to politely excuse myself but the kathoey would not have this.

"Jeff, you know I want you and you want me; let me share with you, my love. Please. It will feel soooo good, I promise."

"No, I cannot. I'm very sorry. I must go now."

"Why not? Do you not find me attractive?"

"Yes, you know I do, but you are kathoey and I'm sorry to waste your time."

At this they became enraged, stomping, splashing, and screaming as I exited the water for higher ground to avoid an altercation. The romance was over.

"No, I'm no kathoey! You are kathoey! You, you! You, not me! F^&k you! F*^ You!"

A close call! I scampered off through the sand, taking a roundabout route to the Y. Not a saint, but I have been reasonably careful with sexual encounters, which has kept me alive over the years.

The next day I hitchhiked to the north shore of Oahu for a few days of body surfing misadventures, great food, and beaches, sleeping in a beachfront park under the stars at night, which further stimulated my appetite for the other islands. My Oahu experience did somehow illuminate the fact that if I ever returned and hustled in Honolulu, working in real estate, there was a small fortune to be made there. Such a desirable location for most all wealthy Asians and Americans, it was bound to boom, which it did with both good and bad effects. But for now, it was time to explore the other islands and their natural bounty.

I had found a cheap, early-morning flight that would land me on the Garden Island—Kauai. The airport buildings there seemed like a collection of huts, surprisingly not blown away by the DC-9's take-offs and landings on the short airstrip. It felt primitive back then, compared to today's monstrous facility.

I set out hitchhiking with a fellow traveler I'd met at the airport. He'd been on the road for over a year, and like me his goal was to see the whole of the island and then the rest of them, starting with whatever ride he could get and moving on from there. Aloha.

It didn't take long before we were picked up by a heavy-set Hawaiian man named Kabuli, who was heading to the south side of the island. He engaged us in conversation right away. Highly animated, he proved to be a wealth of information as he rattled nonstop, getting so excited occasionally he'd spray spit on his Hawaiian shirt, puka necklace, car dash, steering wheel, and windshield while he rambled.

"Love Kauai, man. I'm third generation! Most beautiful place on earth! Aloha! Where are you guys headed?"

"Yah, yah. We are stoked to check it all out. I think we'll go as far as you are going, and you can drop us anywhere," I offered.

"I'm headed to our place. It is a cool ranch and you can grab lunch there. Good timing—we serve Hawaiian-style buffet, and the food is excellent, as you can tell," he said rubbing his belly.

Of course, we took him up on the offer, being the bums we were, and were taken to a breathtaking estate owned, we were told later, by Jim Nabors of *Gomer Pyle: USMC* fame. The buffet was a five-star feast of fresh fruits, veggies, and seafood, which we gorged on, never being able to thank Jim, our supposed host, whom we never saw there. Gomer owned this ranch in addition to his estate on Oahu, adjacent to billionaire tobacco heiress Doris Duke's fabled acreage, hers now a museum. Hula boys who worked in Honolulu at the luaus frequented this compound, which we were told was a secret hideaway where they and others would come and go, living communally, with probably thirty people staying overnight in a main house and a collection of huts on any given night.

In addition to our tour guide Kabuli, other people lived there semi-permanently, caring for the grounds and arranging fascinating trips for guests—floating down irrigation canals on innertubes through the jungle, going out fishing or whale watching on their boat, and other activities, in which we indulged. We hung out there for almost a week, even taking on small chores until it became a little uncomfortable, as Kabuli and some of the others at dinner one night implied that sexual favors were going to be required should we wish to continue the stay. That very night we were both solicited in our separate rooms, Kabuli waking me in the middle of the night, rolling his large frame onto my single bed and nearly breaking its frame, to whisper drunken sweet nothings into my ear.

With no buy-in from either of us, we were promptly booted. At the crack of dawn, we headed out, each wanting to go a different direction. After wishing each other safe, exciting adventures and lives ahead, I headed to Poipu Beach and the glorious Waimea Canyon, then back north again all the way to Ke'e Beach, spending another three weeks on fragrant Kauai.

The next island I jumped to was Maui, which would yield all the beauty imagined, along with another interesting collection of what I call "cultural experiences." Opting to start on the east side of the island's distinct contour, I splurged and rented a car from Wiki Wiki Wheels—a beat-up, sun-blistered bronze Toyota Corolla with a few hundred thousand dings and miles on it for ten dollars a day—which would double as my hotel room when I headed out Hana way for a week. It was the only thing I could find with no credit card, as Maui was an expensive destination. A deal.

I collected some gas and minor provisions, finding a spot to park overnight and sleep on the edge of Paia town, which would give me the entire next day to drive the epic Hana Road. Getting up with the sun, I would have the next sixteen hours to get to Hana, driving recklessly on stretches, known for its 620 curves and 59 bridges, pounding the stick shift, gas, and brakes on the rent-a-wreck, then taking nice breaks on the way, hiking into breathtaking scenery. I liked to drive—like a madman—and loved the tranquility on the walks in between.

Getting to Hana in the night, I parked on the edge of a tourist motel parking lot. The next day, I met a gang of local Hawaiian guys, three or four who befriended me and who I would hang with for several days as they set the pace. Going local.

One of the first activities they invited me to the following night was going to the area tourist hotels, where they would gather with tools to pop out the locks on rental car trunks, stealing all the contents. Since the cars all had stickers like Avis, Hertz, and the like, and those companies advised the renters to lock their valuables in car trunks, it was easy pickings. Duh!! The crew even made a game of it, timing each other to see how fast they could get the lock popped, grab the goodies, and return to the jungle edge to hide out. It was scary, unsavory, and fascinating all at the same time. The booty included cameras, electronics, binoculars, and clothing that was expensive on the island—as everything was imported—along with other goodies. They took what they wanted and discarded the rest in the jungle, then worked their way back along paths to where they lived and my car was parked. They hit several locations, even the one I'd parked in the previous night, and offered to let me to try it, to no avail—no thanks. Just witnessing that one night was enough for me. That night a voracious mosquito came to visit as I slept in my car—biting my face up so badly that it puffed up and the right eye swelled shut for a couple days and itched like hell. I guess that was my punishment for watching the thefts. My new friends thought it was hilarious.

Another day they invited me out, one eye and all, to a boar hunt in the jungle with their machetes and two dogs. We had been out for hours tracking pigs via their prints and feces and were well into the jungle on faint animal paths. Then, in an instant, we ran into a pack of wild pigs or boars, probably a dozen or so, snorting, some with long tusks and probably weighing sixty to eighty pounds or more, all in a sour mood.

All hell broke loose. I felt like my hair was going to catch fire as my heart pounded out of my chest, my blood pressure blasted off the charts. Their dogs defended, but to no avail, and the barks turned into wails as the boars began to tear them to pieces. I caught a glimpse of this, then it was every man for himself as we scattered, me keeping up with the slowest of the gang, lest I get left behind and be part of the boar's feast. Twenty minutes later we got roadside, somehow having made it unscathed. This was Swaney's Hawaii—not Michener's.

My visits with the boys concluded when one night, after attending a local's softball game of rivals, we headed to the bar a short walk away. I was the only white in attendance at the game and watering hole afterward, but continued to ignore the glares I had witnessed on and off all week while in Hana, even though they had intensified at the saloon. It all seemed okay.

The energy in the glorified shack of a bar was off the charts as patrons, who had already been imbibing and smoking the local ganja during the game, and we all were—blasted. Then amid all the commotion, there was a human volcanic eruption. One of the patrons, a giant Disney Moana by any standard, who had been one of the players knocking the crap out of the ball during the game, spouted out.

"Who is this haole?" he yelled, thrusting his finger at me.

This was not good news, especially in this setting, as the word *haole* is not a benevolent term. I could see the crowd roiling up as I attempted to, with guile, to deflect his attack, by smiling meekly. This did not placate him at all.

"Who brought this damned haole in here!!?"

One of my gang went over to chat him up and create an opportunity for me to escape, while another scooted me aside.

"Dude, you need to get the hell out of here as quietly and quickly as you can. Do not look at him or anyone in here again! Follow me."

He took me to the back door and instructed me. "Now, Jeff, run to your car as fast as you can because otherwise, they may beat you to death—I'm not shitting you, and we won't be able to help. Haul your ass."

"Thank you," I yelped.

I busted it as fast as I had run from the boars earlier that week—probably faster, as I'd practiced. The party was over. Dodging a certain beating, I drove to the outskirts of Hana to a secluded side road to sleep uncomfortably in my rent-a wreck at a safe distance. *Mahalo*.

Living truly local is always a learning experience and treat—not anything money can buy—as are all the best things in life for that matter. However, you must abide by a guest's golden rule: never, ever, overstay your welcome.

I had one more island I could hit, as even the cheap twenty-nine-dollar inter-island airfares were crushing the paltry budget. Visiting the Big Island next for the culture and diversity, I rented another rent-a-wreck in Kona, on the island's leeward side, that once again doubled as my motel. I spent the next few days getting my bearings, traveling, and scouting outdoor sleeping spots. This almost got me to Hilo on the long route south through Volcanoes National Park, but I was turned back by a lava flow over the road that nearly enveloped me, as I had driven around "road closed" signs, which were not meant for me, of course. The steam, fumes, and black molten goo with cracks emitting a bright red-orange flaming blaze straight from hell scared me. As I backtracked, I realized the lava had quickly made it over a portion of the section of road I'd passed by earlier. It was nuts, but I managed to avert disaster.

After finishing off use of the car, I hitchhiked and slept in parks up and down the Kona coast. An inspiring visit to Pu'uhonua o Honaunau Park rounded out my Hawaiian Islands sojourn.

I was ready to get back stateside to California for a few weeks to connect with Dad, as promised, before taking off on the next leg of my travel adventure. If not for the fact that I was relishing my planned time that I'd never had with this man, I would've continued circumnavigating the earth, but this opportunity could not be missed. The world would still be there, but he might not. Besides, I was heading to Europe after the brief stateside stint to trek there for months. It was all good.

I had been calling Dad every few weeks at his sister's house in Palm Desert, whenever I could, for short chats. And yes, I'd called Mom from pay phones, too, and have about two minutes for each call, if not calling collect.

"How are you doing, how is Hawaii? When are you coming, Jeff?" Dad asked, every time.

"I dunno, Dad. I like it here. How about another two weeks or so? I'll let you know," I repeated each call. "Do you like the desert, Dad? You having a good time? They haven't told you to get outta there yet?" I chuckled.

"Oh yes, and no, I can stay here as long as I want to, 'til summer starts, but no longer than that. The desert's too hot in the summer, like I told you!"

He obviously did not know the golden guest rule or simply was above it all.

"I'll be there soon, Dad. I'll check the flights and call when I'm on the way."

Dad didn't have much of a role model growing up, being that seventeenth of nineteen in Harvey and Bessie's brood in that Pennsylvania hill poverty. He didn't have any real parenting skills, and I don't think he pretended to. In contrast, in raising my young children I have had the tools of the internet, books on the topic, and friends who went through the paces twenty years before me. Somewhat helpful.

Early on, Mom elbowed him out on the parenting in her overly protective style as he took to working extra jobs and doing his best to not be at the house. I do recall many pleasantries with him when I did see him, along with some serious belt whippings if he came home and Mom had any complaints about me.

The whippings were harsh, and I'd often run, but he'd eventually catch me. This didn't just happen to me, as it seemed to be standard procedure in that zip code. I witnessed kids getting the belt on their naked bottoms in their front yards. Of course, this was back when belts, paddlings in school, and the like were all part of discipline and not a ticket to the county jail, like it is today. My sister and Mom never were subjected to this treatment, thankfully—it was a father-son thang. My children have never experienced this at my hand, as I learned there were no good results to be had that way. Back then, I thought of it as the animal kingdom's mammalian biological process, until this manner of punishment finally ceased.

It all came to a head when I was about ten years old. He had me cornered and was pulling the belt off to give me a good lashing when it hit me. I was going to defend myself. I put up my fists, prepared for a battle I knew I would lose. But I was going to get my pound of flesh. He looked at me, paused for what seemed to be forever, put his belt back on, carefully finding each loop in the Wilbert blue work pants and walked away. No words were spoken by either of us during or after. None were needed.

I suppose every son has his personal story. That was the beginning of a new frontier for us. And the upcoming cross-country road trip was going to be the biggest father-son event since my fists had risen years before.

I arrived in the desert, visited with the family for dinner the first night, and after two days, got set to head out. He was ready, all packed, tank full of gas, car washed, the whole shebang. Seems he had a different idea of what this was going to be about than I did.

It took a day in the car to catch up on stories from the previous few months, and then a night at the first of a few cheap motels on the way back to Detroit. By day two, we had exhausted our travelogues and were driving quietly, just rolling along through America, stopping at some attractions on the way. It was time to flip the switch and engage him on matters of import. We had rarely talked about anything of substance, and he didn't want to share much of his life events with me, which I had stitched together from tidbits gathered from him, Mom, relatives, and other sources. I yearned for this opportunity to break this all down, figure out where he was coming from, where we were and were going to, resolute in cautiously cornering him to get the answers I sought, despite the anticipated discomfort. Taking the lead, I assumed the parental role in this quintessential coming-of-age, father-son confab.

I started out driving the 1966 Valiant down the highway one morning, with him in the passenger seat happy to watch the world roll by. I swallowed nervously as I readied myself to go deep.

"Dad, I'm glad we have made this time together. I have so many questions—some serious stuff. About your childhood.

Harvey. The coal mines. Girls. The War. You and Mom. Mom's crazy family. All that," I spit out.

There was silence. He did not even look at me. I waited for ten minutes.

"Dad, I—"

He turned to me, red in the face. "I don't want to talk about that shit!"

As I clammed up, tears rolled down his cheeks. I held back mine somehow while cruising down the interstate at seventy miles per hour.

"Dad, I—"

"Goddammit, I don't want to talk about this, Jeff!"

He was enraged. Pounding his fists on his thighs in the passenger seat, he began to sob uncontrollably. Now my tears began to fall.

"I'll jump out of this f&^*$king car!"

"Okay, okay. No worries, we won't talk about it. Sorry," I whimpered.

As we continued in silence, calm restored, no more was said about it, kind of like the end of the belt-whipping phase of life. That was it. We went through the motions of gassing up the car, stopping at another historical marker here and there, at McDonald's for hamburgers, and finding another cheap motel.

And then, with None of the Answers, we finally arrived back in Detroit at the family home. I could've been in Goa, India, meditating while riding an elephant or doing yoga on the beach, or in Iran tempting fate while exploring ancient Persian ruins, but this was my choice, without regrets.

After that, somehow our relationship seemed to flower. I would eventually move to Dallas, Texas and make a name for myself, where he became a regular visitor, always keeping it simple. We were at peace with each other. That was all that mattered, and worth more than gold.

These experiences that expanded my horizons and broke me down on numerous occasions would each leave me stronger and wiser. Now again I was poised for new frontiers—a reunion with friends in Detroit and Chicago, to be followed by my first-ever travels to Europe and beyond.

CHAPTER 6

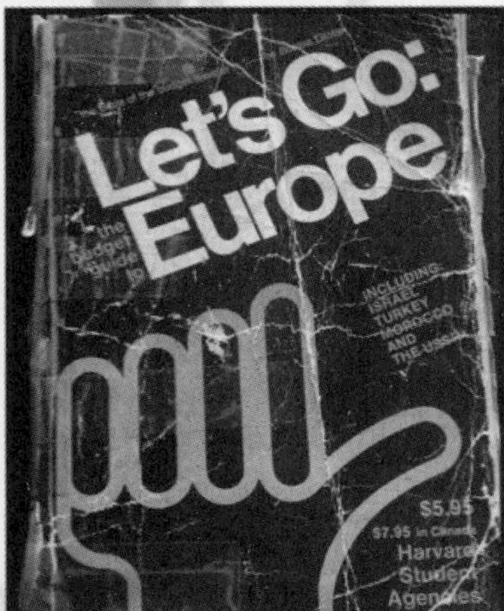

1981

Parthenon - Hitchin UK - Let's Go! - Moscow - Roma

CHAPTER 6

THE BULL BY THE HORNS

From breaking down shamelessly in Hong Kong, where I had boldly struck out and exposed myself to the planet, to finding my Far East family and peace in Japan, the vibe had changed.

Swinging back stateside, I'd had the big father-son talk, although there was not much to it, seemingly coming up empty-handed, but not. I found that our expectations can lead us to disappointment, but in this case, when that fleeting feeling crossed my mind, I wouldn't allow it to win the day. Accepting the experience with Dad was part of growing spiritually as a man and finding my place in this world.

With all that in my proverbial pocket, now I had the opportunity to take what I'd learned, seared onto my soul on that Eastern-leg world loop, and put it to use. By testing ourselves and opening to possibilities in our hearts, minds, and spirit, we become somewhat sagacious and more sternly confident to let it all hang out. Ready to grab the bull by the horns.

After a brief Midwest love fest that included home cooking and connecting with my buddy, Craig, and friends in Chicago for a wild extended weekend—during which drinking heavily all day at a Chicago Cubs baseball game lit the match that left us all inebriated into the wee hours—I would set off to London with Craig for my first transatlantic adventure. He would prove to be a great travel partner, seeing the world through a similar lens due to his family lot in life, engineering education, budget strain, naivety, and zeal for exploration off the beaten path in search of culture, art, and the outdoors. Driven in our quest for adventure, craving all the answers, we were seekers.

We wanted to make the most of our trip, spending little, even making a pact not to utilize a purchased ninety-day Eurail pass early on, holding out to the bitter end before stamping it. Getting around was thumbing time, the Uber of then.

While in London, taking in all the sites, we discussed our course, which we hadn't done so much, keeping things loosey-goosey with budget and goals in mind.

"I'm thinking once we do London, we head out to the countryside and see what we can see," I suggested. "I'll be ready for some air, after chewing the street grime here. Then at some point, we cross over to France and work our way around the continent counterclockwise, taking in everything we can. Of course, we do the Mediterranean to the max, hitting all the big capitals on the way with whatever finds us in between."

"That's what I was thinking," Craig said. "For sure, Italy and Greece are on the got-to-go list, and perhaps we get all the way back up to Scandinavia at some point."

"Perfect. We will do it all and let the current take us. Who the hell knows where we'll be some days!"

Then a hard-smacking, hand-reddening high five, a bear hug, and it was on!

Our trimmed-down, thirty-pound packs held just essentials. Funny how you can learn to get by with so little in this consumption-crazed world, the ultimate freedom I aspire to relive daily. The one luxury afforded was the 1980 version of *Let's Go Europe*, referred to by backpackers as the Bible. The inch-and-a-half-thick paperback was our only travel reference. Nowadays, it sits on my bookshelf looking prehistoric, with its cover tattered and taped together, cryptic notes in various color ink written inside, including how to say *hello*, *how are you*, *goodbye, where is the restroom*, and a few other essentials in ten languages. Its yellowed, flaking pages, now in their maturity, smell like the decomposing wood they were made of, printed with the primitive maps and limited information it contained. What a blessing it was to travel in such a way back then, feeling akin to Columbus, Magellan, Cook, or Lewis and Clark, never knowing what the next turn, day, or night would bring.

London was not a budget-friendly city a la Hong Kong, though the sights were worth the hassle. It was a li'l tricky to hitch a ride out of town with all the traffic and confusing, crazy freeways, and us with no helpful maps or modern-day GPS—just the *Let's Go* book, which was useless for that purpose. After trudging and navigating the freeways and all their intersections, albeit hazardously, we did, however, get our first of many rides on a lorry, which picked us up on the shoulder of a busy northbound highway.

"Not a safe place to hitch here, blokes. Where you two headed?" the grisly driver barked over the noise of the traffic roaring by. *Whoosh, whirrrrr, honk honk, rrrrrrrrrr, ppppppp…*

"North or west as far as we can get," I offered.

"North it is. Get in back—quick!"

We hopped in over the well-worn and rattling tailgate of the diesel flatbed full of tools and whatnot, then sped down the freeway in that open back, white-knuckling it for at least an hour on the way out of town until we got into rural areas, operating at a speed more merciful. There was no way to communicate with the driver. When the ride was over, and eventually it was, we found ourselves in a small, nondescript town an hour north of London at dusk.

"Well lads, here you go, hope you liked the scenery. I've got a delivery to make. Have a good night," he joyfully bellowed, waving as he pulled off.

"Thank you," we chimed as we went in search of some desperately needed food, water, and a cheap bed.

Hitchhiking was a somewhat common mode of transportation back then—seems the world was a little less crazy of a place with a few billion fewer souls. As related, I'd hitched successfully in the States and Hawaii, so I was seasoned, knowing you had to prepare for anything and have an open agenda. In Japan, I recall giving up hitching because the folks would repeatedly just pick me up and bring me to the closest train station. Smiling in a friendly way and pointing to the station as we pulled up, they would even offer up yen for a gratis train fare—which I accepted.

The next bright sunny morning, we walked to the town's edge and stuck out the ol' thumbs again. Ready for a great day to be had, we got promptly picked up by a scruffy plumber who had us squeeze into the cab of his compact pickup that so reeked with the smell of scotch whiskey, I thought I had climbed into the actual barrel. The back of his pickup was covered with a homemade wooden covering that resembled a barrel—hence my analogy—and stuffed with the tools of the trade, which afforded us the VIP seats up front. Yes, he had been drinking and was verging on drunk that fine morning. Apparently deciding to skip his morning work, he took us on a wild adventure into nearby green hills. As we sat in the grasses sharing his scotch well past noon, he vividly recounted various battles from years before involving Scots, Brits, and Irishmen. His passion for storytelling had us feeling as if we were witnessing the battles. We were there years ago, it seemed, or in some Mel Gibson account of those times.

When he dropped us off, he suggested Edinburgh, Scotland, and the International Film Festival and Fringe Festival as a preferred and timely destination, which was a splendid idea. Then he left us off at some intersection way out in the middle of nowhere late in the afternoon with weather rolling in. You must pay to play now or later.

The hitchhiking adventure was about to take a tougher turn. Very few cars made their way by, and we were unable to get a ride as we walked north along a small country road. Hitching solo can be hard enough, but two guys hitchhiking was a taller order. We modified the plan so only one of us would be visible while the other lay hidden in weeds on the side of the road. It looks safer to be just one guy. Then when someone pulled over, we would say, "Oh, and my buddy is coming as well; here he comes now," which over half the time would freak the driver into peeling out, leaving us standing there in burnt-rubber vapor.

After a few hours, it started to sprinkle. The scotch had worn off, we didn't have more to keep the buzz, the sun was setting, and there was no hope of a ride. Walking a little farther alongside a barbed wire fence which met a corner intersection of a smaller farm road, we noticed a large tree inside the fence lines, contrasting with the barren green grass that went on for miles beyond. It looked inviting, so we hopped over and set up Craig's tiny two-man tent. In fact, this would be the only time it we used it, as key parts of it would break while packing it up during what would be a hasty departure.

Inside the tent, which was barely holding up as a downpour began and intensified through the night, we fought to manage the puddles that formed inside, and both inched toward the middle. We were practically on top of each other, but considering the lake forming in there we didn't mind. We had some stale crackers and a couple tins of sardines which, driven by belly-cramping hunger, we choked down. It was just misery; we would have given our souls for just a cup of hot broth. When our goose-down sleeping bags began to get wet, there was not much we could do except pray for the rain to stop.

The next morning, the rain having slowed to a light shower, I got up and made my way outside the tent for my morning constitutional. A bowel movement at this point was going to be a grand pleasure after the grief suffered through the night. I walked around to what was the back of the tent with the fence twenty feet behind me and some cover from the large tree's trunk which was probably twenty feet away as well, and pulled my pants down to assume the position in getting back to nature. Craig still lay lazily in the soaked, bowing, and nearly collapsing tent.

Looking up amidst my healthful release, I spotted a bull not fifty yards away, running across the field toward the tent. I had to blink a couple times, then tensed up a bit as there was an interruption in my business. The beast continued to rumble, closing in. As he reached the front of the tent, with me in his sights, I could literally feel the earth moving, vibrating my bones from the pounding of his hoofs. He must have been well over a thousand pounds, with immense horns twisting out and up at least two feet long, a black glistening nose the size of the largest grapefruit adorned with a shining metal ring of pride about four to five inches in diameter with snot dripping out of it in half a dozen gooey strings of various lengths as he snorted his disapproval of my trespassing.

I didn't move, bent over with some makeshift toilet paper in my hand and half of a fresh turd pile under my bottom on the rocky wet green grass. It was surreal, and I was petrified.

Then the dead awoke.

"What's going on out there?" Craig shouted from in the tent.

The bull's head nodded back and forth and side to side like a bobblehead doll, puzzled at the sound coming out of the tent. I guess he had never seen a talking tent before.

"Well Craig, there is a bull at your front door, probably about a thousand-pounder, listening in. He doesn't look happy, and I'm crouched here with my pants down in the middle of taking a shit and don't know what to do."

"It's probably harmless. I heard some cows, I think it's just a cow, dude. It'll go away or you can scare it off. You're always exaggerating."

"Oh. No, I don't think so!"

The bull just stood there, clearly not knowing what quite to make of this, which was good news since whether confused or entertained, he just maintained his position, so neither of us was going to die just yet.

"Why do you think it's a bull, bro?"

"Well, it's really big, got long curled horns and a nose bigger than your fists with a ring in it and snot running out of it. I think that's a freakin' bull."

"Jeff, you might be right. It could be."

"So, what the hell am I supposed to do?"

"If it's a bull, I think you need to climb that tree or run like hell."

I pulled myself together and slowly wiggled up my pants while getting out of my crouch. I wasn't quite sure that I had wiped my butt, but at that point it didn't really matter, as the bull kept his eye on me watching every move. I had to figure out how to get a clean scamper to that barbwire fence and over it quickly lest the bull gore me.

I took a couple steps to the left as he gracefully countered my move. Shuffling to the right, the bull matched me, staying exactly opposite my position at 180 degrees. A couple more steps and shuffles, and the bull mirrored every move.

I had witnessed bullfights in Mexico, but was no matador and didn't have the experience needed for this dance of death. I was going to have to try to juke him one time and run my ass up and over the fence, praying to not get jabbed. I scuttled back and forth again and when it seemed like I finally had him just a slight hair off-kilter, I made the dash. Taking off as fast as possible —hustling—then up and over, gouging my arms and catching some of my clothing on the barbwire as I flipped over the barrier. I looked back to see if El Toro was going to bust through the fence and mow me down, but he ran right up to it at one hundred miles per hour, then to zero on a dime—digging his arresting hooves into the rain-soaked soil.

He stood there towering over me as I lay across the divide, snorting for a couple minutes, his massive shoulders just daunting. I could smell the sweat and testosterone in that shimmering wet, blackish-brown coat of his.

"What the hell's going on out there?" Craig belted out from the tent. "Are you alive?"

"Yeah," I said, "and so is the beast. I think you need to shut up because he's coming back that way and may stomp you into a pancake."

After nonchalantly trotting back to the tent, the bull circled it, snorting again, and dismissed it. He was satisfied. The majestic and terrifying creature then trotted out to the pasture to check on his girlfriends, never looking back. Craig was silent.

"I'm thinking the coast is clear. He has gone out quite a way now. It's time to get outta Dodge."

"Cool. Come help me get this tent cleared out and taken down, and we can get out of here."

"No way, man. I'm all cut up and I've had my fill. I'll keep an eye out. Just grab the stuff and start throwing it over the fence and I'll put it together, and we can split."

City boys had learned a lesson about respecting a barbed-wire fence line, which we dared not venture past again. We'd had a narrow escape, one of many more to come.

During our hitchhiking trek through Britain, we had more interesting rides, including a wealthy English gentleman who picked us up in a lux Jaguar and, as he enjoyed our banter, brought us to his home—a castle in the country. He had his butler and staff tend to our every need—showers, laundry, even some clothes for us—and had prepared, in our honor, a five-course meal where we were introduced to his three beautiful, giggling daughters who were all a bit younger. We knew we had to get out of there, leaving the next afternoon although we were welcome to stay longer. No caving into our maddening temptations, as that would have probably been met with a loaded shotgun.

Another day started with being picked up by a nun in full regalia on the way back to her convent from a short leave. She fancied me. As Craig fell asleep in the backseat, she glowingly related her commitment to God and her lifelong chastity while she inched her hand over to my leg, rubbing it in a pleasing way while complimenting me on my good looks and sparkle. She wasn't that attractive, especially compared to the three smoking-hot daughters recently left behind, otherwise, deprived as I was, I might have taken the bait. Although I was noticeably aroused by her touch, I surprisingly had control of myself. Holy cow, that was going to be a story—oh boy!—but not. I did charm her into going out of her way to get us to a prime hitching spot so that when I awakened Craig we would be off once again.

In this manner of travel I lived centered and in the moment. Life is a rollercoaster—we G-force in our dips and we get our lovely rises, learning that it's all part of a grand plan. Just like Prof had said in college, there wasn't a free lunch out here. Still, our mantras were Smiles Go Miles and Manna Comes from Heaven—no cares, and worries be damned.

We worked our way on to Edinburgh and the festival, then south to cross the English Channel and the famous White Cliffs of Dover, and on to the European continent. Working our way through France, the Netherlands, and Belgium, then south over the next couple of months, more encounters of the ridiculous sort materialized, with bulls of a different DNA.

We sought out Brugge, that most picturesque and canal-laden city in Belgium, which, like our hometown of Detroit was to the States, was the wealthiest city in all of Europe in its heyday. After enjoying all the city had to offer, we got to the edge of town and began our hitchhiking. A priest stopped and proceeded to play host to us, taking us to his Catholic Church on the edge of the city where no one else was about. As he extolled the virtues of some of the choir boys in their photos adorning the tabernacle, things became creepy, but we continued, as we had him outnumbered. Then we were taken out to the country to his cottage, where he prepared what might have been my best meal in all of Europe: a buffet of the finest meats, cheeses, fresh vegetables, and breads, all served with bottomless Bordeaux of exquisite quality. The table with this sumptuous bounty looked like a Rubens still-life painting, and we gorged shamelessly, wiping our mugs occasionally with the fine cloth napkins provided.

He offered his guest room, which we took despite being concerned about his motives. With a wink, Craig propped a desk chair under the doorknob of the old wooden door that was the entry to the room, serving as a hurdle in case his holiness wanted to disturb us for his pleasure in the night, a la my experience with my host, Kabuli, in Hawaii. He attempted to open it after we had settled, and we explained that no further attention was needed or wanted. Then in the middle of the night, he tried again, waking us.

"I must come in. Please allow me. Please, I must."

"Monsieur, you mustn't. Do not come through that door. We are not interested in visiting with you. We are sleeping, and if you force your way, we will be at the ready."

"Okay. Then I will see you in the morning, if you insist. My room is across the way."

We woke early to depart and found another St. Regis-worthy breakfast spread in the kitchen. We partook, begrudgingly at first, and then, at our host's suggestion, made giant sandwiches that we wrapped up in the linens and stuffed in our backpacks. As we made our way to the door to leave, he offered us a ride back to town, which we accepted. There was no more drama before bidding him adieu back in town.

Excitement and potential trouble always lurked just around the corner. In Amsterdam in search of hashish, rather than the weak pot sold in the coffee shops, we came across a fellow who knew what we wanted. "Follow me to my place, and I'll get this going for you two, no trouble."

He led us to a basement quarter a few minutes from the coffee shop, opening the door to let us in. "My friend has the stuff; I'll be right back; you two make yourselves at home."

At that he left, locking the door. As we began poking about, we found hanging whips, chains, wild masks, and all manner of *Pulp Fiction* S&M gear, and determined we were in a sodomite's den. The kicker was finding a large painting showing boys in stocks, naked, bottoms exposed, and persons wearing the exact masks in line for a treat.

Panic nearly set in as we realized he had bolted the door from the outside. We finally escaped through bathroom window, without a care for the hash anymore; that was enough stimulation for the day.

I had a little black book of names, numbers, and addresses of folks I knew who lived in Europe that I'd collected up in my last year of college. Whenever feasible, we would go out of our meandering way to attempt an unannounced visit—a primitive networking and social media of the times. I had surprising success connecting on over 50 percent of those attempts. One particularly serendipitous encounter occurred in our next stop—Rotterdam, The Netherlands—certainly not a Michelin five-star destination.

I'd met some Dutch marketing graduate students at MSU who had rented a house across the street from our college party house a year prior. They lived a wild life, with keg beer constantly flowing in the kitchen and all their living room furniture on the front lawn, rain or shine. Needless to say, we got along well.

Robert Van Danoker was their ringleader, and I had his address in the li'l book. We worked our way through town and the busy streets of the seaport famous for shipbuilding, finding a four-story building on the busiest of streets.

There was a large metal security door that had obviously taken quite a beating over the years, and on both sides of its weathered panels were black buttons to buzz, in order to be let into the building. Next to each buzzer were little hard plastic scuffed up bubbles with the name of the resident inside, so you could determine which button to push. It was untidy, but after study we did find Robert's name there and began pushing the well-worn button. We got no response, so we walked the length of this building—a large city block long—and looked at other security doors to see if there was another entry, then returned to the first and gave it one last shot jamming on the button.

At that very moment, somebody yelled out of a passing car window. This was to become one of many cosmic intersections ever.

"Jeff, is that you?" It was Robert passing by, slowing from forty miles an hour as I spun around and waved. He turned back and pulled up to the curb.

"I cannot believe this—crazy! What the hell are you doing here, and where are you going?" he exclaimed as he sat there with hazard flashers on.

"We don't know; we were looking for you."

"Get in!"

We jumped in the backseat and drove off as he explained that he hadn't lived at that apartment in over a year. He had just picked up his girlfriend, who was sitting up front in the Citroen, at the airport, and on a lark was driving her by the old apartment. A one-in-one-trillion chance.

As we chatted, he told us that students from around the world were gathering that weekend at a friend's house for a massive weekend-long reunion, celebrating a promotion that one of the guys had gotten working for PepsiCo and running the operations for the north of Africa. He asked if we wanted to join in and see the old crew, and it was on. A whole weekend of hardly any sleep, eating, and drinking in a manner that was a truly Dutch tradition. We had an absolute ball. Drunken, slipping, sliding, storytelling, hugs and kisses, and the hangover to match the next day, waking on the floor in a pile. Of course, the morning cure was breakfast with a cold beer from the still-flowing kegs.

Those occurrences can only happen through divine intervention, aided by a penchant for gathering information, wanting to see old friends, and the extent I would go to do so. Many say this is a most enviable trait. The li'l black book that was useless in the Orient brought joy through connections in Europe—part of making your own luck.

Our travels led us to Paris, after which we bummed through the off-track French countryside, an incredible tourist-free experience. Mixing the art and culture of the big cities with the real life in the small pleb towns and, finally, the Riviera iced the French pastry for us.

We checked off the tourist sites in Rome and then headed out to Tuscany. Florence captured our amazement. Italy had ruled the known world for some time, 'til they decided to give it up for fashion, food, wine, love, and Ferraris. They took the best and left the rest. Marveling at the statue of David under the Duomo, an impossibly engineered structure and one of many, we engaged this culturally stacked town. I believe it was at the

Uffizi where I was stunned to witness the museum's windows left open, allowing pigeons that had served as meals for me in Hong Kong to fly in and out amongst the Italian masterworks.

We got wind of the underground nightlife in Florence and delved in. Hitting the underbelly one night, post-gelato, we bar-hopped, ceremoniously eating patrons' leftovers while quaffing down whatever beverage was abandoned, as was our custom throughout Europe. We discovered the new hot-spot, all-night disco, Space Electronic, where we danced the night away to the throbbing music, smoke machines, and lasers with an international crowd.

As it got late—intoxicated, in need of air, and having lost track of my friend—I hit the exit. Out on the small side street, gathering my bearings, I was heading on autopilot to the ratty nearby room we'd rented for a few nights. Suddenly, passing by an alley, I was pulled almost airborne into the darkness and held tight with a knife to my throat. I could feel the blade, which was about to cut my skin. Luckly, I was so buzzed that I remained very loose, calm, and didn't twitch. The assailant demanded my money, and upon getting the few lire in my pocket, off he ran. Fortunately, he was in too much of a hurry to discover the trusty money belt on under my pants with my traveler's checks and passport inside.

Life on the road in this manner defines adventure and lessons afforded. Boarding a crowded bus in travels, at a time when my buddy and I had been tied to the hip for a couple months, it meant striking up a conversation with a gal who was complaining about her running buddy. I concurred and shared some complaints about my friend that were probably unfounded. As

I finished, out of the corner of my eye between the squish of people standing on the crowded bus, I saw him frowning at me, having heard the whole thing. My heart just dropped, and I felt like a turd. As we departed the bus, he confronted me about it. Of course, I apologized, but he was so pissed I thought he was gonna punch me in the face. We are all human—flawed and subject to acts of stupidity.

With that experience, I figured that none of us can spend too much time with any one person. Too much time by ourselves and we probably couldn't even spend too much time with Jesus Christ. After a few weeks it'd be, "Come on Jesus, you're a cool dude and all, but could you give me a break? Do you have something else you could do? Some miracles, healings, or something else somewhere? Of course, before you leave, you could turn this water into wine for me. I'm ready!"

We are social beings but require balance in our social lives for sanity's sake. So, after traveling for months with my friend, not counting a few short breaks when we'd run off with women we met along the way, we decided to split up and reconnect at the American Express office in the next big city along our circuitous route. First, however, we would hit Turkey and the ancient city of Istanbul. This city that has played such a role in history, certainly delivered on all cylinders, featuring Hagia Sophia, Topkapi Palace, Blue Mosque, Grand Bazaar, and everything in between and underneath the city's labyrinth—hosted by some of the friendliest people on the planet.

We arrived and bedded down in uber-cheap accommodations near the mosque, not the best part of town, but shelter was needed in big cities. The rooms were spartan with nasty plastic-coated mattresses, and a community bathroom and showering area par for the course for our price range at about fifty cents a night. The hot rooms stunk, with floors so greasy you needed to shuffle around to avoid falling, resulting in patrons there dragging their mattresses up to the rooftop via a ladder and stuffing them through the roof hatch to escape the heat and stench and sleep under the stars. Sweet.

Next day, in the early evening on the first floor, we discovered a simple open-air bar with a little twelve-inch-diagonal, flickering-black-and-white TV pinned up in a corner at ten feet, and a collection of locals with wrinkled happy faces, stained and missing teeth, and ragged clothes chewing khat while smoking hash and drinking heavily. There was a limited selection of libations at the bar, all local and unfamiliar to us.

The popular-at-the-time TV series *Dallas* was showing on the tiny, rabbit-eared television. The local Turks, in considerably higher numbers than we'd seen at the bar at any time, were pressed out onto the sidewalk, eyes glued to the show, giving it the feel of the event that it was. I found the scene humorous and the energy compelling, so we slid in and asked for a drink at the bar, pointing to the liquor that the locals were sipping. It was a strong, bitter brew. A couple of the guys made us some space as we were the only Yanks in the joint, and suddenly we were attracting as much attention as the show.

"Do you like *Dallas*?" one of the patrons inquired.

"Yeah, I like it. I think I'm going to move there when I go back to the USA. For some reason Dallas is calling to me."

At that point, it seemed all the guys in the bar turned and looked at me. Hoped that was a good thing.

"You are going to Dallas? You going to be like J.R.! You are going to be rich and be with all the beautiful girls!"

"Well, I don't think so, but I'm going to go to Dallas to work."

"No! Everybody in Dallas is rich—you will be very rich! We will come visit you there—we want to go to Dallas."

At this point, they all started to get out papers and pens, sharing them around and writing their names, addresses, and phone numbers. The one ringleader who had the better command of English collected them all for us.

"You must call us from Dallas. You must have us come to Dallas—we want to visit you there."

"Okay, I will, I will. I promise," I replied, feeling no ability of ever being able to comply.

Politely, we finished off the episode, and the drinks that kept coming gratis. We passed on the khat and other goodies afforded us, as we had seen the movie *Midnight Express*, which tempered our desire to partake of such in Turkey.

"We will come to Dallas! And we want to see the Dallas Cowboys football! Go Cowboys!" they yelped, raising their glasses to us as we went back out into the night.

I had seriously thought about going to Dallas to start my career. Craig was going to Houston for a job he already had nailed down. Dallas was the magnetic epicenter for young, post-college talent headed down from the Midwest and its long economic drought. Texas's booming, diverse economy, sunshine, and pretty girls had proved alluring. The state that had it all was then rumored to want to secede from the Union, and the idea has bubbled up again now, forty years later. The encounter in that bar in Istanbul is what got me more committed in some way to a Dallas migration, and indeed that's where I ended up starting my career. More cosmic directive.

We had spent several nights in remarkable Istanbul, being very careful about what we ate to avoid the bug. If it wasn't peeled, dried, factory-packaged, or boiling hot, the rule was to avoid it and any resultant gastronomic explosions. In doing so, we maintained our health, until the last night when, in a celebratory mood, we would become overconfident and fall off the tightrope. Drinking heavily, feasting on every food-cart item we'd been smelling and salivating over for days, we gorged ourselves to the delight of the vendors before heading back to our rooftop hotel. Big mistake.

We contracted what I'm sure was amoebic dysentery, or worse—to this day the most abominable sickness I've ever suffered. In the middle of the night, we woke guts a-rumblin', to rush to the communal toilets which were a collection of Turkish-style, squatter toilets without separation, in a large antiquated bathroom. The toilets afforded two porcelain foot pads rising above a hole in the depression between the pads, where we proceeded to vacate bowels—and tummy—since once we exploded, it was coming out both ends nonstop. In between our moans and begging for God's mercy, we expelled side-by-side on what ended up being a very convenient fixture, perhaps designed for these very moments, splashing everywhere. I was so sick I couldn't make it back up to the rooftop, so I had to go to the room and flop on the box spring, which I think we did for a day and another night, hoping pre-purchased tickets for the magic bus to Austria would be honored a day late.

I do not know how we made it to the bus station in delirium, unable to muster a shower —dehydrated, splattered a bit in dry shit and vomit, and preserving every ounce of energy for the trip. Boarding the bus packed with humans and animals, including a pet goat, as well as myriad taped-together boxes and bags inside and strapped on the roof, I attempted to sit upright but could not. Ending up lying on the floor while people stepped on and around me, jabbering in an array of indecipherable languages, made things most nightmarishly surreal. My friend Craig, seated nearby, was in a daze and unable to help.

The bus ride to Graz, Austria took thirty-six-hours. Had it happened today at my current age, I would've certainly died in route. No exaggeration. Luckily, I didn't have anything more to vomit or poop, so I just lay there on the filthy rubber floor mat in the dilapidated bus, vibrating for a day and a half, sleeping on and off. The bug in my bowels was outlasted and died of dehydration and starvation.

Don't break the food rules in the Third World or they will break you.

The magic bus finally chugged into its destination in Graz, Austria, after many stops, including one at the conscientious Turkish and Greek border that caused a five-hour delay and almost got the bus turned back. In Graz, Craig helped deposit me outside the American Express office where I was to rendezvous with my college sweetheart, as he headed off on his sojourn, as planned. We would reunite ten days later in Germany.

Hours later I woke to see my college girlfriend, who arrived via London where she had been studying.

"You look like hell!" she exclaimed. "Aren't you going to get up and give me a hug? Aren't you glad to see me after I've come all this way?"

"Yes, yes, of course, but I am very sick," I moaned.

Somehow, she guided me to a hotel room secured and nursed me back to health, allowing us to trek through Austria and Bavaria together for the next days of a fabulous interlude.

After reconnecting in Germany with my buddy, the two of us headed to Copenhagen, with plans to conquer Scandinavia. Chatting with students in a bar, we learned of a tour group that was taking students to Russia. American students posing as Danes could go.

This was the time of the Cold War, with Reagan and Brezhnev dancing the final rounds of the conflict that had started forty years before. The USA was ramping up weaponry under Reagan's direction, to overwhelm the Soviets psychologically and financially, which it eventually did, and Americans were forbidden to go to the USSR or its satellites. The prospect of illegally going to Moscow and beyond was alluring, and we were able to get ticketed on a weeklong trip that was leaving in a matter of days.

A group of about twenty of us gathered at the prescribed time, we being the only two Yanks, and embarked on the overnight train to Moscow. Upon arrival, we were then bussed through town, viewing the never-ending stream of gray apartment buildings on the way to our just-as-drab hotel. Paintings of the Soviet leadership and historical figures as propaganda posters on the sides of the buildings showing workers bearing giant sickles provided the only splash of color and life to view.

We had dinner, met with our tour leaders, and received all the extensive rules and regulations that went along with being a visitor in the USSR. We bedded down, and then the next day headed off to sight-see around the Kremlin and Saint Basil's Cathedral, the most prominent sites in the city. In the afternoon we were given some free time to wander, with explicitly limited boundaries. Of course, we didn't like being confined, so we decided to check out the off-limit subway system, which we'd heard doubled as a bomb shelter, finding that was true—with many sets of escalators leading down deep into the earth to the subway trains.

On those escalators, we were approached by two Russian gals who immediately began to chat us up. They were very cute and they had all the trappings of Russian privileged hipster society—the Levi jeans, the Marlboro cigarettes, and all the other accoutrements that were the fashion of the day. We quickly found out that they were daughters of Politburo members, with one of their fathers an admiral in the Russian Navy and the other's an ambassador to a handful of South American countries. Elitist and wild, it didn't take long before we were under their spell. They suggested that they take the reins and function as our tour guides for the time we were there. Sounded good—real good, and it was while it was.

Going back to our hotel that night, we promptly skipped back out with them as a novelty that helped them push the limits, something their rubles couldn't buy. Looking back forty years later, details are a little sketchy when we bailed on the tour group and didn't re-connect 'til we saw them in St. Petersburg at the Hermitage Museum days later. In between, we had a near run-in with the KGB at an underground bar one night, as one of the young agents approached the gals about two American students posing as Danes who had gone AWOL, suspecting we were the two. While the one gal chatted up the agent, the other one suggested we head out the back door like I had in Hana, Maui bar months before to escape the irate softball players. We were off and running.

At this point, as it had been apparent from the beginning that the tour group leaders were not well organized, we figured we would just reconnect in St. Petersburg per our tour agenda and pretend that nothing had happened. So, we went to the Hermitage at the designated time with the gals, spied the group going through the place, and followed them, staying a room at a time behind them. Eventually, I got the attention of one of the other students on the tour and he wiggled back to chat with me.

"Where the hell have you guys been? They have been looking for you everywhere. You are in some deep shit," he nervously exclaimed.

"Don't you think we can just feather into the group? They will not know what is going on."

"Oh no, they know everything about you, and I think if you are caught you will be in the Gulag for sure."

The Gulag, which was synonymous with Siberia, was the old system of Soviet corrective labor camps, where the patrons toiled for up to fourteen hours a day doing punishing physical labor with little rations, and where most died.

"Holy shit! Well. I guess we need to go to Plan B then. Whatever you do, do not tell the Rooskies that you saw us."

"I won't, and you need to get out of here."

So now Plan B was in effect, although we did not know what Plan B was. After noodling madly, we realized our only option was to show up at the airport at the time of departure and try to connect there and just slide out of town. The gals agreed. When they got us there, they wished us good luck and goodbye. They'd had their fun.

We found our way to the tour group, which was preparing to have baggage checked and be shaken down at the airport departure counter. We worked our way into the group holding our fingers in front of pursed lips as some of the students looked at us, indicating we wanted them to stay cool, which they did. It only took a few minutes for one of the guides to see us, point, and grab a couple of guards who immediately apprehended us, pulling us aside as the head tour guide began berating us.

"Where have you two been?" he shouted, with the veins on the side of his head swelling. "Do you know you have broken the rules? You are in some serious trouble now!"

We just nodded. He went back to talk to some of the other fellows and his superior who berated him in turn. It was obvious that they could not decide what to do with us, and of course we were fearful we'd be eventually sent off to Siberia, deservedly. As the other students were being cleared and starting to head toward the departure area to fly back to Copenhagen, the increasingly frustrated tour operators had still not reached a decision.

Nervous as hell, we stood there trying to look calm, as they came back and went through our bags keeping anything that had a Western flair, which excluded our Russian hats, trinkets, and vodka. Then the leader stomped around, getting in our faces and waving his finger at us with his final decree.

"You are fortunate that you are not going to be sent off to work camp. It is your lucky day. You two are being thrown out of the USSR, your names and information are going to be kept, and if you are ever found in a USSR territory you will be apprehended and will be punished to the extreme. Do I make myself clear? You are permanently exiled!"

"Yes sir, yes sir, we understand."

"So, take your bags and get out of here, you dogs!"

Sweating like pigs, rather than the dogs we were, we picked up our bags and briskly walked to catch up with the others. I often wonder if we are still on the expelled list, now managed by one Vladimir Putin.

Grabbing the bull by the horns and pushing the limits, riding the wave of outrageous adventure with all my polished talents, was a rush, but grabbing the Soviet bull was not wise. They were not to be messed with, and we finally crossed the line between carefree and careless, probably dodging the biggest bullet of our lives.

It was on to Scandinavia.

The salesperson/trader learns how to survive with no cell phone, employment, or bank wires from a wealthy family, executing international goods trading sans tariffs. Bartering frisbees and jeans in Turkey for tapestries, folk clothing, spices, and cash, and purchasing vodka in the Soviet Union on the cheap, which could now be sold illegally outside the Swedish liquor store in downtown Stockholm for a fortune, made for some memorable hauls. If caught here, I wouldn't be going to Siberia, but would probably just suffer a hand slap or confiscation.

Several Swedish customers took a pass on my vodka, thinking it was a rip-off, but the smartest gentleman looked at the bottles, checked the caps, and knew a deal when he saw one, buying it all above the asking price. It was always just a matter of supply and demand. Many times, I'd sell all my clothes and belongings and just be down to my shorts and a T-shirt before buying the local clothing, and then selling it again in the next country and buying theirs. Everything always for sale made for some interesting, clashing, juxtaposed fashion.

The trading, charity, and sleeping outdoors kept the poor Detroit boy in tall cotton. Sleeping outside, when possible, in any place not stinking of urine or too brightly lit, would do, and those included cemeteries, which became one of our favorites. They were quiet and rarely bothered except on one occasion where I made the mistake, not purposely, of sleeping directly atop a man's grave in Bergen, Norway. I would realize my mistake when I woke up the next morning.

"Craig, help me—I can't move."

My neck was so tight I couldn't even turn onto my side to get up.

"Dude, I'm paralyzed. I don't know what's going on, help me."

He came over and helped me up, and wow, was I ever in pain—I never had neck pain like that ever in my life, and never have since.

"I think I pissed that dude off! Did I sleep right on top of that guy's grave—what is his name? Lars? Shit! Damn I'm sorry, Lars! I think your claws must have come out in the middle of the night and ripped my neck muscles out."

And there it was. Despite trying everything including Bengay, ice, massaging it myself, pounding with my fists, and begging others for a rubdown, for the next three to five days I could hardly move my neck—not a frickin' millimeter. I couldn't even get my shirt off—a total mess. Cemeteries lost some of their allure after that, and if it was the only option, care was taken to never sleep on top of a grave again. Happy to have survived the Grim Reaper, you realize not to mess with the dead.

Fantastic, otherworldly, fjord-ridden-postcard Norway led back to London, and then back to the States via Boston. Upon landing, on to the domestic terminal and gate area for the flight back to Detroit that would wrap up over a year of travel for me. But when I saw the Boston skyline out the Logan Field Terminal window, it called to me, either because there was still a travel bug, or, unlike my friend, there were no concrete commitments to face the real world, whether that be good or bad.

"Wow, look at that! That's Boston! One of the most amazing cities in America! What history here, and all those great schools—Harvard and MIT, Tufts, and more! Never been. Have you ever been to Boston, have you?"

"No."

"Well, hell, I am going. I've never been this close, and I'm not gonna miss this opportunity."

"Jeff, are you crazy? You are never going to stop!"

"I might not."

We chatted for a while longer as Craig waited for his flight, previously our flight.

"Jeff, let's make this backpacking thing an annual event. It's just toooo good!"

"Bro, for sure! Luv ya, man!"

And with a big hug, Craig was off to the workforce and I was Boston-bound.

And so we did, as agreed—and it would continue for over forty years, with an ever-changing cast of characters and destinations worldwide, some of the best memories and experiences of any lifetime.

In Boston, the little black book came back into play, and I found an old friend of a friend attending dental school there who let me sleep on the floor of his small apartment above a loud, raucous bar called the Bull & Finch. The bull theme continuing, I either attended the bar late at night or otherwise lay there on the floor above, listening to and vibrating with the noise. Little did I know the bar would become famous as the inspiration for the sitcom *Cheers*.

I saw all the sites, visited the universities, and was even recruited by L. Ron Hubbard's Scientologists, whose cult I found to be a very interesting lot, although it was not a long-term life choice for me. Not accounting for my study of Eastern philosophies or my true out-of-body voyages, this was the first spiritual, quasi-organized "religion" blast point since the Lutheran school and church days.

It began downtown Copley Square, made famous by the Boston Marathon, in the shadows of the looming, recently completed Hancock Tower. A brisk fall day with trees popping autumnal colors around the park framed a perfect New England October. Crossing one of the streets amidst the swirling leaves, honking, diesel fumes, and unfiltered noise, I noticed and ended up jumbled in a group on the opposite corner that I thought

I could "swim" through. They were passing out leaflets to the captives, and chatting up whoever would slow to listen. You see folks like this on corners in every major city around the world, even more so these days, some holding up signs that might read "Whales for Jesus" or other compelling slogans.

"Hey man, how are you? How's the day, brother?" asked a kind of hippie-ish-looking guy dressed in that fashion with a splash of tie-dye, loose-fitting, thin cotton pants, Birkenstocks, and teeny-lensed spectacles. Normally, after traveling for so long, I'd either just wave, smile, or plain ignore these folks, but this guy was particularly, compellingly cool with his energy.

"You know, dude, it's going really well—diggin' the city."

"Well man, you know, what I see is a beautiful soul in you, man—I'm feeling it—and if you're interested, I'd love to turn you on to what we are here about," he said as he handed me the pamphlet on Dianetics and Scientology. I looked at it, folded it up, and shoved it in my pocket.

"I'll have to give it a read, man."

"Dude, it's like so real and so true. If you want to, we're going back to the house in a bit to grab some lunch, and you're welcome to join us—no commitment, no pressure."

"No thanks, I've got some things I wanna see, and it's all cool, bro."

"Cool. Have a great day. If you want, you can come back anytime, we're here every morning."

I gave him a thumbs up and he reached into his bag and gave me the book entitled *Dianetics: The Modern Science of Mental Health*, which seemed a prize to him. I had zero books in my inventory, having finished the last on the plane ride from

London, so this was good fortune—a nice, thick, dense one. For a solo traveler, a good book as a companion was a necessity and even doubled as a good pillow when wrapped in a jacket.

Over the next few days, I read the book, which proved to be incredibly intelligent, and really was a bit of a game-changer for me, as touted. It had truth on so many levels, but at the end of the day funneled everything into an organized program that felt more like a cult or money-making gig than that absolute truth. The promoted history of an ancient spaceship and all the other craziness likened to von Daniken's *Chariots of the Gods*, was too much to swallow.

Ready once again to move on, this time to warmer climates, referring to the black book again and recalling a friend had moved to Miami. A real wheeler-dealer in college, like myself, Steve was an ultra-hip cat. I called him in South Beach.

"Steve, it's Jeff. What's up down there and how are you?"

"Dude, I'm great! Miami is just rocking. I'm killing it down here selling condos! Come get rich with me in thong central!"

A place in time in the boom-and-bust recycle of the Miami market.

"Dude that sounds so good; just what the doctor ordered. I'll have to hitchhike down, so it might take me a couple or few days."

"Not to worry. Write down my address, show up whenever you want. You will dig it. Babe-licious!"

The next day in my wanderlust was a blast for Miami. I worked my way to the interstate and began to head south. Presenting in a sketchy freeway location with no takers, finally some guys slowed down to pull over, looking like a bunch of gangbangers in a beat-up car. When I began my approach, one of the guys brandished a gun. Sprawling to the pavement, covering up as it went off, I hoped he was just shooting it into the air to scare the crap out of me, which he did. This wasn't hitching in Europe, Dorothy. They sped off.

Finding myself scraped up, worn out, broke, and disillusioned, I realized it was time to go home—wherever that was—and on to other challenges. Miami would have to wait. The bull had gotten the best of me that day, and I was done!

CHAPTER 7

Kids -2020

Swaney & Cuban crew -1985

Cowboys

HP Days -1983

CHAPTER 7
PICK A TEAM

Dallas, Texas was everything that Detroit, Michigan was not at the time—sparkling, vibrant, sunny, friendly, flush with cash, with high-paying jobs and beautiful maidens galore. I got my parents to cosign on a car for me—the cheapest and best Nissan stick-shift a little money could buy—and packed up whatever I could fit in the hatchback of that thing heading south from Detroit to the land of milk and honey.

I felt it was a calling, with clear visions of me moving there, as corny as that sounds. My connection to Dallas, Texas started with the Kennedy Camelot saga and assassination—JFK was shot on my fifth birthday. November 22, 1963. I was a very highly energetic and self-assured five-year-old, always seeking the center of attention, and my birthday was going to be a coming out of sorts. Mom made a special cake in my likeness, down to the detail of the hair, blue eyes, and outfit. In addition, there was a punchbowl full of sweet juice with floating orange slices, festive paper plates with matching napkins, balloons, banners, and all the decorative trimmings in the family dining room. Several neighbors and relatives were invited over to celebrate. I was pumped up.

During the day, my parents kept the JFK thing on the down-low, but as folks showed up that evening for the festivities, they all focused on the little black-and-white TV blaring in the dining room—much like those patrons in the Turkish bar would, years later—watching over and over the footage of the shooting and associated commentary, kibitzing about the assassination, a few of them teary-eyed. This was not going to work for me.

"Everybody! It's my birthday today!" I announced, banging on the table to get their attention.

They looked at me in amazement. This was sacrilege.

"Hey, we got cake, punch, and all this great stuff. I'm here and I'm ready to have fun. Games to play! Do you know those people on TV? You do not—but you know me, so let's turn that off and have some cake!"

It worked, and the party got started. Who shot Kennedy, or who shot J.R. in the *Dallas* series for that matter? Who cares! We rolled on.

The drums beating for Dallas and my connection continued as a young sports fan. Every boy in blue-collar Detroit was a rabid sports fan from birth. Detroit was Hockey Town, so that sport was the religion. Detroit Tiger baseball was hit and miss, except for the dream season of 1968, and basketball's Pistons were mediocre, excepting a spurt of The Bad Boys. The pitiful lot of the bunch were the football Detroit Lions, paving the way to root for the Dallas Cowboys, "America's team" and my favorite. There was an allure to their success, and following that was undeniable, and that further watered the seed for a Dallas move.

The Cowboys and J.R. Ewing in the TV series symbolized the city's can-do attitude. The image of Pegasus, the winged horse that flies above the city, further characterized Dallas as a mystical place that made something out of a vast prairie of nothing, that defied the odds beyond all expectations—which resonated deeply with me. Years before, John Nealy Bryan had founded Dallas with a cabin on the Trinity River and miscalculated dreams of wealth and success. He ended up piss broke in an insane asylum in Austin, but my destiny was going to be much different.

I arrived without a nickel in my pocket, sleeping on friends' couches and borrowing money while searching for a job. The nighttime party atmosphere was intoxicating, and my friend, Rick, who managed a successful restaurant, partied like a prince every weekend, with limo service and VIP, red-carpet attention. I was surprised to see some iconic Dallas Cowboys players indulging into the wee hours at the after-hours gatherings we attended on Friday nights, wondering how they could perform the following Sunday. It was a work-hard-play-hard city of youthful exuberance.

A vibrant downtown area, full of that youth and energy I had envisioned, below the red shiny neon Pegasus, a horse not yet refurbished, just didn't exist. Apart from a few noteworthy structures, the dilapidated core of downtown had been vacant for years and was now populated by zombified street people. In time, that changed for Dallas, in small part due to my efforts along with many others, and a calling would be fulfilled. I had told the guys in Istanbul that I was going to Dallas, and they predicted my good fortune correctly. Dallas was to become a perfect fit, melding into a symbiotic relationship.

With my booming confidence, I ended up getting five job offers within a couple of weeks, often just showing up at company offices, asking for the top dog, and getting an audience. Long-ago extinct companies such as Harris, Wang, DEC, Datapoint, and others tendered lucrative offers; but the offer with Hewlett-Packard company, which that year *Forbes* magazine lauded as the best company to work for in the world, was the prize. This was what I had bargained for and worked towards, salvaging my college career and GPA, with that visit to the professor's office long ago.

Happy people, the HP way. Everyone there was euphoric, it seemed, drinking the company Kool-Aid and rolling in the dough. I recall the HP interview as the manager looked over my pumped-up resume, questioning me about it while boasting about what a great company it was.

"Of course, it's a great company; that's why I am here," I declared. "You have a lot to offer, and I have a lot to offer, and no doubt I'll be extremely successful here. I like the culture—this is a good fit."

He had very few questions, it seemed, so he passed me on to the district manager for the next interview. A definitively gray-haired man with an abrupt, stern manner, he waved me into his squeaky-clean office and motioned me to sit down while he glanced at my resume. Then he gave me a good looking-over. A delegator with an intimidating glare and me the pissant. This was new to me in my two weeks on tour.

"Mr. Swaney, it is, right?"

"Yes sir."

"Well, you finished school and decided to go traveling around the world for a year goofing off. Now you think you can land a job like this one?" he asked as he cut to the chase.

"Well, it was the only time I had to do such a thing. I learned a lot, and now I'm ready to get to work."

"Mr. Swaney, I think that was totally irresponsible of you. It was a bad call and poor decision."

"Sir, I respectfully disagree. I know my experience abroad will bear fruit. But we are both entitled to our opinion on that, and I'm ready to join your team and contribute here."

"Well, we will see," he grumped.

With that, he sent me out. I thought that opportunity was over, but I'd had to stand my ground. I was not in the game to be beaten down, and a strong-willed man would never respect a wimp. Besides, I had other offers, and if that was the real mode here, it would not last, anyways.

The next day I got a call from the subordinate, who invited me to join the company. Meeting him later that week, deftly negotiating my pay, explaining that upfront money was needed and some time to get settled.

"We are not in the habit of negotiating these offers with fresh college grads, Jeff, and we don't offer any advances. If you're hired, you come to work next Monday."

"I don't think that'll work for me. I'll need a few weeks to get everything sorted out, but I'll give you my all when I get here. Promise you that."

Ended up landing my advance and pay increase, along with three weeks off before having to show. That required signing a non-disclosure agreement and a personal promise to not disclose my terms. I got my advance in two days, opened a bank account, cashed the check, and it was party nonstop for the three weeks before the start of work. Spent all the money and was back to broke.

Sucked it up and showed up for work at the prescribed time, began my training, which included six months of flying to various HP sites and side trips to San Francisco, Tahoe, Carmel, Yosemite, and other glorious locales that I had never seen. The training was followed by a three-year successful sales career there.

They liked me a lot, but they didn't love my expense account, which during my tenure was the highest in the entire office. I remember having a meeting with management over it. As a top performer, perhaps there was some kind of leverage, pointing out that the company policy stated to "spend as you are accustomed to." Checkbook register in hand, I related that I spent every penny of my pay, had cashed out my stock options every quarter, and was planning on burning every nickel in my twenties. With little responsibility in life except to schlep our products, I had no interest in saving anything. That's what I was accustomed to, a position I held until my thirties. Never had any money in my life, and dammit, I was going to enjoy this! The case was begrudgingly closed.

In my second year, during a management luncheon held in the Dallas office for about thirty people, honoring top producers like myself, an opportunity arose. The COO of HP, Dean Morton, who eventually became co-CEO, was the guest of honor, which was a big deal. I entered the room and noticed that none of the people looking for a place to sit had taken a seat next to him. I jumped on it and sat down beside him, engaged him, and within minutes we were discussing world travel, which was a hot button for him, firmly negating local management's presumption in my first interviews. Over the course of the luncheon, much to the dismay of local management, I monopolized the conversations with Dean. At the end of the luncheon, he handed me his card on which he scribbled his personal secretary's (as assistants were referred to back then) private phone number.

"Give me a call next week in Palo Alto, Jeff. I'd like to chat again."

"I will do it. I appreciate it. Have a safe trip back."

That call resulted in an offer for a full ride toward a Stanford MBA degree. Oddly enough, I turned it down, as the thought of having to go back to school, even in the Silicon Valley "club," was distasteful. An amazing opportunity, but no regrets. I felt I could always connect with Dean later and revisit the option, but never did.

Another interesting life intersection of my tenure at HP occurred when one of my party-scene friends among the fourteen-thousand-unit, Village Country Club apartment-complex dwellers where we lived needed some special HP computer cables, which I could provide. Mark Cuban, now an international household name due to his *Shark Tank* fame and other ventures, needed a small favor.

Mark and I had met as we both habitually roamed the town on the weekends, and could be found at the hottest bars in town drinking cheap champagne directly from the bottles, always with a crew and beautiful women in tow. Working and partying hard, by weekend day we were poolside, and weekday nights after his job at a local mom-and-pop PC consulting company it was party every night at the bars. He was positively always positive, with a big broad smile baring long bright white teeth, dark eyebrows that jumped up and down with his changes in facial expressions, and a happy little snicker that accompanied every conversation. He seemed like a cartoon character of himself.

"Swanes, I was wondering if you could help me out with some of those kooky proprietary HP PC cables. They're a pain, but I have a client who needs a bunch."

"Sure Cubes, just get me a list and I'll see what I can scrounge up at the office."

And so, a friendship flowered. I'm often described as an uber-persistent individual, but in my life I have never met anyone, ever, of literally tens of thousands of people, that fit that bill like this guy.

At a friend's bachelor party in Ensenada, Mexico, drunk as skunks after staying up all night, he asked a question as we wobbled—nearly starved from lack of food, with empty champagne bottles in hand—toward a local taqueria.

"Swanes, I'm curious. If you had the choice to be rich or famous, which would you choose?"

At this point in our young lives, I think we both fit in the infamous category.

"Well, I don't know. I've never thought about it, bro."

"I tell you: I will be both, and one day I'll be in the BBC."

"I don't doubt you for a second, Mark. You are on your way. But what's the BBC?"

"The Billionaire Boys Club, Swanes," he exclaimed with a grin. "The BBC!"

I've thought about that many times, and never truly had the fierce appetite for either fame or fortune. Happy where I was in life then, and now, despite travails aplenty, yet having fun every day and living a comfortable life. This early awareness of gratitude in later years would become a mantra. It has been great watching Mark beat the odds and continue to be popular even with his ofttimes brash personality and risk-taking. As a sports fan, it was also a thrill to see him take the NBA Dallas Mavericks from cellar dweller to competitor and then champion in a very short time. Shows you what drive and confidence, with unrelenting perseverance in life, can do. What you can dream, you can achieve. This guy was—and is—the poster child for that theme.

After my stint with HP, I had a brief gig with a high-flying switching company creating brilliantly conceived and desperately needed computer-switch mapping products for the industry. The company promised richness beyond imagination, but the products didn't function correctly. I even recall being told to intercept and spray-paint the scratches on a used switch, sold as new at the delivery dock for a customer data center at General Dynamics corporation in Fort Worth, Texas. I was sweating. Think about it. This was a big-time government defense contractor. When the

SEC had some issues with the company shortly thereafter, it was time to cut the cord or go down with that Titanic. That worked fine, as I was about to radically shift my focus.

I had accelerated my time living the nightlife scene, having found the spark of the beginning of a scene new to Dallas. A long-neglected area east of downtown, referred to as Deep Ellum, emitted raw, artistic energy. Established in the 1800s as a freedman's town, it became a nationally recognized center of jazz and blues music in the 1920s and '30s, featuring such notables as Columbia Record's Blind Lemon Jefferson. But the area declined sharply in the years following World War II, with businesses and residents moving to the suburbs. It became a boarded-up warehouse district where the city's homeless constituted the majority of the populace. Eventually, artists, attracted by cheap rents, moved into fixer-upper buildings, and a few underground punk and alternative nightlife venues and galleries sprung up in the stew.

Having grown somewhat disenchanted during my last year with Hewlett-Packard and the switching company after that, I was burning the candle with a blowtorch at both ends. My life had then been corporate by day and Ellum by night. I yearned to make my mark on my adopted city, but it had become evident that I could never be part of the Dallas scene working for a company or companies out of state. So, it was time to strike out. I could always go back to the corporate world—heck, I was only twenty-six years old. But of course, destined to be an entrepreneur, I never would, and that would be the last time I ever worked for anyone again.

I was drawn to Deep Ellum irresistibly. I had ideas about the when, where, and why. All I needed to figure out was the *how*. At HP, I had picked my corporate team; now it was time to build my own team.

CHAPTER 8

The first dollar made: Concept Nouveau, Inc. June 1985

First Dollar - Clearview - 1985 - Flip Phone

Loft Home - The Biz

CHAPTER 8

STEP RIGHT UP

It was time to get involved in the fledgling Deep Ellum world, an area seemingly a wide-open palette awaiting new directions. But with limited money and time. Strained by only a modicum of savings, I had continued my young life's program of spending every dime I made.

Then a revelation jolted me. The *how* was going to be a series of roving warehouse parties, as witnessed in Los Angeles while visiting hipster friends. To orchestrate late-night events with varied locations, fresh themes, and outlaw to the marrow, these would be parties related through a network that was not cyber-influenced—just word-of-mouth guerrilla marketing, utilizing little business-card-size flyers handed out by a small army of vigilant volunteers. The venture would meld the highest degree of difficulty with the broadest exposure by having new partners for each party, each with a distinct following of their own. Although I wasn't sure why I came to this conclusion, it would become apparent later. Kinda how life works.

Taking stock of gifts, I suddenly discovered who I was: a yearning artist anxious to fill a niche. Rolling out these parties, akin to the rave events of now-past decades, felt just right for me. Creating a unique world, with pieces assembled along the way, and populating it with a diverse group of wanting, wonderful, and wacky people intent on reinventing and impacting a scene in its infancy, was the task at hand. Mixing it up with freaks, yuppies, misfits, and all in between, facilitated and living in a home-cooked version of pop culture.

In building a network, way before social media existed, an expressiveness and ability on the social front to flow effortlessly as a chameleon—the result of survival skills developed at a young age—would serve well, especially when coupled with viscerally laced world travel experiences.

For my first event, I tapped Mark Cuban and some mutual friends, and picked an abandoned louver window manufacturing facility. It had the blessing of a few working toilets and some pirated electricity, which was an advantage over other locations. The Clearview Louver Window Company, birthed in Art Deco Miami, had boomed in 1940s and '50s Dallas, then petered out in anonymity as the deco craze faded. I snuck into the hard-to-secure and immense property one day to find it was in abject disrepair with a leaky roof, which had gaping holes in places, a multitude of water-pipe leaks, and feces and food scraps swirled with other assorted unmentionables left behind by the "homeless" who visited or lived there. From a short distance, I saluted the few characters I saw camping out in the shadows.

Making contact with a well-known, flamboyant, and controversial Dallas real estate tycoon, the late Louis G. Reese—who had built a portfolio of warehouses in the area with visions of turning Deep Ellum into a Dallas SoHo—was key. Things weren't going well from the real estate perspective in the neighborhood, or any neighborhood globally at the time, since the country was then in the throes of the 1980s Savings and Loan Crisis and global financial meltdown. Most of the properties were on the verge of foreclosure and all in ramshackle disrepair due to the crisis. Lou Reese and his team were interested in having me jump in and try to help kick-start the struggling area with my ideas. The meltdown, with all its pain, had also created opportunity, as it has in most all economic slides historically—including this S&L crisis, the global recession of 2008, and the COVID-19 pandemic. The party and booze businesses thrived as other businesses suffered. My timing—luckily, rather than by plan—was good, even if the footing was rocky.

Meeting with Lou was always an event. Arriving at his offices, which were decorated with a knockout collection of modern art and furniture, was like entering a mini-Tate Modern in London—very impressive. Real estate brokers often sat in a waiting room outside his office waiting to pitch him deals, many of which he acquired with his group's insatiable appetite and financing schemes. The suit-tie-and-briefcase-clad broker yupsters were rolling in as I sat waiting for my time slot in my trademark barefoot, shorts, and T-shirt garb. I had been one of those suits in my previous gigs, but I sure wasn't anymore.

"Well, come on in here, Mr. Swaney," Lou beckoned warmly. "I've heard a lot about you. I'm excited to meet you."

He was a big man—head, torso, feet, and all, well over six feet tall with humongous hands that would famously gobble pinkies up with the greeting. I survived the handshake.

"Come on and sit down. Let's chat. I hear you wanna rent some of my warehouses to throw parties. I am delighted to work with you on that."

"Yes, I think the one I'd like to tackle is the old Clearview factory. It's not very secure, and I was able to take a walk through it, but think it would make a great space."

"Well, we have lots of spaces like that, and so I think we can equip you for a while if you want to bounce around with your scheme."

"Cool. Let's get after it."

I left the office with a grin, realizing I now had a landlord who understood what I was doing and that we both needed and could benefit each other.

So now it was going to be off and running with none of the necessary know-how, systems, insurances, or proper permits and licenses to operate whatsoever, planning on selling beer and champagne illegally at these events that started late and ended when the sun came up. Looking back, it was an insanely high-risk and foolish endeavor, but I really had nothing to lose. Or so I thought.

The first event at the Clearview building was a great success, not so much financially, but it produced a huge buzz, so I forged on with others. We didn't do much to clean up the place. As we just utilized the entry, offices, and showroom spaces that were ragged but serviceable, we simply gave it a solid mopping with bleach and kept it dark at night, using only some basic lighting supplied by the DJ, together with multicolored plastic gels taped to some of the working lights, a disco ball, smoke machine, and strobe light. The operation was ultra-low-budget.

Over the course of that year, I would host over a half dozen events with my various partners, all on handshakes, mind you. The menu expanded as the parties progressed, with various forms of entertainment, art, dancing, live music, and bizarre environmental displays, which were the talk of the see-and-be-seen crowd. The gatherings grew and became obvious, hardly underground anymore, hosting a couple thousand patrons each time, which eventually drew the ire of some local businesses and the authorities.

Finally, there was a raid at one of the last events at 2 a.m., with the police and fire marshal, who was awakened by phone in his suburban home and looked the part in his PJs and slippers. The lead police officer cornered me with his lieutenants in one of the small, quieter rooms of this sprawling warehouse down the street from the Clearview facility, which in the '90s would become inhabited by several retail spaces, including my friend's famous Curtain Club.

"Just what on earth do you think you are doing here?" he bellowed.

"Having a party. It's totally under control here, guys," I answered.

The authority figures just stood there with me for the longest while, in a semi-trance, sizing up the storming energy and revelry going on in the cavernous adjacent rooms. Answering their walkie-talkies, amidst their floating daze, they communicated with other officials to determine if backup was needed to squelch the buzz. It wasn't.

While being held captive in the smallish room out of the main fray, my staff of volunteers and some friends who were patrons kept checking on me.

"Do you need any help, Jeff? What should we do?"

"Carry on guys; it's all cool. Take care of our guests. I'll sort this out with these gentlemen," I assured them.

Abruptly, at about 3 a.m., the fire marshal announced, "Mr. Swaney, I'm going to ask you to shut this circus down because I'm going to head home. If not, I think the officers will do that, and then will need to take you downtown. It is your call, young man."

"How about another hour? Everyone is having a ball here. It's good clean fun."

"No. Did you hear me?" he said. "I mean *now!*"

With no other options, we pulled the plug, asking all the revelers to leave. The party was over. The building went from a throbbing rave to empty in ten minutes. It felt like falling off a cliff into the void.

I would have to wait for another day to have the next party and hopefully not have these uninvited guests again. The plan for the next extravaganza had already been laid a few weeks before. It would not come off well.

The word had gotten out about the previous "bust," and the police were at the door as we opened for business that night. They brought with them officers from the Texas Alcoholic Beverage Commission to oversee the event. These good ol' boys did not seem to like where I was headed with this event, though oddly, they were not concerned with any license except for a dance-hall permit. That was surprising, as we were illegally selling keg beer and wine coolers, but that didn't seem to register. They explained that the party could go on this time but with no dancing. When I asked for a definition of dancing, they brought out some city code book that defined it as "a swaying or swinging of the hips," reminiscent of the early Elvis Presley years when The King was demonized for that wild rock 'n' roll dancing with the Elvis pelvis.

The dancing ban did not go over well with the patrons, as the DJ played non-danceable ballads while the Billy Bobs looked on to ensure that there were no hip movements as described in the archaic code. Eventually, the few people who had come left early—a disaster that left me flat broke and needing to cancel my next event. It was all over. No more!

So, I had to question myself. *Where are you headed now? Jeff, you passed on a Stanford full-ride MBA to do this? Really? Are you nuts?*

Hey, a voice from the future answered. *Elon Musk only lasted two days at Stanford, I heard, and I think Steve Jobs was a college dropout, too, so maybe you just saved yourself some wasted time. You are twenty-seven now, you can do whatever you want to.*

Post-party-bust, I had to come up with grocery money, so the following week I went to one of the warehouses solo, as the volunteers had now scattered, and posted garage-sale signs on the road. I would sell off whatever I could. That weekend would be remembered as one of the dreariest of my life. I had few takers, but did manage to scrounge up a few hundred bucks selling some odds and ends, together with a few broken vintage vending machines, one—an Adams gum machine—which I kept, and I have to this day in my office. The next week, I returned to set up for another weekend garage sale and discovered that someone had broken into the place by driving a truck through a pull-down, heavy-duty, corrugated-metal industrial garage door, and had stolen everything of value.

Now what?

I'd gone from corporate high flyer to nothingness in eighteen months, having to hide the car for fear of it being repossessed, witnessing tow trucks circling the condo which I'd purchased with a down payment from the computer-gig monies. Fortunately, there was rental income, courtesy of my roommate, which covered the monthly mortgage and bills. Beaten down but not out, proud and undeterred, it was time for another comeback-kid chapter to add to the repertoire, a la my fave actor Robert Downey Jr.'s incredible career. I'd had a taste of entrepreneurial freedom and was not about to go back the corporate grind.

After a few days of thought, a return to the Clearview space was the answer. Everyone loved that vibe. The media had dubbed it, "Raw Inspiration—hard to come by but this place has it." They were spot on.

I tapped my friend, Steve—who I had partnered with on one of the previous parties, in fact, the one that got busted—pitching him the idea of opening the Clearview space on Saturday nights with some makeshift permits, quasi-security, killer music, and the bigtime underground promo. If he would fund it with profits he was making from his margarita-machine rental company, he'd get paid back and we could eventually end up with a legitimate nightclub.

"Steve, with your network of friends that are so enthusiastic and inspired by the whole scene, and both of our hard work, I really think we can pull it off, bro."

He paused, thinking for a moment.

"Cool, Swaney. I like it. Let's do it; we'll have a ball!"

Steve was the coolest of all the warehouse party partners I'd enlisted for my roughly half-dozen individually distinct events. He had a nonchalant demeanor and a quick sarcastic wit about him. His group of post-high-school friends, collectively referred to as "the family," a fitting name for them, were the most happily crazed volunteers ever and really helped make it all hum. Let's send out thanks to Chris, Palmer, David, Mark, John, Ann Shannon, and all the others for their help in unknowingly launching an entertainment career, as well as all the wild, wacky, selfless blast enjoyed in the earliest years.

A handful of my other one-night warehouse party partners had been less congenial. Several accused me of stealing money, which never happened, as I rarely even covered or kept track of my expenses, let alone my time and effort, working night and day tirelessly for my newfound passion. At one of the jams, one of the partners took all of the money at the end of the night. I called him the next day after figuring out what he'd done. "Hey, my friend, all of the money is missing, every cent—and I didn't see you when we were closing. Someone told me you had it and were handling it for safekeeping, which is fine. We do need to get together and get this sorted out."

He listened, then angrily replied, "Listen, Swaney, don't call me again. I need this money more than you do, and it's mine now. If you call me or bother me again or show your face at my home or restaurant, I'll call the police, the IRS, the state, and the alcohol board and make sure you are screwed."

"Wow," I muttered as I hung up the phone. I always took the high road, as I aspired to do more than make money, and let karma handle others' misdeeds.

Another group I worked with that owned a bar in town decided to take off with my one-hundred-fifty-pound drop safe that we had kept hidden at that warehouse party's premises the night of our event. When I called Sunday after the night's revelry to have them join me at that location and divvy up the proceeds, they wouldn't answer. Perplexed, I drove to the party location and found that the safe was gone. As they remained unresponsive by phone, it was on to their business, which they had suspiciously closed for the day. I finally got a hold of them on Monday morning.

"Hey guys, been trying to reach you. The safe has been taken. I'm supposing you have it, so what's up?" I asked pointedly.

"We heard about you and don't trust you, so we have the safe, and if you would come and open it and give us our money, you can have it. And no funny business!"

"Okay. I'm on the way. But I think you guys got the funny-business category cornered already. Really disappointing, guys!"

When I arrived at their pub, we split the monies as agreed. It was brusque business with four of them hovering over me. They had somehow damaged or dropped the safe, in the process bending the combination dial so it wobbled like a car's flat tire when spun. To my amazement, it still worked to open its door and count the cash. Oddly enough, this same safe would be installed in the Clearview location Steve and I were now working on, as well as the spot we would move to down the street. Over its twenty years of service—two at the original spot and eighteen at the second one, the dial still wobbling with every use—it would be bolted to the ground, as it held millions of dollars in cash over the years, and would survive two more heist attempts.

One thing I learned from the party, booze, and club business was that partners seldom ended up as friends. Imagine a lot of the attitudes were a carryover from Prohibition and the days of Al Capone, which spurred cutthroat tactics. So, I chose more carefully after experiences with some of the warehouse-party partners, and it worked to good fortune, with no one in our mix ending up hating each other or getting killed. I'm most proud of the fact that I'm still friends with all the partners of my twenty years in the Club Clearview business.

I also discovered that a flamboyant style and rising high profile, which served well in some ways, seemed to evoke distrust with others who did not truly know me. Good to know.

We all get more of what we focus on in life, and I was going to take the lessons and make a big run. None of the negative experiences inherent in those warehouse parties throttled me, so in late summer of 1985, the aptly named Club Clearview was hatched with partner Steve. Within a few months, our endeavor had exploded into a blasting underground scene, legitimized to a degree, and put on steroids.

We needed a beacon to direct our patrons to their destination, since at that point the neighborhood had largely been undiscovered. So, we commissioned the iconic fifty-foot-tall Clearview neon sign to be repaired to working order, with the brightest red neon that could be had adorning the ninety-thousand-square-foot concrete behemoth of an edifice. The building consisted of about five different "rooms"—one somewhat recognizable as an entry lobby, offices on two levels, showrooms, three restrooms with showers, and a cavernous backspace, which was a raw concrete two-story structure, constructed with twenty-foot-thick concrete slabs, and comprising about seventy thousand feet of space. The factory and loading docks had been located in that area, which was coated in thirty-plus years of grime, resembling a Batman or Terminator movie set.

We utilized all the smaller spaces and then simply cyclone-fenced-off part of the factory area needed, cutting the total club space to about thirty thousand feet, with the ability to expand on a whim by rolling out more fencing for growth or larger live music acts. With an increasing need for electricity, we opted for straight-off-the-pole-and-grid complimentary power with no circuit breakers—as is done in many Third World countries. A risky endeavor, we would later find out.

Historical on-site features included men's, women's, and colored bathrooms, something I had never seen before or since, and a relic of Dallas's deep-South history as a hub of the cotton-picking business. All our bathrooms were unisex anyways, so the separate-colored bathroom's existence was ironic since we catered to a mixed clientele of all preferences, colors, and descriptions. "Love All, Serve All."

We allowed staff and friends to live in some of the run-down, former ivory-tower second-floor offices, providing built-in late-night security. Before long, we were hosting up to three thousand guests on Saturday nights 'til sunrise, and in no time we were on the international circuit of the coolest clubs worldwide. All on a shoestring. We had pulled off the impossible by transitioning to a fully permitted and licensed establishment, which should have never been allowed as we utilized altered photocopied documents, charm, sleight of hand, prayers, and bribes of free entry passes to high-demand concerts with comped bar tabs to officials, to get everything in place.

Late every Saturday night in the club's infancy, a graffiti vagabond would emerge out of the shadows, spray paint images on club walls, and, like a ghost, slip back undetected into the party crowd, leaving fresh art and toxic odor of spray paint in his wake. I instructed the staff to find this guy and bring him to me. A plan was hatched.

Finally, one night they caught him, and we got to meet. He was noticeably upset and thought there was going to be some major trouble.

"What's your name?" I asked, flanked by security, as I firmly but kindly confronted the bandit.

"Clay, and man, I'm really sorry about this. I won't do it again, I promise. I love your place and I can't help myself, you know…I just can't!"

"Well, I understand. I know passion and impulse myself. Hmmmm. I have a proposal for you, Mr. Clay. I'd like to hire you on here as the artistic director. Do you think that would be something you'd like to do? Admittedly, we love your stuff."

I regularly would engage folks to be part of the group, to sink or swim. Unbeknownst to me then, this man would be a fixture for twenty years.

"Oh yes, yes, totally; it'd be like a dream, dude. I'd love it. I have lots of ideas for this place!"

"Excellent. I'm sure you do, and I'm going to give you a lot of license, but we will probably do our painting during the day, if that's okay with you. And we can meet to discuss your nuggets prelaunch."

"All good; no doubt!"

"Okay, so let me buy you a drink and you can hang out. Bouncer Whitney will introduce you to the crew here at the club. We'll meet next week for our first go-round."

"Yes, cool. I'll have a Jack and Coke, and thank you very much, Jeff. You won't regret it—this will be great."

That was the beginning of a beautiful relationship. Clay created environments in different rooms of the building and became famous for his themes, installations, black-light room, and black-light go-go dancers whom he painted live, entertaining more than a million patrons over twenty years. He had other unique offerings as well. Knowing some of the homeless people in the neighborhood who were cool, he built a quasi-camp in the larger back space of the club, with the cyclone fence expanded to gobble up more of the yawning factory space, where patrons could walk through along a lit path in the darkness and witness different spot-lit "scenes" where actual homeless people were live participants. He created a fishing hole (complete with a broken-down boat that became an instant hit, with patrons photographing themselves in it), a campground with a fake bonfire, a bedroom scene, a junkyard, and various other always changing "environments," as he called them, that reflected found objects thrown out in the trash in the district that he would drag back to create his masterpieces. "Working with what we have" was an unspoken mantra we both shared. I rarely censored his or anyone's work at the club—whether it be music, art, or anything else—and pretty much gave Clay carte blanche. His creations, which were often photographed by patrons and the media, became backdrops for films, and even hosted engagements and one wedding.

It's seldom said, but Clay was the heart and soul of the place. Always having a beat on what was hip and edgy and loving what he was doing, this highly intelligent, gracious, and just plain brilliant man was integral to the club's birth and reincarnations. His dancers, the homeless, and his other subjects who loved him were stoked to participate, enjoying chatting up the patrons as well. To this day, I have some of his eerily beautiful pieces of art—deconstructive, '60s pop and social satire, incorporating discarded material—adorning my Bend, Oregon home. I've collected many artists' pieces from that neighborhood, whose works now hang in museums around the globe, but none sweeter than Clay's.

Interestingly, we would get visits from other club owners in town who, despite spending millions on their dance clubs, attracted limited attendance. On arrival, they'd wander about scratching their heads.

"How do you do it?" they would ask. "You're in a dangerous location. No AC, flooding bathrooms, no parking, and overcharging for cover and drinks."

"I don't know," providing them with a drink. "It's the secret sauce—hard to figure it out."

The people made the place at Club Clearview—staff, entertainers, and patrons alike. High IQs, loyalty, hipness, and a sharp sense of humor defined employee DNA, and we nurtured a culture of diehards that became family. A family that really loved each other and still do. If a new hire didn't fit in, they usually left in a week, via a collective silent lynching. For me, it was part of a constant reinventing of a family of choice, which continues to evolve to this day.

Despite all the love, however, in the early years, the business side of things was mismanaged. Neither Steve nor I had any appetite for management. In fact, we loathed it. My strengths were in the hosting, creative, and marketing side of things. The money we collected at the front door in the early years, literally thousands of dollars, got thrown helter-skelter in an old wooden drawer, often falling on the floor underfoot. After finally getting licensed, we found on our first audit by the Texas Alcohol Board Commission (TABC) that 40 percent of booze revenues were unaccounted for, which we attributed less to dishonesty and more to the free for all. During the audit, I had to provide the club's and my personal checking account information to prove we hadn't skimmed. Since the allotment for spills and comps was only about 5 percent, we clearly had to get our act together and dance to TABC music. The auditor was very cool and only asked for $2,500 when he probably could've asked for well over $100,000. In addition, he gave us six months to pay.

In getting reorganized post-audit, Todd emerged as the man with the plan. For the front door, the five-dollar bills go here, the tens here, etc., etc. We would do drops into the safe every half hour and promptly fill out log sheets. A clicker would count the number of patrons entering, independent of the cashier, for checks and balances. Liquor had to be weighed in and out per bartender station, and beer and wine were not bought in mass kegs and big bottles, but rather individual bottles for a more exact count. Under Todd's tutelage, aided by his banking background, and my systems engineering degree that I finally used, we went from worst to first in management. The club grew in sales and profits while our wild-and-crazy environment still maintained its edge, even though the apparent chaos as witnessed by the patrons now belied a back-of-the-house employing the most sophisticated home-grown systems. We had the secret sauce now on every level.

I learned to delegate by accepting the golden rule of entrepreneurship and enterprise management—finding people in each aspect of your business who are better than you, and giving them the reins. In my situation, as the master of nothing, that was easy.

As we pressed along with the club, I knew nothing about the real estate, planning, zoning, or other particulars concerning the neighborhood. We were focused on operating our monster and keeping things fresh, as we were in the big time now, and the music and club scene was exploding around us as other competitors entered the market. I knew that would eventually make for a bigger pie for all that survived. Still, we had to jump the hurdles of temporary sales drops and escalating costs. As my good friend Greg, the GM at the groundbreaking Dallas institution the Starck Club, shared with me, "Jeff, we are only as good as our last Saturday night."

The explosion in popularity of the discovered district strained the area with new problems—parking, public safety, trash removal, and the new reality of what a mixed-use district would look like. On that note, the building directly across the street from the club's front door, with our club being a loud bustling spot 'til the wee hours on the weekends, had been beautifully renovated into the residence of a local architect, Brent, who was a partner of one of the largest architectural firms in town and involved civically, as well as being a lecturer for students at UT Austin. The area's rezoning would allow residential, nightclub, restaurant, and similar uses in proximity. Other big cities had done this, but these ideals were experimental in Dallas.

I'm sure the vision manifested in the regulations did not foresee the dynamic that was then unfolding. Brent was always very cool about things and would ask me about trash, parking, and trying to figure out how to get the sound from reverberating and rattling the windows in his home until 6 a.m. on the weekends. I always worked to accommodate him, at one point installing sound abatement along the entire front of our two-story building at great cost and effort. His wife, who was also a partner of the firm, was less enchanted with this situation, understandably, but their son loved it because he could sneak out and come over to the club at night, which he did regularly as a VIP. I'm sure his parents thought we were a passing fad, but as we got entrenched and the crowds grew to an enormous size, we became an increasingly undesirable neighbor.

The tension finally came to a head one night when Brent and his wife returned from a black-tie function well past midnight and barely squeezed into their garage to park. They then came across the street and asked for me. The place so packed, it was hard to even get to them. Swimming like a struggling salmon through the thick crowd, we connected. He was noticeably upset, and his wife was just plain pissed. She ended up popping a rivet, yelling at me in her finest Neiman Marcus dress, then walking out in the middle of the street, where, to my dismay, cars blew horns at her and patrons heckled. At this point she threw one of her high heels at me from the middle of the street, proceeding to fall, skinning her knee badly, which put her into a rage. Screaming at me and her husband, who was standing by my side, she finally scooted bloody into their house as Brent looked at me in a daze. I really felt like hell about it.

"Jeff, we are going to have to figure something out," he implored with surprising calm.

"Yes, yes. I feel like shit. Let's get together this week. I'm so damn sorry, my friend."

So began the collision of the reality of what a newspaper article referred to about another tussle that developed down the street as "the nightclub next door." You really had to have thick skin to live in a neighborhood such as this, dealing with all the moving parts and everyone's independent and vigilantly defended positions. Deep Ellum was a place of opinions. Strong opinions. It still is, as is the case in many funky bohemian neighborhoods that gentrify, but perhaps Deep Ellum takes the cake.

Years later in the 1990s, I would renovate a loft in a 1920s two-story building above a former family grocery store. At the time it was perfectly situated on the edge of the entertainment zone, and a bit quieter and more suitable for living, yet a short walk to the action. After residing there for several years as peacefully as I had envisioned, with the area's growth, I wound up having to deal with some of the same problems that Brent had—but on a more challenging level, as the neighborhood by then had fallen into dangerous times, with high crime and gang violence prompted by other landlords' poor tenant choices on a grand scale. Gun violence and even murders in the streets became commonplace. It was a different world. I was regularly exhausted during the day thanks to the nuttiness and literal gun battles in front of my door at all hours of the night, seven days a week. Eventually, eyes crossed and in desperation, I would relocate to the suburbs to avoid permanent sleep deprivation.

Thankfully, that level of violence was not anything I had to deal with while running the Clearview. As wild as the indoor and outdoor entertainment was in 1980s Deep Ellum, the area was incredibly safe to visit in those times. Seemed there was a certain level of respect and tolerance—even with all the diversity—that waned in the late '90s and beyond. Oddly enough, considering the area and how we were operating, even our club was pretty darn safe at a time when so many were not.

Fire had catapulted illegal nightclubs—and even legal ones—into the national headlines after deadly fires one year killed hundreds. In the wake of those tragedies—one in New York and another in Miami—that swept the news, a nationwide detailed inspection of all clubs resulted. Fortunately, we knew our inspectors and passed with just a few minor additions of exit signs and fire extinguishers, with still no notice of our pirated electrical use. Being trapped there by fire was not probable—the club had very little wood and flammables, and many points to exit—but there was another lurking possibility much more lethal.

The infamous, ginormous back room at the original Clearview played host to some big national acts, including, just before they became world-famous, Edie Brickell and the New Bohemians. One overcapacity night, with the toilets overflowing as they did when we got busy, the New Bo's were rocking away while the rabid fans were dancing wildly, sloshing in the nasty water hemorrhaging from the bathrooms in front of the stage. It wasn't enough that the building came with ancient, marginally functional plumbing, but we had also found out that some patrons, or perhaps competitors, exacerbated the effect by jamming toilet paper rolls in the toilets and flushing them repeatedly to create a tsunami effect which had people wading in the putrid waters. Ironically, that seemed to be sort of an attraction. The waters would then cover most of the back area of the place until the morning, when they would subside, ready for another round of mopping and disinfecting.

The night of this show, the waters had reached unprecedented levels. For some divinely inspired reason, I was standing by the side of the stage watching the patrons and band. It was great—almost electrifying. Stepping out of the nasty water, I glanced backstage and noticed the main power cable that had been hacked into the power company's grid and the thick rubber-coated snaking cable that ran to the stage—along with the raw metal coupler used to connect the two—lying on the ground directly in the path of the inching water. There was no way to stop the water flow from ultimately reaching the coupler, so with no time to reach our jack-leg-rigged electrical disconnect at the building a full fifty yards away—which probably would have arced and killed me if done in haste—and absent another plan, everyone standing in that water, including me, would be electrocuted. I couldn't call out for help, as no one would hear thanks to the joyous but deafening pandemonium. I spied my dear friend and soundman Arthur and motioned to him, but he didn't see me. On my own with no time to spare.

Locating a nearby tattered old chair with an orange plastic seat cushion that would not conduct the electricity from the coupler, heart racing and mind razor sharp in clarity of purpose as the brain dumped its fight or flight chemicals into the heated bloodstream, I wiggled backstage. Setting up the chair along with two nearby plastic trash cans, grabbing the rubber housing on each side of the coupler, careful not to electrocute myself, and pulling the assembly away from the water, it was secured to the chair pinned with the cans. The vibration of the raw throbbing and humming power in that cord, feeling like something from a Marvel Avengers episode, was terrifying.

I stood there guarding the wildly imperfect setup and watched as water inched under the chair, all too aware of how close we'd all come—and still could—to being toast. Luckily, Arthur finally saw me and came over to ask me what was going on. In the full-blown madness, I pantomimed the situation we faced, knowing he was familiar with our rigging.

"Dude, don't move; don't touch that thing!" he yelled as he pulled his thick curly hair skyward, rolling his eyes and moving closer to hear me.

"No shit! I get it, Art. I guess we will be right here for the night. When the band quits, do one short encore and shut it down. Just keep people away from me here and don't tell anyone.

It will just freak them out, and if they scatter like rats, we'll all be screwed."

It took a couple hours to get the club cleared out at 3 a.m. and to finally get the pirated power shut down. We survived.

We would have to find new routing for our bandito power cables—above, secured, fastened, and out of people and water's way by the following weekend. Art and I worked solo on the project for the next few days, figuring out how to suspend our big mama source. Even so, we never would completely solve the power puzzle at that club, and the risk remained.

Meanwhile, Edie Brickell would go on to incredible fame, eventually marrying Paul Simon, an icon from my youth. That would have never happened in the event of our mutual end that night. Good juju reigned.

The party raged at this original Clearview factory building for well over a year. We made front-page news on a regular basis. The articles always featured mixed reviews, but we bought into the adage that any press is good press, as the controversial edge kept people coming back for more. To that effect, I'd always tell it like it was with no fear or filter, which kept me on the media's shortlist when they were looking for a story. A supercharged earthshaking Club Clearview story was now brewing with headlines.

The S&L boondoggle-fueled financial crisis of the '80s, with roots in Dallas-Fort Worth, had deepened, while Speaker of the US House of Representatives, Jim Wright of Fort Worth, assured Congress that everything was just peachy in his backyard—"no problems here." This was far from the truth. Consequently, when the shit finally hit the fan, the Clearview building and a slew of others nationwide fell into foreclosure as banks failed and the government took over.

Clearview landed in the hands of the property's noteholder, an elderly heiress of the McCarty-Bush fortune. She was taken on a tour of the building by the Baptist Foundation of Texas one morning on a Sunday after church, as reported by a manager who lived upstairs at the club and woke hung over to greet them. The folks walked her through the facility to show her what exactly she owned—the devils' workshop, an underground club seething with all activities unwholesome and unholy. I can just imagine what they saw with people passed out in various rooms of the building, broken bottles, and who knows what paraphernalia. I'm sure it was disgusting and she was aghast, which resulted in the immediate deeding of the property to the foundation, which in turn moved to evict me as a tenant.

Within days, this made the *Dallas Morning News*. "Bar and Baptist Group Are Bad Mix" headlined the front page, accompanied by my photo. It was juicy news for a Bible Belt city, where a beleaguered religious organization was prepared to go toe-to-toe with a young man operating a wild underground nightclub in a questionable but increasingly high-profile area of town.

Wheeeew! I really didn't want to wrestle with the Foundation and was uncomfortable with the idea of being portrayed as an enemy of church and state. As it turns out, the Foundation having its own internal struggles and scandals exposed added to the unfolding. We went to court on the eviction process, represented by my good friend Ken, a died-in-the-wool Texas attorney and veteran in the courthouse. Although the judge was humored by it all and obviously liked us, even beating down the Foundation's lawyer, there was no legal basis to grant me a favorable ruling. In a courtroom packed with giggling, clamoring press hounds, the judge, after listening to the Foundation's lawyer extol the purity of the Baptists and decry my disgraceful persona, explained to the Baptist's attorney with a smirk that he was Catholic—not a Baptist.

I lost the case, as anticipated, but bought time to file an appeal, prompting a deal with the Foundation. I just had to pay them five hundred dollars and move out within sixty days. After we had all signed off on the agreements, I realized that I'd forgotten to mention the massive Clearview neon sign restored to its 1950s glory, an irreplaceable relic, which we'd planned to move down the street to a new location already scouted and leased. With construction already underway, unable to fathom them wanting the sign, and being a forgiveness-rather-than-permission guy, we hired our sign company vendor to dismantle it, move it, and attach it to our new home ASAP.

Behind the wheel of a massive crane truck, the operator showed up to start the job, which would take most of the day as the sign would have to come apart in three pieces.

As the crane operator cranked it up, I walked to the new locale down the street for renovation meetings. Within an hour he called, telling me to return now as a man in a suit and tie representing the building's owner, looking very official and ready to call the police, was demanding that things cease immediately. Unshaven, barefoot, and in shorts and a T-shirt, I walked back down to meet the clipboard-toting and assistant-accompanied gentleman, who would eventually become a city councilman in a neighboring district. He was furious and immediately got in my face.

"What in the hell do you think you're doing here? We had a deal. You're supposed to be out of here!" he shouted.

"Yeah, no problem. I just forgot the sign and we're just picking it up today and that'll be the end of it."

"Oh no, you're not taking that sign. That sign's part of our property. It's real property that's attached, and we own it, so you need to get out of here or I'm calling the cops."

"That sign means something to me and nothing to you. It's also the insignia of the devil's workshop that was here, so I would think you'd want to be rid of it."

He turned to the crane operator. "You need to detach that crane, or I will have you jailed. I'm a representative of the Baptist Foundation of Texas, the owner of this building. Do you understand me?"

The crane operator was a big, burly, hairy bear of a man, a real in-the-flesh Grizzly Adams with whom I'd worked before and had hit it off. We clicked. He looked at me and I looked at him, then we both looked at our adversary.

"Sir, respectfully, I don't know you. I work for Jeff, and I've known Jeff for a long time," the crane operator said. "He's a good man. Whatever Jeff says, that's what I'm gonna do."

"Thank you, my friend. Please continue removing the sign."

"You got it," he replied with a smile as he continued to raise up the top section of the three-piece sign with his monster eighty-foot crane.

Trapped by my logic and befuddled by the worker's resolve, the Baptist official ripped off his tie, threw his clipboard down on the sidewalk, smashing it, and stomped around huffing and puffing. As we watched him, awaiting his next move, his assistant slunk off from the scene.

"You can have your ridiculous sign, but that's gonna cost you another two hundred dollars," he finally spouted. "That was not part of our agreement!"

"Done! No problem. I'll go and get you the money and be back in a flash."

Minutes later, he pocketed the cash.

The sign presided over the new, soon-to-be-legitimately-permitted Club Clearview when it opened to major fanfare four months later. Just two blocks away from the original club, it would last an astounding eighteen more years at that location and remain after the club's closure. Take the high road, persevering, and the cards will fall in your favor.

The club's move heralded the start of something new to come, but in its newness, it would still exude that radical '60s spirit and early Ellum groove that we had captured organically to take things to the next level. Yes, the '80s nightlife scene was wild in Dallas and other big cities. There was fresh art, a feel of somewhat reckless abandon, punk and alternative music, avant-garde fashion, designer drugs, and all the rest. This energy was a kind of last-ditch pushback against the feeling of being drawn into a corporate- and government-controlled lifestyle, a push that mirrored the '60s revolution. And the new Club Clearview embraced it all.

CHAPTER 7

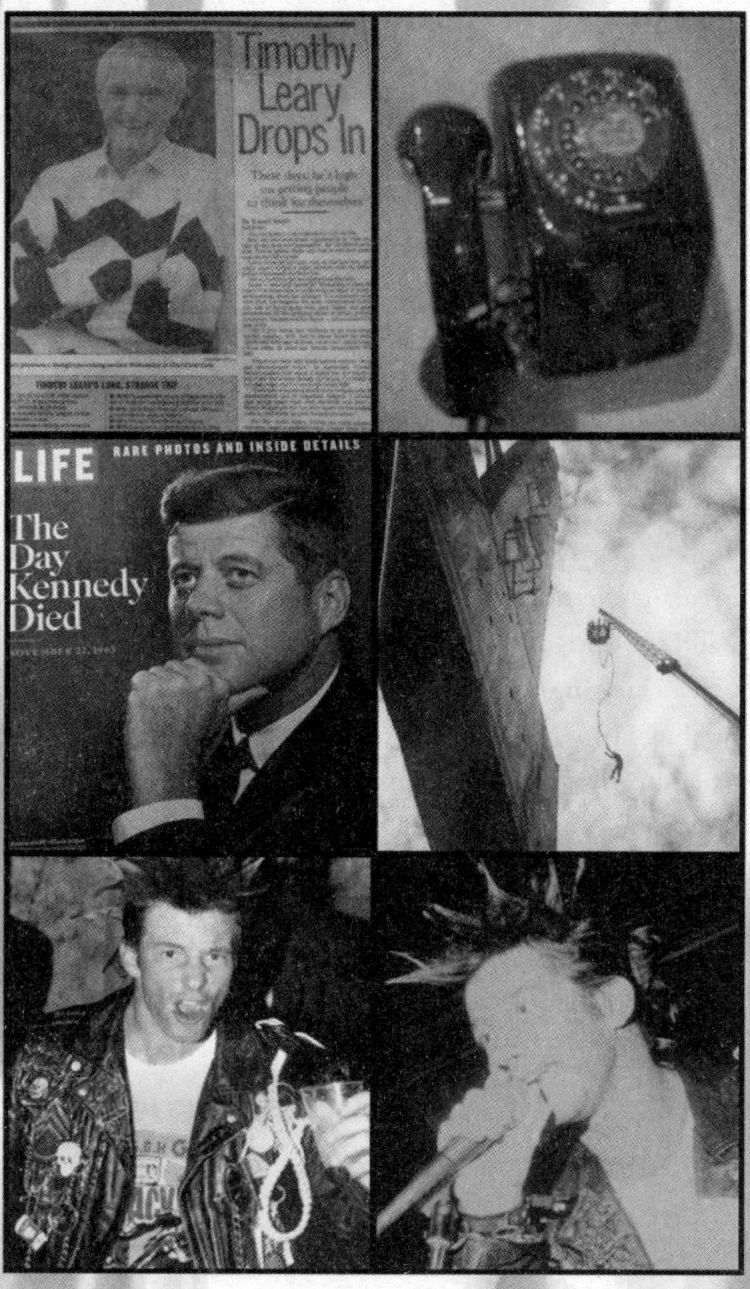

Influencers - Phone from Jail
Bungee at Club - Jeff as Punk MC

CHAPTER 9

TAKE ANOTHER STEP

The eviction was a blessing in disguise, as the front-page news stories of the Baptist's ownership and tussle with them rocked the allure of our joint and brand. Controversy sells. Stepping back to see a glass half full was an acquired skill, wrought through experience. This was one of those.

It was time to get down to the first orders of business. After lease-signing on the new location, which in its last iteration had been a large auto repair shop, we had all the key staff involved in the initial visits, design, and plan for the new facility join in multiple free-form, on-the-fly meetings, and we toiled seven long days and nights every week. The now-famous, glowing red neon sign, attached as a priority, rose high above the other single-story 1920s- and '30s-era buildings, and signaled our new home was happening to throngs that strolled the area on weekend nights, chomping at the bit.

Another useful relic recovered from our prior home was our old beer cooler—a ten-by-twenty-by-ten-foot insulated box, formerly the back of an old 1960s refrigeration truck, gifted to us by our dear friend and Anheuser Busch alumnus, Cliff. One cold Saturday afternoon, we entered the old building through its back factory doors, which we found flung open as the homeless residents had multiplied since our departure, rendering the building accessible to all. Our mission: to relocate that beer cooler to our new establishment. A parade of cheering staffers and others watched as we chained the one-ton hulk of a metal box to a hefty car and dragged it down the concrete roadway. Its thick, multi-layered metal bottom absorbed the punishment, sparking, screeching, scraping, and gouging the public and private pathways en route to its destination two blocks away, while we carefully maintained momentum lest it melt and fuse to the road. The cooler relocation's music was nails on the chalkboard times a hundred, until we got it settled into its painstakingly calculated location at the center of the building. We were still low-budget, scavenging, seat-of-the-pants operators—committed enemies of waste, amid a deepening S&L-sparked recession.

We proceeded like ants or honeybees to build the interior hive of the operation around the beer cooler relic, which would serve literally millions of patrons in its extended life, rivaling the floor safe in its longevity. As much as the previous club had started off as an operational disaster, this one's nerve center was going to be customer-service-oriented and ultra-systems-efficient in funky style.

With the skeleton in place, it was time to conjure up the vibe and raw elemental energy of the original location and get the venue open. We thought and worked hard to avoid sterilizing the concept to be birthed in the ten-thousand-square-foot bland box we had adopted, which was going to need some magic. The property itself had very little charm except for one area with old white hexagon floor tiles and a decorative iron pole on the street corner that apparently had been the shop office entry. We knew that area had future promise as the club spaces would morph almost every year, but for our initial design it would serve as our club's combination onsite premise office, band dressing room, and storage area.

The eventual floor plan we noodled up for the rest of the venue featured a series of different-size rooms and passageways to create a circular motion in the interior's perimeter and provide alleys in between. With high ceilings, there was also an opportunity to go to two levels in some places. Flow and the ability to serve patrons were paramount. We also needed adequate bathrooms, placing them in three different locations throughout the building. Patrons waiting in line either for entry, bathrooms, or drinks was lost fun time and lost revenue for us. The layout and back-of-house machinery needed to be invisible and even confusing to the casual observer; the decor, however, needed to be as attention-grabbing as the infrastructure was unobtrusive.

As a result, the rooms were carved out to be themed into unique environments, each one vetted by our most brilliant group. We knew what worked from our experimentation at the original location and from spotting current changing trends. Of course, we got Clay's input during and after group tribunals, and then cut him loose to do his thing with whoever volunteered to work with him. He adorned the property with textures, colors, found objects, day-glow paint, and everything in his unusual and expanded toolkit.

What sprouted from his creative genius was marvelous to behold. In the various themed rooms, throbbing, swirling, pounding, whirling, and blasting lights, color, smells, and sounds gripped the patrons packed in like lemmings on the opening night, writhing toe-to-toe in ecstasy. Moving from one room to the next, if they chose, would scramble the synapses, bouncing like a bubble in the energy's wake. The vibe changed in each room, distinct from zone to zone, and from minute to minute.

Contrary to popular belief in Deep Ellum clubland, I did not come from a moneyed family, having been slugging it out starting from my Detroit roots—so there was no money pot to draw from. Paul, a patron who had witnessed our path and become an investor, partner, and ultimately friend, plopped down a modicum of cash to make the whole move happen. He was a straitlaced, reserved, and very bright fellow who understood the promise of this venture and was thrilled to dip his toe in the funky sauce.

The opening was a bang, and the energy continued for years, with dynamic nights often being influenced by the live music performances and DJs of the evening. Our new place was just as successful as the old funky one, perhaps even more so. Paul would wind up lauding me as a great promoter in a newspaper story, saying, "You take a talent like that, and he could make millions in real estate but he wants to do this." Perhaps he was right, but I was following my heart, having learned long before missing BikeCentennial to honor that tune and dodge future regrets.

Paul was not our only supporter. Everyone I partnered with I learned from, and valued those relationships to the roots of my soul. It was another case of me subconsciously wanting to create the family I didn't really have, to everyone's mutual benefit. We can all find egregious differences with anyone in this world, but better to brazenly nurture what we have in common. Those who focus on differences end up being castaways on islands unto themselves, places where we as social animals cannot survive.

Our new club certainly gave people a spot to congregate and indulge in that social need. The place had opened with that bang, and the crowds grew every weekend. The A-to-Z clientele seemed even more varied this time—hippies, yuppies, trendies, punks, and fashion victims of all pigment, social status, beliefs, and sexual preferences, melded together in a stew that was truly new to Dallas. It was utter perfection, providing experiences for people that they never would have had otherwise. Clearview had the allure of a combined Woodstock, Rainbow gathering, and Burning Man festival every weekend. In fact, since we had all missed the '60s, some weekends and months we pushed a psychedelic atmosphere with the music, art, and poetry. Whatever came into vogue or was on the cutting edge, we adopted in our own versions, inviting artists, musicians, DJs, speakers, and absolute nutballs to come and spray their potions.

With dance music pulsing in part of the club, and varied live shows in other rooms, it was difficult to capture the blended or sometimes clashing vibes that emanated from the structure any given night. On some evenings, bands diverse as Front

242, Ministry, Skinny Puppy, Mudhoney, The Dead Milkmen, Divine, Reverend Horton Heat, Husker du, the Butthole Surfers, and the late Mojo Nixon, to name a few, performed in wild, sweaty, pounding, ear-splitting madness. On the mellower side, we hosted the Neville Brothers, Burning Spear, Pato Banton, Yellow Man, Chris Isaak, Buckwheat Zydeco, The Dixie Chicks, Sara Hickman, and more. The diversity kept the club fresh and exposed constantly to new clientele, as well as always keeping everyone on their heels. If you know the music, imagine it in the setting we invented, and you are there.

The press chronicled many of the shows, but a couple of them stood out.

The Red Hot Chili Peppers played their first of two shows at the club in 1988, long before sold-out world tours, groundbreaking MTV videos, and the bestselling, revealing books *Scar Tissue* and *By the Way*. Their music and showmanship blended perfectly there. In their first appearance, they would take the stage—naked. Halfway through the set, they donned their traditional socks, but bassist Flea stayed completely nude during the entire set. Jack Iron sent one drumstick after another ricocheting off the drums and into the crowd, which took the blows without major injury. Later, our staff collected more than ten drumsticks, including one wedged into the makeshift drop ceiling.

The Beat Farmers and their late lead singer Country Dick Montana were Mojo Nixon and Clearview faves. In a late '80s concert, Dick, dressed in a black duster, ran through the bar with a five-foot inflatable phallus, jumped up on the bar guzzling down a whiskey, and then led the crowd down the street in a conga line, inflatable toy in tow.

It wasn't all fun and games dealing with the bands and their managers, however. Sometimes excessive drinking, heroin, and guns would get in the mix, making things a little messy.

Mother Nature didn't help. I recall an ice storm in Dallas in the '90s one February, when the roads were impassable. We seemed to have one ice storm every January and February, which made booking expensive bands a bit risky during those months. Regardless, we booked a Seattle grunge band prior to them becoming a phenomenon, Soundgarden, for a then-hefty fee of $3,500 to play a few weeks into the new year.

The band called me the day before from San Antonio, one of their tour stops, fully aware of the stormy conditions in the Big D. Bands always knew when a concert was going to bomb, and ofttimes it was all about the money.

"Hey man, we're coming, we're coming, no fear we will be there."

"Guys, the roads are impassable here. You may wanna save your gas. I don't know if I can get any staff here; if so, it'll be a skeleton crew, and we've only sold about thirty tickets. You've got the deposit; we can just call it even."

"No way, dude, we're playing—we're there and we're getting paid!"

"Okay, well, I may be the only one there, but I'll meet you tomorrow. We'll work it out."

As it turned out, after barely making it to the club in my Volvo and slipping around in the parking lot on a glazed sheet of ice an inch thick, with the entire city paralyzed, only myself, a bartender, and soundman Art had arrived to represent the club. There I stood alongside the band, the manager, and seventeen patrons, watching them play with the arena sound system they had brought with them, in addition to ours that skated into the venue. I watched painfully, my whole body shaking with the blasting sound waves, thinking I was going to bleed internally as well as financially. At the end of the night, they got their full fee and would go on to chart double platinum records and Grammy Awards, selling thirty million albums worldwide.

Sometimes, it's all about making accommodations. Back in those days, we got popular booking numerous reggae bands through a promoter in Washington, DC. They drew well, and for the most part it was a good relationship, even though a few of the managers carried hardware to ensure their payment. I remember meeting with one of them in the office before a show. He pulled out a gun and set it on the table close to him, making sure I saw it.

"Hey mon, we're going to have to get paid before we go on, you know, bra. It's the way we do it."

"Well, my friend, we typically pay the balance after the show. You already have a deposit, and you need to put the gun away; that's not something that we do here. Go put it back in your tour bus and come back, and I'll pay you in advance—this time."

He looked at me, grinned, and did just that. It was not the first or last time I'd have guns pulled out or brandished. I continued to take the same kind of bold stand, having more balls then than I do now.

Having become a brand and a novelty, we hosted all-night-long weekday parties for bands pausing on their world tours or wrapping films—two of the better events being a Pink Floyd world tour, where they sold out three Texas stadium concerts back-to-back-to-back on my birthday week in the '90s, and Oliver Stone's wrap party for *JFK* (yes, there are those initials again), which would require two to three days of recovery time. We offered a relatively uncensored, inspired environment for artists to showcase their craft, and Hollywoodies loved to carouse and cut loose without being hassled. Hence their affection for our place.

Whether you were famous or not, being at Clearview on any given night was a memorable experience and a gift from the cosmic beyond. The media loved it as much as the regulars, who were compelled to attend every weekend. The newspaper and weekly's headlines—always adorned with colorful photos, as the venue art and clientele were a photographer's kaleidoscopic dream come true—offered descriptions such as:

> "Clearview is one of the last vestiges of funky Deep Ellum style, as if a cave was graffiti-ed by Neo '60s flower children."
>
> "Speak softly and carry a heavy club."
>
> "In the Deep Ellum night a funky refuge from slickness."
>
> "The writings on the wall at roomy Club Clearview—it's art meets disco at Deep Ellum bar."
>
> "Through the years, blearily. Club Clearview's twenty years of existence encompass a lot of funky history."

Yes, indeed.

There were quite a few characters on our staff/family who collaboratively breathed life into the venue and were a germane element of the brew. Many stayed on for over two decades. Too many geniuses to tag.

A position of import and requiring a special skill set was that of music director. I had been the original music director and set the pace early on, but I had a hard time keeping up with the scene with all that was now on my plate. I recall doing some intros for bands and fancied myself a young Bill Graham of San Francisco fame. A dream gig, it was a hard privilege to let go of and pass on. A youthful, passionate, high-energy lady by the name of Robin took over for me, and did a great job booking the venue before pursuing her first love and family's business of polo.

So, the search was back on for a new maestra. It can't be understated how relevant this person is to a venue, especially in what was becoming an explosive and competitive music scene, where local bands were getting signed by record labels monthly, becoming national acts, and being loved in that community was key.

We were blessed with the arrival of Lisa Oldham, a hard-charging, bright, independent woman with a personality and bosom that could fill an entire zip code. She nurtured many genres there and brought us much success with her brash, boisterous, fun-loving style. An incredible hoot, she could hobnob with the best of them, and with her significant other Brad—a talent in his own right and brother to Dallas's fashion designer to the stars, Todd Oldham—Lisa brought a lot to the table. The story she loves to tell is the time she booked the band Green Day, before anyone knew who they were, for $3,000, and had them crash at her pad in exchange for them building her bookshelves. A character not to be forgotten, she was one of many who consistently gave it their all and made us the success we were.

But we offered much, much more than the best music and art commandeered by the talent directing it. We were always open to trying new things. While some fell flat, quite a few were spot on:

- Bungee jumping in the middle of the night from a construction crane mounted to a truck, fifteen stories above a concrete parking lot—squiggling free-falling bodies dropping to the screeches of a thousand onlookers below.
- Slam poetry that covered all manner of sociopolitical themes, politics, sex, racism, harmonizing chants, and angry, spitting, raging, ballistic rants.
- The renowned Miss Galaxy outdoor, over-the-top, runway fashion shows (thanks to well-connected creative staffers David, Brent, and Dale), where contestants would dress and be styled as parts of planets, nebulas, and other spaced-out themes.
- The Brothers Grimm—now called Hellzapoppin' and still out there—a bizarre new-age traveling freak-show troupe. An actual mini-circus featuring fire-breathers, a wolfman, a serpent lady, and more, who interacted with the crowd both thrilling and scaring them shitless.
- Micro-crafted pub beer, way before it was a thing, as well as incorporating Virtual Reality, which became one of the hottest commodities—both in their earliest manifestations.

We were most raw and elemental in infancy, and maintained that thread while becoming the conduit of cool in the '90s.

Rather than call it "selling out," in the trendy world of fashion, art, and music, you either get with it or you are a dinosaur. You'll be a fossil overnight. We were always ready to accept risks and damage incurred or give someone a shot—that was how the stars were born.

Detractors in the area noted, "The guy knows what's coming on and knows what people want, but it's driving too much business here, and we want to avoid tour buses with blue hairs in the neighborhood." The tour buses with blue hairs never appeared, but the area certainly grew in popularity. That was not always the easiest thing to manage.

While we mostly maintained a diverse crowd (minus blue hairs) swimming in wild energy, there were some minor brawls on occasion, and some patrons had to be denied entry, cut off, ejected, and/or jailed. The security staff was very skilled at handling people without throwing punches or using weapons. Most of them had been trained in martial arts and could easily take people down using a person's own aggression against them. No matter what incidents occurred, and there were a few, the party always raged on at the club.

One night a drunk patron got in an upstairs, off-limits area. Wandering around, he moved some barricades and continued to walk out onto a paper-thin drop ceiling, where he immediately whooshed through and onto the shoulders of a bartender fifteen feet below. Debris and metal track flew everywhere and liquor bottles went airborne, busting on the concrete floor behind the bar. Amazingly, no one was seriously injured. There were nine other service stations in the complex, so things just kept rolling, and within fifteen minutes the bartender was all set up and back in action.

Another night there was a scuffle on the jam-packed dance floor, with a girl crumpling to the ground after being shot in the abdomen by her boyfriend. Security got there and quickly summoned an ambulance that took her to nearby Baylor Hospital. She miraculously suffered no injuries to any organs, with the bullet going right through her. The shooting prompted a few dance-floor patrons to briefly pause, but then they popped back into a full-on blow. Most were oblivious to the mishap.

I wasn't present that night but was notified and went down in the morning to survey the situation, in case we were summoned by whomever to give our side of the story. I saw the blood traces on the dance floor and wondered where the bullet might have ended up. I had planned on meeting the DJ that day, Mark aka Mookie D, so I called him on the phone and asked him what he remembered about the incident.

"You know, it was weird, Jeff. I heard something and then there was a whistle sound and that was it. But it was the strangest noise."

"Hmmmm," I said. "Thanks. Let's plan on getting together here later as planned, to talk about programming."

I hung up the phone, walked back out onto the dance floor and then strolled over to the DJ booth. Walking behind it, I surveyed the sheetrock wall. In a small indentation, I found the mystery bullet. After sizing it up and its possible trajectory, factoring in the whistle that Mookie had heard—I realized then it must've gone right by his ear. Just an inch over it would've spelled the end for my friend. I carefully dug out the bullet and kept it in case it would be needed later. Of course, when I met with Mook, I showed him what I had discovered.

"Holy shit, Jeff!"

He truly dodged a bullet that night.

All of these mishaps would've closed a normal club, but we knew how to manage insanity and keep things going while providing the best outcomes for everyone, incorporating warts and all. In the early years, I worked there every night, staying up late and attending all the after-hours parties, then sleeping until noon or later the next day to start over again.

At age thirty-two, six years after throwing the first warehouse parties, I finally began to delegate more, to create other opportunities for myself and get some sleep. Doors had been flung open, and I needed to take advantage of the options. Things I could never do or even dream of as a kid had become part of my newfound domain. I had never seen a pro sports game as a VIP, only as a high schooler scalping tickets with my friend and riding to the downtown venues on Detroit city buses. Now, it was limos as the standard ride, VIP at the Dallas Cowboys' fifty-yard line for classic unattainable San Francisco 49ers playoff tickets, and more, which seemed unreal. VIP access, A-lister parties, private boxes, you name it—for years it was there for the taking, with the privileges and money pouring in.

Being considered a Dallas underground trendsetter of sorts, I was often asked to speak or opine on various topics of the day, both on and off the record, which led by default to some heavyweight sponsors. One of my favorites was Stanley Marcus, world-renowned retailer and creator of the legendary Neiman Marcus high-end department store chain. In a stunning slide, the company was forced into bankruptcy in 2020 after he passed. Thankfully, he did not have to witness that—it would have prompted him to shred his suit or tear what was left of his hair out. On that topic, we both had our hair and nails done at the famous Highland Park Village Barbers, an old-time barbershop perched over the most prime piece of real estate and boutique shops in the city. It was laid-back and inexpensive, yet catered to the A-list clientele of Dallas. I had the good fortune to see Stanley there many times as we sat in our "regular" chairs that were by happenstance next to each other. He loved to pick my brain in his forward, classy, unrelenting style.

"Jeff, I know you have your fingers on the pulse in this town."

"Are you kidding me? That's you, Stanley," I replied.

"Well, that's flattering. But I'm troubled by some things I see. With your influence, can't you help this generation of kids and show them what to wear? Why is everybody wearing jeans? We sell them, but there has got to be more to life! What is wrong with a nice designer suit?

"I'll see what I can do my friend," I responded, of course knowing I had no influence whatsoever in that world.

He was an inspiring, tell-it-like-it-is person, and he invited me to speak at Neiman's acclaimed Inner Circle club for their elite members. I remember honing some speaking skills with my polished club partner Jeff during a shtick we did together, which was a lot of fun. As a byproduct of this, I was often asked to mentor and serve on area boards. With success came notoriety and eventually some semblance of responsibility, even if I was of the Charles Barkley, not-a-role-model ilk. Our success certainly eclipsed what anyone could have ever imagined, leading to a certain amount of celebrity for me, my partner, and our venue.

D [Dallas] *Magazine* created a special issue for its thirty-fifth anniversary. It identified the top thirty-five moments in Dallas history. Among those were its founding by John Neely Bryan and his cabin on the Trinity River, the JFK thang, the first Neiman Marcus store founded by my friend Stanley, the Dallas Cowboys history, and more. "Club Clearview rocks Deep Ellum" was #17, which was elite company, rarefied air, and perhaps manifest destiny.

On the flip side, in my submersion into the Deep Ellum area, I had found myself neighbors with what folks referred to as the Dallas homeless population. The authorities would regularly run any "undesirables" from under the freeway in the downtown area to our neighborhood, which became known for this mix. I got to know a few of the characters and even hired some of them to do odd jobs or work with Clay. I'd chat with them to garner an understanding of who they were, and even help to get them on track and stay out of trouble if possible—sometimes with good effect and sometimes not. I found many of these people to be brilliant, some not so, and plenty of others in between.

One was a character by the name of Johnny, a drifter from Arkansas whom I worked with, befriended, and helped for many years. He lived in the purgatory of, by his own admission, being not quite right enough to function in society, yet capable in many ways. He became somewhat of a charming celebrity, and I mentored him for several years. He was hired as a janitor's helper of sorts at the club, as well as a helping hand for anyone who needed one. I would drop everything to help him, and worked hard to keep him housed, fed, and sober, something of a challenge in our environment. The club staff wasn't happy with him at times, but I stood by him and he was a fixture. Seeing Jamie Foxx in the movie *The Soloist*, playing a skid-row homeless violinist discovered by a Los Angeles columnist, reminded me of my special friendship with Johnny and my aspirations for him to star in a book I would never write. Later in life, and closer to home, I had the pleasure of meeting and becoming friends with Ron Hall, an acclaimed art dealer and writer of the book *Same Kind of Different as Me*. Ron's story of his friendship with Denver, a homeless man he befriended, which changed both their lives, and became a major motion picture released by Paramount, touched me in the same way. There is a lot to learn from these types of relationships that few are privileged to experience. However, my friend Johnny's charm was often lost on others, especially when he performed spotty work, misbehaved at the club, or got into booze or drugs.

I recall my club manager, Dale, at the Club Clearview requesting a conference with me.

"Jeff, I need to talk to you about Johnny," he said.

We strolled over to the small, unadorned office on site, walked in, closed the door, and sat in the shabby seats, inherited from the former auto repair warehouse.

"Johnny is just not cutting it. Getting lazier and often drinking too much, finishing customers' leftover drinks during cleanups, and getting smashed. Gurgling and ogling the female customers in an uncomfortable fashion. I cannot deal with this anymore."

"Well, I'll talk to him about this. I remember drinking leftovers in bars when I backpacked the world, so I'm guilty too," I said grinning.

"Jeff, this is not the same. I'm at the point where I say, let's just pay him to not work here. I will even contribute."

"I will discuss this with him, and we can even reduce his duties or hours somewhat. We will work it out," I said. And we did.

In my quest to understand, develop the compassion I now have, and assist with the "homeless" problem in the city—both out of my caring and necessity as it impacted my business—I joined local boards to help address these issues, which were common in all the big cities in the country and still are today and ever-increasing. I found the catchall phrase of "homeless" to be very misleading, as very few of the folks I had contact with even wanted a home. They just wanted to have their freedom and roam, kind of like I did. Many had mental illness issues or addiction issues like Johnny, or both, or even worse, were lifetime cons. Being in the big city, the concrete jungle, didn't help matters, and I was a proponent of various ideas, including a central point to screen folks to figure out who they were, if they were wanted criminals, what type of issues they faced, and whether they needed or even wanted help or simply rejected it all. They could then be directed to the proper resource rather than pinballing between various shelters, food sources, disjointed agencies, downtown church organizations, and the like, which was the status quo. Knowing the habits that most folks did not, I was a promoter of orderly triage.

As I lived in the urban core, I was often asked to assist suburban church groups—well-meaning folks, many of whom lived far from the urban center. They had similar requests. "Hi Jeff, I know you're down there and my church group would like to help some of the homeless people. We would like to come on a Sunday, perhaps use your parking lot at your home there—just the parking lot—and we could feed some of these people. We've got a plan."

"Thank you, that is very well-intentioned, and I get those inquiries all the time. I must decline. Feedings in my parking lot just puts me on the map with folks neither one of us knows or knows anything about, which typically results in me picking up a lot of trash and feces afterward, and even witnessing skirmishes and then receiving unannounced return visits from these strangers randomly. This is not voicing a lack of compassion, just real-life issues here."

"No, we would take care of everything," they would assure me. "Trust me, we are good."

"Well, I'm sure you are, so I have something for you to ponder in earnest. This environment down here is not very hospitable for folks on the street, so perhaps you could come down, engage a couple of these souls, and take them up to your area to help them there? That might be best. Just a couple who are willing."

"Oh no no no no no! We don't want to bring them up here! No, no we are happy to help them down there."

"Exactly. But that's my suggestion. In your backyard, helping folks one on one. In a more agreeable environment. Think about it."

I never got a return call after these types of exchanges. There was an acronym created for this sort of thinking. NIMBY—Not In My Backyard.

During my tenures on various boards, I suggested many things and helped with many initiatives. One vision I had was utilizing areas south of town that had grass and trees on massive acreage for housing and maybe even communal-style farming. The land could have been bought for pennies and would have offered those who would have welcomed the opportunity an alternative to life in the scorching heat and cold shoulders of the concrete jungle.

People might not have embraced those visions of mine and my solutions, but they did continue to flock to the wildness that was our ever-evolving club. We kept reinventing constantly, keeping competitive, and working to incorporate the neighborhood at large.

One of the more ambitious projects we tackled that lit up the area was a hundred-yard-long and thirty-foot-tall mural, which wrapped around the entire outside of the club and an adjoining building. It came into being thanks to twenty-five artists going at it in a two-week-long painting competition. There was a lot of pride involved, and they took it very seriously. I witnessed fierce battling in conjunction with camaraderie. The contest became an instant twenty-four-hour-a-day scene in and of itself, prompting local, regional, and even national media photographing, videotaping, writing feature articles, and even doing live coverage of the event.

Day and night, artists would arrive and go up and down ladders with their paints, stencils, sponges, and even toilet plungers. There were no office hours, just a two-week window to get your work done, with a judging party comprised of staff together with local art aficionados and celebs for the finale. As fate would have it, Clay won the contest, even though none of our staffers were allowed to vote for him.

One typical weekday, during the fest, I stood out in the parking lot surveying artists, many good friends of mine, working on the walls. I loved going there every day to chat and watch them create and interact, and watch locals and tourists alike photograph them with glee. I was in my P.T. Barnum self. That day, I was approached by a neighboring club owner who was curious about the details.

"Wow, Swaney, this is quite a spectacle," he said. "Did you guys get permits for all this? And what kind?"

"Are you kidding me?" I responded. "It would never happen if that was the case. You can't deal with that bureaucracy. Let whoever wants to hassle us tell us to stop. That'll just get us more attention. We are making headlines every day here—the media loves it."

"Well exactly, it's so wide open. Aren't you concerned about getting into some shit? Why not clear it up front somehow?"

"It's not in our historical DNA! Besides, it's 'forgiveness not permission' in this world. At City Hall, the answer is always *no*," I spouted.

"How about insurance? What if one of those guys falls off a ladder?"

"Well, we have insurance—I don't know if it would cover it, and I'm not gonna worry about it. I'm not gonna live in a bubble. And I luv ya man, but don't jinx us, please. Let it roll and enjoy!"

Not long after, the same guy enlisted artists to muralise his outside club walls.

Our twenty-four-hour-a-day mural party rocked, creating the largest mural of its time in the state of Texas. It set the tone for even larger and celebrated painting efforts years later, where some of the same artists would paint an underground tunnel from the 1920s, which was the entry point to the neighborhood slated to be torn down to make way for roadway changes and further redevelopment. Current developers in Ellum continue to tap some of the same artists we promoted to great effect, in particular renowned artists Greg Contestible, the late Mosquito, Brad Smith, and Frank Campagna, the latter who may be the Godfather of Ellum mural art, depending on whom you ask.

Since art had been a central theme in the old club and continued to be so in the new one, it was only natural that we would birth the concept named The Art Bar, a project that put us over the top. It was a calmer, mellower bubble in the scene, hosting art openings and sales, with several pieces being purchased by Dallas and Fort Worth museums, myself, and other collectors. We would theme some of the shows, including our famous "Images of Big Tex," an annual long-running show during The State Fair of Texas each fall—Big Tex being the fifty-two-foot-tall, talking cowboy icon who welcomes over two million visitors annually to the nearby State Fair. Art Bar was that reprieve, a place to chat apart from the interconnected, throbbing, and sometimes chaotic insanity of our main club areas. The creation of Art Bar made business sense, as the competition in the club business was heating up, and we needed to downsize the live music and DJ dance floors and carve out some space that was connected but could stand on its own. It succeeded and ended up being our higher-end clientele's go-to.

A few years later, we took the redevelopment further when we invited our friend Jeffrey Yarbrough to join us and incorporate his funky-cool New York-French bistro concept into our facility. Jeff had been a co-promoter of a few fashion parties at the club, through his work in Dallas, New York, and LA with *Women's Wear Daily* and *Scene Magazine*. Christened "The Blind Lemon," the bistro became an instant hit, filling a niche for food and drink and late-night dancing to funk and house music there.

I've always believed in the following advice:

> *Be Aware. Reinvent yourself and your business—or stagnate in this world. Be grateful and thankful, and follow blessings bestowed to fulfillment.*

I followed that advice in every possible way, which kept the media spotlight on us. Jeffrey and I grabbed those media opportunities as they came and were dubbed "The Jeffs" or "Jeff and Jeff." The monikers caught fire, often confusing others to the point of people asking me in later years about my wife Tara, who was Jeffrey's betrothed, or asking him about some of my past exploits he knew nothing about. There was a particular moment in the Jeffs' history that rings a bell.

I recall being contacted and asked to be interviewed for *The Dallas Morning News* "High Profile" section. This was a high honor in town—akin to receiving an Oscar award there—and few got this privilege. I was excited about the possibilities.

I asked the writer, "Do you want to do just me or the Jeffs?"

"Not sure about that, Swaney. Hadn't thought about it. Let me vet that with the group."

They took it to their committee, then answered back, "We want you at the minimum, but it's your call."

Since our enterprise was on the verge of expansion, it was best to put my ego aside for the good of the business and team. In all honesty, there was a lot to say on a huge platform, but wise to quell that urge.

For me, it was never about visibility, but more about the club's, an approach that contributed to our success, although not apparent. Never fancied myself a "club owner," a moniker with dubious distinctions; rather, more interested in creating, making the scene, and making people think. For ten years we hosted the hoi polloi—rock stars, politicians at the highest levels of government, designers, artists, urchins, freaks, the quirky, the filthy rich, and the filthy—all our clientele. With our undeniable draw, if you had not been, you simply hadn't lived. There was an air of chaos, fun, and barely controlled madness, all managed by a security team that was Zen. It was *the place* to be for any big show or weekend night.

I recall a conversation with a fellow club owner, Blake Woodall, one of the heirs to the Vent-A-Hood fortune, as he walked through the club one night, a drink in one hand and scratching his head with the other.

"Man, I'll tell you what, Jeff. This is really something you've got here."

"Well, I really appreciate it, and coming from the guy that has the coolest club in town, that means a lot."

Blake and some of his well-heeled friends, including heiress Christina de Limur, had opened their club a year previously on the other side of town. He had brought in designer Philippe

Starck from Paris, who at that time was not quite the universal household name he would become. Starck, for whom the club would be named, created a very slick, minimalist, velvet-roped, black-marbled, white-sheered, glammed, co-ed bathroomed, see-and-be-seen venue that Dallas had never witnessed before. Sleek, chichi, uber-stylish, and legendary on a global scale. An absolute 180 of our place in many respects, except for the ever-elusive cool factor. We considered it our sister club, despite its being built and operated at a hundred times our budget, and many of our staffers had friends there. We had an excellent relationship, uncommon in the club world, with each offering something beyond country and disco, and eons beyond anything that Dallas, Texas had seen.

"I'll tell you, Jeff, if you ever get some real money, there is no telling what you could do."

"You know, Blake, really wouldn't want to compromise things, especially in this club. Love where we're at, working with what we have—funky and elemental. And honestly, we don't know how else to do things."

He nodded his approval and vanished into the crowd.

I had come a long way from my humble beginnings. But, no pain, no gain. Amidst the glory, there were some bumps in the road.

When you get bigger than life—you are a target. Success and notoriety breed this. I wasn't always ready for that and sometimes didn't handle it well. But when club wars erupted and neighborhood competitors seemed to have it out for us, I maintained cool with them, even though I knew they had called the police on me, bad-mouthed me to the press, and were guilty of other sins.

It was okay with me—they were good for the hood, and I could survive that and others nibbling, attributing it to just good fun.

One day, I found painted on a key side-street building wall—competing places being on Commerce Street in the area and mine on Elm, two blocks over—a giant, ten-foot-tall tag about forty feet long that read:

~ STYLE ——————— SUBSTANCE ~

Style being the direction of our offering on Elm Street and *Substance* towards Commerce Street.

I couldn't tell if the big graffiti was meant to be a slight but believe the unknown purveyor got it right. While we each offered both, I'd always give others the nod on being and staying rawer. This is what attracted me to the area in the first place—they had more than what they knew. We would not have been what we became without the influence of our neighbors. Many years later, we would all realize that and come together in the making of a documentary film on the Deep Ellum scene, with a working title of *Round Pegs in Square Holes*. How appropriate.

Even though pushed by some populace and media, I never spoke ill about other operators in that neighborhood—it hurts your business, and friendly competition makes the pie bigger. Besides, patience results in a big piece of a bigger pie. Global trade partners have witnessed this truth. Our clubland tussle microcosm and its outcomes reflect these findings that may keep our world from self-destructing if we can all, or at least some of us, practice patience.

Yes, patience and keeping calm win the day, but sometimes that's easier said, than done.

One night I was out dining in the area with a well-known freelance writer, his girlfriend, and mine. He was going to write a piece on the hood and wanted to hang out with us to get an insider's perspective—and he did.

After dinner at the area's first fine-dining joint, The Deep Ellum Café, we walked down the busy streets and sauntered by the club, only to witness a police raid in progress. Some five police cars and at least a dozen officers buzzed around the club parking lot at the front entry. That wasn't particularly bothersome to me, since things were almost always cool there. Besides, my staff knew many of the officers and could handle any situation.

"Jeff, don't go in there," one of the members of my party said. "Just hang with us; walk right by and keep going."

"Of course," I readily agreed. "No need to get into that mess."

Then I saw something I couldn't stomach. An officer had one of the barmaids pushed up against a squad car, arms behind her back by the wrists and cranking upward, jerking repeatedly as she screamed out. Ironically, this gal was a goody-two-shoes—didn't drink, do drugs, or anything of the sort, and just was a special human. A nanosecond after seeing that, bolting from my group, found me running headlong for the offending officer. I torpedoed him, launching myself at full speed, airborne, knocking him off the barmaid and off his feet with a reckless body blast. We both flew tumbling onto the pavement as more officers came over and subdued and pounded handcuffs on me, face ground into the concrete and contorted every which way to induce discomfort.

"There's no way I was gonna let you do anything more to hurt her. That totally sucks, dude. No way. That was total bullshit."

They didn't respond, but rather rifled through my pockets, finding my ID as the officer got on his walkie-talkie to contact the lead in the raid.

"We have man down on Elm. ID is Jeff Swaney."

"Jeff Swaney—really? Oh, that is great. Bring him to me!" the lieutenant growled with an elated Darth Vader tone. A captive prize.

That started my journey to the police station downtown, the same station where, in 1963, Jack Ruby shot Lee Harvey Oswald point blank—flashing back to more Camelot story from my past. I was unceremoniously escorted up from the underground parking garage, remembered vividly from the world-famous photo of Ruby firing on the accused assassin. After being roughhoused up the stairwells, arriving at a lieutenant's office adorned with 1950s furniture and room dividers, I was plopped down and handcuffed to one of the wheeling green-and-gray-padded throwback office chairs. Little did they know that their 1950s office motif had come into style—however in more juxtaposed moderation. We would use similar styles in the artsy real estate office a few years later.

The setting made me feel as if I was in a period movie. A "B" movie.

Sitting silently for over an hour as officers came and went, I started developing an urge to go to the men's room, which was managed until it needed to be taken care of—right away. Another officer walked into the cubicle.

"I am going to need the bathroom here at some point. It's been a while, so if you could help me out with that, I'd appreciate it."

"What? You're not going anywhere. You're staying right there in that chair."

"Well, I have some news for you then," I said with a grin.

"And what exactly is your news?"

"Well, I have to pee really, really bad, so if I can't get to the restroom and I'm cuffed here to this chair, my only choice will be to do it right here and flood this joint. I don't think you guys are gonna like that, especially the smell it will leave behind for probably years on end, my friend."

Occasionally, obstinacy can be an effective weapon.

He glared at me in disbelief and then hopped up. "Okay, let me get the keys—hang in there."

Which I did, barely making it to the urinal, and what a relief that was. Apparently, this put some wheels in motion to move on and hopefully out. I was taken to another room, stripped, dressed in inmate wardrobe, and moved to an iron-barred holding cell, all the while realizing they had never read me my rights. I still remember the yellowed and chipped beige enamel paint on the one-inch-thick bars that comprised the fifteen-by-twenty-five-foot confines, grimy from years of neglect. And hey, look here, I got a bonus—a new roommate! The slender, wrinkled up, gruffy, unshaven, BO-laden character paced the cell and mumbled to himself nonstop while I kept in a corner. We were cordial when the food trays with the stale raspberry Danish or cold hot dogs got slid under the bars and when using the stainless-steel, lid-free toilet bowl.

This was clearly my punishment for torpedoing the officer at the club.

I had already called my manager Todd on the pay phone with the permitted single phone call en route to the jail cell. He said he was planning on bailing me out with others who had been taken in from the club that night. It had been a long night, but now in the morning, it was time for my next call to try and get out again. Luckily, unlike today, back in the '80s people still remembered up to thirty people's phone numbers.

Ring ring ring. By good fortune, I caught him, as cell phones were rare back then.

"Todd, man, you gotta get me outta here. It's not going well!" I pleaded.

"Where are you? I tried Lew Sterrett Justice Center and they said you're not there. Everyone else, eight of the staff, I already got bailed out last night."

"I'm in here! You've gotta come down and get me out, my friend."

"Okay, I'll do that if I can. You weren't on the log—we looked hard. I'll try again."

"Call's up," the jail guard announced with a smirk.

Then it was back to the cell to hang out with Looney Tunes. This sequence repeated itself for over two days until I finally popped up on the inmate list and got bailed out.

In the end, I was never charged. The plan had obviously been to punitively hold me, crammed into a cell with an insane inmate. That was my first experience in a jail and one I've never repeated. I was cured! Pick your battles.

On the legal front, all the cases were dismissed, as the raid had been botched. Truth be known, I had a case for an unlawful arrest and holding, but I've never had an appetite for courts and lawyers, as I'd much rather make my time in life productive. I was never jailed again and avoided the courts, even leaving money on the table when I had done no wrong, until thirty years later, when I would be forced into a courthouse where, much to my dismay, I would be forced to grind unhappily for years on end.

Little did I know that my soon-to-be friend, Timothy Leary, had suffered a similar fate, being put in a jail cell in Folsom Prison next to an infamous wackadoodle, Charles Manson. Tim described this as a tough point in his life that, like me, he lived full-on. I had yet to find my bottom in life's sine wave, but that would come.

I met Tim booking him on tour doing speaking engagements across the country. The timing was good, as we were about to launch a new look for Clearview, and Tim's schtick would fit in perfectly.

Of all the reinventions, reincarnations, directions, presentations, fads, and trends, Dr. Tim coming to town and the launch of Cyberium at the club hit the collective public nerve. The Cyberium term we coined would blast us off into the '90s, and a club facelift with virtual reality machines and all the trimmings that really took us to the next level. It caught the uncontrollable interest of the media and became a huge promo from our then-perch of 1988. With the VR, smart drinks, and techno-rave beats to match, it was the next wave, and the media buzz from this one effort probably added ten years to the club's life.

The virtual-reality headgear back then was very primitive compared to today, but was state of the art for back then—akin to a grainy, first-run color TV these days. I checked it out, but it wasn't a very pleasant trip, inducing vertigo and nausea for me. It was nothing like the Oculus and other products out there today, which I'm not a fan of either, since I'm far more interested in being outdoors than having more screen time or virtual anything—a Thoreau, Muir, Ed Abbey guy, all the way.

It was a smart move to take the Cyberium ride, and the best part was having Dr. Tim coming in from LA to kick it off. He returned to Dallas many times to visit, hang out, and speak at the club. I loved chatting with him and attempted to capture his genius dialogue's twists and turns, occasionally offering up a nugget of my own.

After we solved the world's problems late at night, Tim would quip, "Love you, Jeff, you are a very alive spirit. Good stuff."

And I'd respond, "I love you more, my friend—keep rockin' 'til we meet again."

It was different for me to hear and use the word *love*—even felt uncomfortable, as I'd never heard that in my childhood. But he really taught me that—to use daily, without fail.

Much of Tim's philosophy was akin to mine—and what we were doing at the club: expose, expand, and invite people to think.

Funny, I remember interviewing for a summer internship with IBM in the late '70s and seeing the plaque on the interviewer's desk that read, *THINK*. IBM at that point had become an organization where the employees all dressed in lookalike dark blue sport coats, buttoned-down, starched white shirts, with yellow polka-dot or blue-and-red-striped ties, and black wingtip shoes. Not exactly an army of thinkers. I had learned freshman year from that college professor the difference between truth and bullshit. The company that I witnessed literally giving Bill Gates the keys to the kingdom in the greatest business boondoggle of all time wasn't thinking. They even tried to best that mistake by exiting the PC market prematurely, and then after a prolonged courting, passed up buying Apple for a song in its dark days. Still, *THINK* remained their motto for decades. IBM's THINK was bullshit, but Tim's and Clearview's were truth.

People from his camp and mine expressed worry about me hanging out with Dr. Tim.

"Oh my God, Tim's gonna be hanging out with Jeff Swaney; they're both going to get all messed up on drugs."

Nothing could have been farther from the truth. Tim had a busy travel schedule, and I was working on the club's needs and my real estate foray, spending a good bit of time, and piling up thousands of dollars in bills, on my ten-pound boat anchor of a cell phone, with no option to be screwed up every night. For me and Tim, excessive hard partying was rearview mirror material. Been there, done that.

Dr. Leary was often misunderstood and misrepresented, and I could relate—being defined by conflicting sound bites at times—which perhaps explains why we hit it off like fire. Tim got busted for minor transgressions which would be legal these days, and suffered harsh punishments in Folsom Prison and Afghanistan, as the establishment wanted to make an example of him. There was a transcendental connection with this guy who thought religion should be disorganized and was truly high on getting people to think for themselves. That was his religion.

Years after he passed of cancer and in 1995 and was granted his wish—ashes to be shot into outer space on a Spanish rocket with other famous souls—I read Ram Dass, Tim's Harvard partner in crime, friend, and ofttimes adversary's book, *Be Here Now*. It was another game-changer, so awe-inspiring, absorbing Ram's transformations brought to life in the illustrations midway through that book. A true top ten of all time. I saw where Leary and Dass came together philosophically and kept focused on that intersection. Vibrations. I've read many of the great philosophers of the ages, but for some reason, these contemporaries seemed to strike a chord, resulting in being spiritually redirected.

Back on earth, there was more to do.

CHAPTER 10

Making it in Big D

1980s Rolodexes

CHAPTER 10
MY WAY

I've never been one to settle for a single option with life's open buffet spread out in front of me. So, during years managing the club, I also tinkered with band management, worked on a treatment for a film to satisfy filmmaker aspirations, became the owner of an art gallery and a collector thanks to our Art Bar venue, and even toyed with the prospect of becoming a full-time art dealer. It was hard to keep up with many aspirations, and time to decide on a wise choice at this juncture. I had followed my P.T. Barnum heart to get on top of the scene, but now it was time to focus my energies on a concrete plan for my future. The signs pointed in one specific direction.

I had launched a real estate company in 1987 and now had five people in that office. In need of a place to park money being made at the club, over time I had purchased various properties in the neighborhood with a couple of other landlord partners.

It was a way to realize a long-term benefit while continuing to influence the area positively. Besides, approaching forty after spending nearly every dime in my twenties and into my thirties, you don't want to end up empty-handed years later.

Real estate, as Paul had predicted, held the most promise financially. I liked renovating historic properties on a small scale, and shepherding a healthy tenant mix in the neighborhood. Our club and restaurant business were set to expand beyond Deep Ellum, and I was a key man in the construction management, budgets, and investor relations. It was going to be a big move and a multimillion-dollar investment for us and our newly minted investor group, with significant risk, but we were ready to forge into uncharted waters. My idea was to get the new venue and management team stabilized, then return to the real estate world in Deep Ellum to shore up and expand my interests, taking a more advisory role in the entertainment business and mentoring others who aspired to succeed in that arena. If the new entertainment expansion proved to be as successful as we hoped, we were going to take our proven concepts and management national, with the real estate company taking the lead on the property side of the equation.

Those were the grand plans. Plans change.

We tried our multi-concept show in a north suburb of Dallas where we started off strong but then petered out, probably due to a combination of mismanagement, B location, and serious competition. I always put my all into a project, and as fellow author David Rosell says, failure is not an option; but that's where it was headed. *Ugggh!*

My partner Jeff and I were taking our personal money from the profitable Deep Ellum location and endlessly pouring it down the drain in the new north Dallas location. If that wasn't bad enough, we had to deal with 167 part-time employees who were disgruntled, and to face unhappy investors every quarter. I had busted my butt to build, launch, and fund the massive four-in-one-concept—club, coffeeshop, restaurant, and art venue—and was exhausted reaching the end of the rope. There had to be a way to make this work, but it wasn't going to be with the company democracy we had structured with a consultant's help. *Good Lord, how did this happen?* I asked myself one afternoon as I made the drive from south to north.

I set up a meeting with my partner Jeff to discuss the situation.

"Jeff, the inmates are trying to run the asylum here. They are pitting us against each other and making this situation worse for both. I'm concerned that not only is this bad for a business that's in trouble, but it's also stressing our friendship, brother."

Jeff looked at me and paused. Being from a small town in Texas, he had some very down-home, yet sophisticated delivery in his thinking, speech, and anecdotes.

"Yes, I agree, and I understand completely."

I presented my solution.

"Well, I've thought about it, and think the best way to move forward here is for me to buy you out and take this tiger by the tail. I can straighten things out, but the only way I know how to proceed here is via a dictatorship."

"Well, I agree—sorta," he concurred. "I think it makes more sense for me to buy *you* out, Swaindog. I married the founder of Chili's restaurants' daughter, and I'm president of the Texas Restaurant Association. This isn't all a coincidence—its destiny. Being a restaurateur is my life dream, and I want to continue with this. You've got your real estate you can work on, and that probably makes sense for you."

I felt punched square in the gut, and I'm sure my face dropped. Deep inside it offended me that anyone could think they would be the logical candidate to run the show I considered my baby. I can still close my eyes and visualize that moment—giving up the glamor and excitement of the entertainment world to focus on bricks and sticks. In hindsight, he meant no ill will and he was right; but initially, it was hard to swallow.

Still, I knew deep down that I had to get out of the ego. It was time to let go.

"Well, let me think about that. In any event, we should sort this out in short order," I responded after a long pause.

The resulting buyout that we papered up within thirty days was one of the best decisions I ever made, however reluctantly. Losing a dream meant having to reinvent and redefine myself in a totally different arena. But it also meant letting go—my first time to do that, although certainly not my last. I would have to do that many more times going forward, on bigger stages with more at stake.

The business baby I'd birthed had been fused to me and had absorbed me for fifteen years, through my late twenties and all of my thirties. And now, that extension of me was to be severed—mine no more. That included the staff who, along with other industry relationships, were like family. Losing a huge part of that family I had chosen, nurtured, and needed all those years was perhaps the hardest part.

There is physical pain and mental anguish in life. I have witnessed physical pain watching my children's mother writhing in agony while giving birth to my daughter au natural. I have experienced physical pain with my many surgeries—back surgeries, repair of broken elbows, ribs, ankles, wrists, fingers, teeth, and more—due to my recklessness and DNA. I've suffered multiple concussions, and, the most painful of all, an outpatient posterior hip replacement that left me literally chewing leather, sweating profusely, crying uncontrollably, pissing myself, and slapping myself in the face to regain my composure. The mental pain of separating from a groundbreaking entertainment creation was the equivalent.

We must realize that all things in this world are fleeting. Everything has its time and place. Wisdom is attained by following the paths divinely revealed, then detaching with love when necessary, and by luck, sober thought, logical assessment, or some combination, finding a fresh prescribed path.

So, big changes started. I needed to focus on my fledgling, band-aided-together, neglected, mini-real-estate empire, which I'd collected in my "spare time" in order to direct its growth. I did have the blessing of hiring one of the best employees we ever had at the club, Miss Marianne, who ended up being my right hand and confidante for many years, and even served as the trustee for my estate and my children's interest in later years.

I hadn't exactly had any training when it came to an entrepreneurial career, which had begun at seven years of age and rolled on from there. The parties and club had been started on fumes and a dream, much like the real estate career. I just had to figure out how to make them work—and did.

I was once asked to teach a class on entrepreneurship at SMU business school, and passed. Often asked, "How did you start a club, a restaurant, a music enterprise, a real estate company, and get into oil and gas, venture capital, and angel investing?"

My answer is simple and Yogi Berra-ish. "I never knew nothing about what I was doing. I just done did it."

Learn by doing. That's hardest sometimes, but it's the most fun and best way. Like Sir Richard Branson's take on the Nike anthem in his Masterclass, "Screw It. Let's Do It!"

So, it was full time on the real estate career started during the great Savings and Loan crisis, of which Dallas was the epicenter. Back then, local real estate brokers were starving.

"I'm going to jump in and get my real estate license now—feeling it," I exclaimed, all bright-eyed and bushy-tailed, to a friend in 1985.

"Really? All the realtors are going broke. That's the stupidest thing I've ever heard of."

"No, timing is good now for the contrarian. Things are cyclical. It's a seven- to ten-year cycle. I'll ride this up to the moon."

And did, making my first sale within three months while co-commandeering the entertainment company. Little did I know that would be the first of four boom-bust, high-intensity waves to surf, in a storied real estate and investing career.

My real estate license wound up being parked with one of the few surviving brokers during the S&L debacle, and wound up being largely unsupervised and freewheeling under my broker Reggie, a bright guy always buried in paper stacks three to five feet tall, creating a maze surrounding his desk reminiscent of a Moroccan souk. He was mummified in paper, it seemed, trying to dig out of the S&L morass with his bloodshot eyes behind bifocals, just happy to make his cut of a couple coins from my efforts should I score. It started out with a few lease negotiations, which were a lot of work for little pay, knowing the real money was in brokering bigger sales and eventually in ownership and establishing "turf."

I printed some business cards always kept in my pocket, prepared in a flash to provide my expertise should a potential investor wander the neighborhood or find a chance to make any deal materialize. The hood was still predominantly boarded up, filled with throngs of homeless folks pushing shopping carts and baby buggies loaded sky-high. It was certainly on the fringe and struggling in transition, with high crime and other maladies, so investors weren't exactly flocking to the area.

At that time, we had our club offices in a multi-tenanted, single-story building on one of the main streets where Reggie also rented space, which he and his partners had owned and renovated prior to losing it in foreclosure. I had talked to the building's then-owner, a gentleman by the name of George, about purchasing it and had gotten a price and terms that seemed to make sense. The guy did not have a lot of faith in the area and was happier toting notes than dealing with the noncredit tenant mix. I wanted to buy the property but couldn't convince a financial partner. So, I decided that if I could not purchase it myself, I'd make a fee on my first sale.

The Main Street in the area had been closed for over a year due to an improvement project that included fancy brick pavers, cute shrubs, ornamental cast-iron streetlights, and various other improvements. The city's effort—designed to encourage investment there, which was desperately needed—would begin to pay off after this prolonged construction on a then-dirt road. I would witness that one rainy day as I was sloshing down the street in shorts and T-shirt, the rain resulting in a chocolate-almond slurry of mud, and spotted two guys in business suits with umbrellas, walking, weaving, and pointing. I approached them.

"Good afternoon, gentlemen, how are you? A great day to check out real estate down here, yes?"

They looked at me in amazement and didn't respond for it seemed like a few minutes. The rain started to come down a little harder, but I stood there patiently, umbrella in hand.

"Well, in fact…hmmmm…we are interested and looking around. Uhhhhh, what did you have in mind?"

"I've got a few things that you might be interested in. My name is Jeff Swaney," I said, handing them my business card.

We arranged a meeting for the next day, at which time I told them about a couple of properties, including the one where I was renting office space. They seemed to really like that deal, a slam dunk in my eyes, and told me they would have me a contract the next day, which they provided. Clean and simple. Little did we all know that years later I would broker it for them, for a profit to them of more than a million dollars.

I called George, the owner. "George, I've got a written offer for your property. I want to bring you and discuss."

"Okay. Is it legitimate? If so, come to my office tomorrow. I'll take a look at it."

I arrived at the office, a very modest fifteen-hundred-square-foot, dated building from the '50s, with decor somewhat reminiscent of the police station I had visited a few years back, in another questionable part of town. The office had that old lived-in smell, like Grandma's house—not stinky, just the odor of yellowed, decomposing paper you notice when cracking open an old, classic book. It was a comforting smell and scene compared to the glass high-rises, mostly vacant then, that had grown like weeds from S&L money in Go-Go Dallas.

George was a somewhat crusty, old-fashioned character. He was friendly enough, but a grumbler who didn't seem to trust anyone or anything, initially reminding me of the cartoon character Mr. Magoo, without the bulbous nose but with his manner of speech. Over time, I'd catch him grousing the same refrain, "Damn taxes, tenants, and always more problems!" C'mon, man—he was doing very well.

I produced the contract. He donned his reading glasses and immediately dropped the paperwork back down on his desk. He removed his glasses and slapped both hands on the desk. Thought he was pissed.

"Do you know this guy?"

"Well, not really. I just met him a couple days ago and I got the contract yesterday."

"Well, if he is who I think he is, he's the son of one of the biggest bankers ever in the history of Dallas. I worked for that guy for many years in the basement dungeon of their thirty-story downtown office sorting coins. Is that who the guy is?"

"I...ahhh...I don't know," I blabbered, wondering what this was all about.

"Well, tell him I'm interested in the contract, but I want to see his financial statement and I'd like that I see his dad's, too."

I had my marching orders and ended up obtaining the statements in a sealed envelope, which I brought back to George the next week. He practically salivated when handed the envelope. Turned out these people were exactly who George thought they were.

"I'll be damned!" His eyes bugged out. "I can't believe you met him just walking down the street in the rain. That's unbelievable! Come here, I want to show you something."

He pulled down a book from his bookshelf, a recent one that also adorns my library today, entitled, *Trammell Crow, Master Builder: The Story of America's Largest Real Estate Empire*. He thumbed through the pages rapidly as I sat in wait like a schoolboy.

"Here's a picture of my former boss making the first loan to Trammel Crow for the first Dallas Market Center. You know, Trammel Crow is the biggest real estate developer in the world now. Here, look at this—the Market Center today. And there's more," he exclaimed eagerly.

He worked through more pages and photos, pointing and remarking with exuberance.

"That's really something. I guess that's my good fortune to have been out in the street that day!"

He paused, looked at me, and smiled. "Yes, it was."

The deal went through, and George became a good friend and subsequently a business partner for many years. For over fifteen years, I played tennis almost every Wednesday with him, his son, and some friends in his backyard—our own little country club. It was something I looked forward to every week. As the years rolled on, I ended up meeting and befriending Trammel's three sons, as well. The world had gotten smaller, finding open doors via cosmic connectivity.

George may have been thrilled with the sale, but my broker Reggie was not happy when he got the news.

"Why didn't you tell me about this? We spent a lot of money on this building and were planning to buy it back!"

"I didn't know. You didn't say anything. I do have a commission check for us coming though."

"Shit! Yeah, that is just freaking great!" he snapped, throwing his hands up in frustration as his pen and white-out flew off behind him and became lost in the maze. I backed out of the office.

That's how I rolled, fearlessly willing to strike up a conversation with anyone, polishing my timing and delivery by trial and error over the years, all with heartfelt, authentic good vibes. That led to my meeting many of Dallas's movers and shakers despite my lack of roots there, or access or birthright to the good-old-boy network. In all my endeavors, which subsequently included many far-flung ventures in music, energy, banking, advertising, high-tech, and more, I did things my way. Put yourself in a direction, keep it simple, be patient and resolute, meet the right people, and then go get it.

The sale caused Reggie such indigestion that we had to move on. You were required by law to do two years as an agent to become your own broker, so I had to find another broker to hang my license. It was slim pickings, and there were many rascals in the Dallas mix. I worked with a few of them, some of whom stole my information, went behind my back, or lied to me, the latter causing me in one instance to fly over a desk and nearly rip off one of the guy's shirt collars in front of a family member. That was my last day in that office. Somehow, I survived that two-year period and got my own license, eventually having others work for me with some of the same resulting heartburn. This was a gig not for the faint of heart.

After getting licensed, I moved into an office with Dan, my club landlord, a former insurance salesman, and another real estate owner who had once been a partner of Reggie's group and had inherited a slew of trashed-out buildings, such as the one we rented from him. In this incestuous mix, and wanting to build as much equity as possible, I was bringing partnership deals to both George and Dan, who would manage the properties in their own way. They were two of the good independent guys in the neighborhood oligopoly, I thought, especially compared to others, including a couple of old used car salesmen—literally professional repo men—who were hoarding the S&L leftovers, making poor choices, and many times devouring people's entire lifetime net worths and dreams. I met all these real estate mongrels, maggots, or slumlords, it seemed, and many times had to deal with them sporting a smile to cover a scowl.

In the wake of my entertainment company sale, I prepared to focus on my real estate company and do things my way. That meant sorting out ownerships with George and Dan, and bringing what would be my properties under my umbrella, to consolidate and manage my holdings. I would then seek to purchase more property with other eager partners where I controlled the direction and management.

In anticipation of this, I purchased that two-story building to be my residence above my ground-floor office. I worked hard to revamp it into a showpiece for the area and wound-up winning awards and being featured in articles and tours touting downtown Dallas living.

Wanting the split of the properties with Dan and George to be amicable as possible, I approached them both and related the plan to consolidate and go out on my own. I suggested to each that there might be some natural divisions relating to the tenants, the proximity to other owned properties, the outstanding debt on each, and other factors. They both independently agreed to noodle on a fair split.

George and I got together first, in that same lived-in office where we had first met. "George, I've come up with which properties might be yours and mine, some valuations considering the debt, and some monies to equal it out," I said.

"Well, let me show you what I have calculated."

He presented me with a paper pad of notes, and I did the same. As the pads crossed his desk, we both looked up at each other.

"Oh my God, George, we basically came to almost the exact same conclusion. I think with just a little fine-tuning, we've got it!"

"Jeff, yes, it makes sense. Let's hammer out the details and paper it up."

It was that easy, and in thirty days it was all done.

"Good luck, Jeff," he said in closing. "You know I'm always here for you and always ready to look at a deal. I'll see you at tennis next Wednesday."

This coming from the guy who at his seventieth birthday party, speaking before a sizable crowd, pointed me out sitting at a table and told me I was like a second son to him, which made me tear up. Loved him.

The negotiations with Dan did not go as smoothly. Dan had a schoolteacher persona, country-smooth and brimming with charm, but with a different inside. Like George, the packaging didn't mirror the man inside.

I met with him in our mutual offices with a similar notepad outlining fair deal points as a starting point. I told him I had struck a deal with George in about ten minutes.

"Well, that sounds great. I agree; I've always seen George as a reasonable guy."

"Dan, what are your thoughts? I have some ideas here that I think make sense."

"Jeff, I've thought long and hard about this, and I think the best move is for me to make the decisions that'll be in our best interests."

"What do you mean? I was thinking, worst case, one of us could suggest two equal collections, and the other one could pick one or the other. The fairest way of all would be to let one person make the groupings, which we can call *the piles*, and then the other one can pick the pile they want. I would even defer to you if you wanted to be the pile maker or the pile picker, so to speak."

"No, Jeff, I think what we should do is I'll make two piles, and then I'll pick one of them and give you the other one, because, truthfully, I've been in the business longer and I think I can make a better decision for the both of us."

"So, you want to be the pile maker and the pile picker? That makes no sense whatsoever."

"Well, that's the way I see it, Jeff."

This negotiation went on for many months, with us officing in the same building despite the underlying tensions of an unresolved business conundrum. In the end, in the interest of side-stepping the aggravation and moving forward, I probably left $250,000 on the table. I was not exactly happy, but it was kind of my template for how I rolled—not a weakness, but just not wanting to be in conflict and always feeling my time was better spent making my next move. After the sorting was done, my enterprise went on a thirty-five-year run that continues today.

I remember someone telling me, "Jeff, if you can survive the way you have in that Dallas, Texas real-estate shark tank (this not Mark Cuban's TV shark tank—but the real beasts), with those stakes and the greediest unethical slimeballs ever, you are going to be incredibly successful." As things rolled on in life, it would get worse much later in the slimeball front—icing on the dirtbag cake—so that training would come in handy.

To rise above the muck, and create the financial firm ground that would carry me to the present and through all that mire, would require focus on the re-creation, re-branding, and fresh re-launch of my real estate company. With purpose. All that would start with a new name.

The naming had flowed back to ancient Greece and my obsession with Dallas's rising-above and high-flying symbol despite its disrepair—Pegasus. In my research done at the downtown library—customary back then before many of those institutions became glorified homeless shelters—I had stumbled across the legend of the Oracle at the ancient site of Delphi.

In its time, Delphi was considered the center of all knowledge in the universe, the *omphalos*, the navel of the world. A beautiful site perched high above the Corinthian Gulf, with stunning views among the pine and olive trees, it was a magnet for those VIPs the world over who would journey long distances by land and sea seeking divine guidance and predictions for the future, which were provided in riddles. Ofttimes the travelers misunderstood the answers gleaned, and their corresponding chess moves would spell disaster and even death for them and theirs. Sounded like the real estate business to me.

My enterprise would provide expert guidance in what we called "solving the real estate puzzle," our tagline and ode to the obscure. We took pride in guiding people in their decision-making, with a nod to the future and honest, inspired, and straightforward solutions. Unlike the Oracle, the company's advice was never cryptic.

The Delphi brand was my brand. My way.

After my consolidation and re-launch, the company's first biggest clients were the Resolution Trust Corporation (RTC) and Federal Deposit Insurance Corporation (FDIC). At that time, as the government had closed most all banks after letting them run rip-shod wild, the RTC and FDIC owned an unimaginable inventory of real estate, the most on the planet. So, even though the paperwork was torture, it was a bonanza for those who scored them, especially since you had to battle all the other starving brokers to win these agency listings. Unfortunately, agency policies lead to overreaching and overreacting—destroying investors' holdings and the entire industry practically—but you either got in with them or you were left on the sidelines. With a local's knowledge, absent a slick presentation, I got in. Eat or be eaten.

These agencies were run by some of the same folks who had caused the crisis, then jumped the fence to be government employees. The RTC gobbled up all the real estate it could, mindlessly foreclosing on owners at first and pricing the assets at ridiculously high prices to keep them in-house. A couple years later, for whatever reasons, they let it all go in a blowout of fire sales for pennies on the dollar, at the taxpayer's expense.

That is what happens when big government oversteps its bounds and makes radical swings in policy. I saw this being repeated during the COVID crisis, lining the pockets of Big Pharma and the folks sucking down PPP money they didn't need and promised to pay back but didn't have to, screwing the rest of the populace. The government had no vehicle to get paid back those monies, so, as foreseen, forgave all the debt, just printing more money and kicking the can down the road.

An apolitical No to Big Government didn't work in USSR—doesn't work here. As Thomas Jefferson supposedly said, "A government big enough to give you everything you want, is big enough to take everything you have."

As the RTC and FDIC liquidated and wound down, by necessity, I ended up partnering with many Dallas icons to work on real estate projects too numerous to mention, as well as growing and managing our own account. Becoming a key participant in the complete revamping of downtown Dallas, imagined upon landing there in the early '80s, was remarkable. Working on the boards downtown, brokering, partnering, and consulting on many projects—including the transformation of Class B and C vacant downtown office towers into residential units, and the planned relighting of that Pegasus atop the old Mobil Oil building at the center of downtown that occurred with fanfare on New Year's Eve 2000—took things right over the top for your friend here.

With all that, the proudest accomplishment in Dallas had to be the pro-bono championing of an all-encompassing, connected, twenty-eight-mile biking and hiking trail around the city that I lobbied for in Dallas, Austin, and Washington, DC. Fifteen years of melding love of biking and solving constraints for creative bikeways in a car-centric city, with all the political challenges, made that tough but rewarding.

The Dallas experience and the real estate career weren't all about money, fame, or fortune. Just like the club, it was rather about being creative and facilitative. Got into real estate because I had figured out that I did need money to survive long term, but didn't have to sacrifice creativity or anything else—made a lot of other people money and benefitted the city, and got my nickels, too.

A case in point was a close-to-my-heart purchase of an entire two-block area in Old East Dallas that was the haunt of Jack Ruby, the famous nightclub owner whose club and supposed brothel were included in the purchase. Jack gained eternal infamy by shooting Lee Harvey Oswald, the man who supposedly assassinated JFK. Whatever the JFK reality, stumbling on and owning those Jack Ruby-tinged blocks of real estate was yet again a surreal Camelot connection that was meant to be. Heard stories of the mob, with whom Jack purportedly had ties, owning a sausage-packaging facility in one of the buildings purchased, where unspeakable things occurred a la *The Sopranos* TV series. It was all fascinating. Dealing with what was there, I worked toward turning that neighborhood into an eclectic, funky, mini-art scene. It was one of the more fun hands-on projects, yet one of the least financially successful. Go figure.

Having survived and thrived again in a major endeavor, making the real estate climb with Delphi Group, perched as a leader of that respected stable enterprise, I could once again move on to other endeavors. But at this point, the most important task for me, where many never venture, was taking time to re-explore and re-invent myself.

I had come from nothing and seemingly accomplished a lot, but it was just the formation of the base and midsection of the Maslovian-needs hierarchical pyramid. Now it was time to climb that triangular rock. Step one involved determining what you stand for and believe in.

I've had many conversations with journalists, espousing my Swaneyisms. The approach was always unrehearsed and came from the heart; hence the themes were consistent, even though the dialogue was a bit kooky when read in publications.

I met one writer for lunch at Sambuca, a hip Mediterranean restaurant and jazz bar our real estate company represented. The journalist presented me rushing in apologetically with pager, cell phone, and PalmPilot III jangling from belt loops, unkempt in jeans shorts, a rumpled shirt, and sandals. That was my style—or lack of it—absent an uptight business function or black-tie event.

"Jeff, thanks for making the time, I know you're a busy guy."

"All good. Sorry I'm a bit late; a meeting ran over; they wouldn't quit." Panting.

"It's okay. I know you have a lot of irons in the fire, being the mayor of Deep Ellum and all."

"I'm not sure I'm the mayor, but I'm doing my part."

"Jeff, it seems like everybody's got an opinion about you, and I mean Everybody. Some like what you're doing and say you're benefiting the community, and some see you as a greedy, self-promoting, sell-out opportunist. A yuppie who is ruining the neighborhood for artists and musicians."

"Well, I gave up trying to please everybody a while back. It's a fool's endeavor—a game you can't win. I do the right thing, supporting a ton of bands and artists down here, getting the right tenants to move in, and working for several charitable causes. All things I'm proud of. That's why I do this instead of making millions doing land deals in the suburbs. At the end of the day, we must follow our hearts."

"I see," he said, seemingly convinced.

"I suggest we just put everything on the table and let people make their own decisions if they care to judge, and leave it at that."

I did many interviews, and everything seemed to spill out the same, like the ingrained particles of spiritual magic in my conscious capitalism. Always driven to do something fresh, cool, meaningful, and to make people think was innate. Many people gravitated toward the messages channeled about compromise and re-using rather than tearing down buildings or others.

It took years to capture the path yearned to be on, regularly being bounced between the guardrails and veering into mishaps. But it was—and still is—all a work in progress. Luckily, I followed some ordained route, rather than running off track through the rails and into walls, although got close sometimes. It was taking life's experiences and evolving into a more spiritually aware, still-hungry-for-answers soul. Seekers keep seeking.

As a seeker and budget world traveler, I inhabited the streets, meeting numerous folks espousing their discovered truths, some in what many considered cults. In Tulum, Mexico in the '80s, way before the tourist invasion that ruined the Mayan ruins and everything else there, I stumbled upon some simple palapas (open-sided dwellings) on the beach with communal showers, healthy food, yoga, and more for five dollars a night. Pure heaven! Unbeknownst to me, I was at the "oasis" of Bhagwan Rajneesh, aka Osho, where I would learn about "The Long and the Short and the All," his Jain- and Buddhist-tinged expose on the human condition. Like the Scientology I had discovered in Boston upon my arrival from Europe, Osho's precepts explored man's inner being and fundamental inquiries into the "self," much being borrowed in bits and pieces from age-old philosophers and religions. These beliefs were brilliant; however, like Scientology, and similarly the Transcendental Meditation movement of Maharishi Yogi, scandals would rock the enterprises, and what started out as golden nuggets of shining truth ended up being bastardized as the organisms got too big, too complicated, ordered, and monetized. Kind of applies to all facets of life, including the world's many organized religions. As my friend Dr. Tim said, "Religion should be disorganized." Beliefs are personal.

With that in mind, however, some organized form of governance allowing freedom of religious belief, at minimum, must be in place, and we must submit to that, however imperfect, and constantly work to improve upon it to avoid savagery. But in the spiritual world, we need not be boxed in, and our experience should be individualized. Hopefully and thankfully, knowing deep in our hearts good from evil, then if we carry on peacefully, we can follow our own drumbeat to shine our unique bright light. We are all beautiful souls, Tim—no need for intense conflict.

All our individual beings' energies are connected via cosmic strings, all defined by a Higher Power. So, to that end, we do have a say, as we can tug the strings and create tiny ripples into the unknown. I had always theorized that if every soul on earth focused on one particular action at any one time, mountains could be moved. With today's communication, it seems that things could be synchronized and that could happen—for better or worse.

For us, the biggest realization of all is to own the fact that we only control our own attitudes and actions. Focus on that first.

I had a need for order in the chaos early on in life. A slippery slope in a speed-of-light, quantum-physics cosmos, finding fleeting handholds in the rocky pyramid for spirit's nourishing climb. I had acquired self-esteem and relinquished the demons of any shame, guilt, jealousy, or other of what I call "wasted emotions," somehow manifesting a resiliency that became a strong suit.

I learned to share values and knowledge, but not be a preacher or politico. One can make a difference without adapting, adopting, or pushing a political or religious agenda. It's wise to be your own person and to encourage others to do so—to think for themselves.

I had achieved a fine balance tying up the loose ends from childhood, making some sense of my success in the physical and biz world, with the natural world loved, and wired connections in the spiritual realm, finding myself at peace. This anchoring, with faith in a Higher Power indescribable and myself, would be needed in the future.

CHAPTER 11

Foolhardy

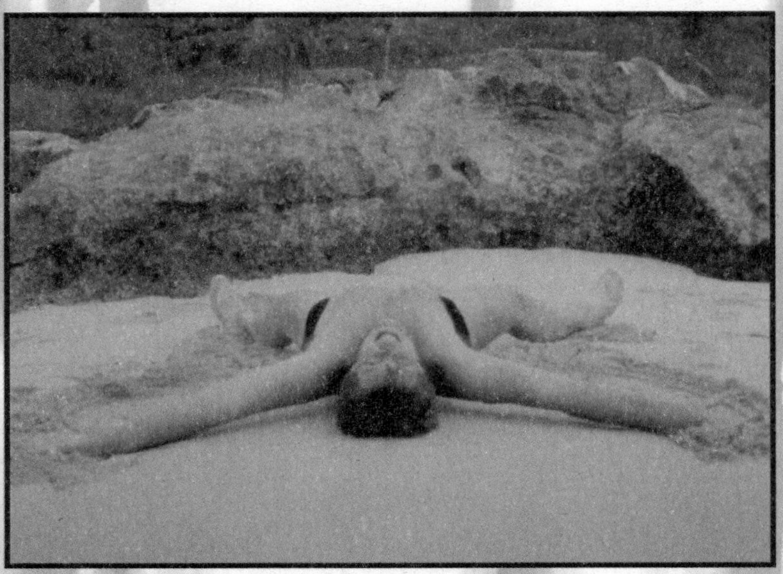

Alive on Molokai

CHAPTER 11

CHAOS ON THE EDGE

Living a life of adventure despite being inexperienced, ill-prepared, and lacking in knowledge, was the M.O. both in business and pastimes. That included some wild outdoor exploits.

Since Big Bend National Park in South Texas was a favorite of mine on earth, I'd made annual pilgrimages there for twenty years. The allure of Big Bend lay in its vastness, starkness, and quiet. Spending most of my young life sheltered in suburban Michigan, I had pictured deserts as dead—empty square miles of impassable sand dunes bearing witness to photos and films depicting Lawrence of Arabia's Sahara. I came to find out deserts are much more. The colors—every imaginable blended shade of red, orange, blue, purple, and green melted in whimsical grainy textures—were mesmerizing. The desert plants like the ocotillo, the yucca, barrel cactus, and prickly pear, which appear dead most of the year, would perk up and flower in the late spring or after a rain and dazzle with their blooms.

The ghost town of Terlingua, today with a population of just over a hundred folks, is a tribute to the area's remoteness. I fell in love with it and met many of its quirky residents, and even fancied becoming a citizen. One harebrained scheme hatched with Glenn Felts, the then-owner of the Terlingua, Texas RV park and famous La Kiva underground restaurant next door, would have had me trading my Club Clearview interests for his property. We negotiated seriously, as he loved the raw Deep Ellum of the day, but the deal did not come to pass. Glenn did pass, however, as he was murdered in 2014 in an after-hours bludgeoning at his restaurant that was never solved. Conversely, I survived Big Bend and Club Clearview, despite several hair-raising experiences that could have wrought my demise at either location and various others, in the Texas desert and beyond.

Backpacking solo in the park on one of my first visits, under the glowing sunset of the desert sky, I set up camp off trail with my small one-man tent. When I woke the following chilly morning and crawled out of the tent, reminiscent of the greeting I had from the bull in Scotland, I was welcomed by a pack of wild javelinas. A passerby in their world, standing still with skin on fire, my only knowledge of wild pigs gained from that mishap in Maui where the local dogs got torn to shreds by a pack of piggies—I froze. Staring out at the mountains beyond, I ignored them, wisely; and fortunately, after about ten minutes of rooting and sniffing me out, they moved along. Over time I learned the differences in wild pigs—boars, peccaries, ham and bacon—and knew that, in general, catching any wild animal's gaze, even if they have poor eyesight, or running from them, was a no-no—and only a last resort.

Unqualified, I took small groups of folks out to the Big Bend on epic hikes of anywhere from thirty to seventy miles or more, bushwacking much of the time without any high-tech phones or GPS navigation tools. On one occasion, I took a girlfriend and another couple from Colorado out in the time of severe summer heat, topping 120 degrees.

We headed out one day after sunup, planning to complete our fifteen-mile trek before the searing blaze of the afternoon would fry us. Unfortunately, I was unaware that half of our route down from the Chisos Basin plateau there had burned in uncommon raging wildfires the previous year, and the semblance of a trail was black and scorched, with not a green spec for miles. This would make for an oven-like effect, as the ghost of a trail was reduced to a three-mile-long decent over flaky, slate-like, sharp-edged, thin black scree that was difficult to navigate, steep, and slippery. Even though we had not seen another soul all day, we decided to forge on rather than double back, as we had left a car on the other end of our trek.

Time was not our friend. We got to the bottom of that plateau after many hours of baby steps, slides, and falls, and scrambled to finally find some modicum of shade in the valley below, consisting of mostly two-foot-tall sage bushes that required us to practically curl around to block the blistering sun. We would assess our abrasions there.

"I'm sorry guys, I had no idea about this condition. We're way behind on time and it's just gonna be getting hotter now since it's about one o'clock."

The Coloradoans—Mike, and his girlfriend Rita—looked at me. Then my girlfriend blurted out, "Jeff, my feet are bleeding—look at my socks! It hurts! Oh my God, Jeff, this is terrible!"

As she pulled off a bloody sock, I could see that her toenails were going to be gone. All of them.

"Don't worry, it'll all be good. We will get through this. Here guys, here is a pear and banana—a little beat up—and my last bit of water. Why don't you three stay here huddled up? I am pretty sure there is a water cache down the valley a way. I'll either find it and return here with water or bring help. Just stay put. Worst-case scenario, if I don't come back, you should walk out only after sunset when cooler. It's a straight shot of about four to five miles to the car. Adios and sorry—I will return!"

Sure enough, I found the cache after about forty-five minutes of brisk walking—about a hundred milk jugs and other containers, jumbled up, mostly fouled, presenting an array of colors, brown, green, black, and the three colors combined—some, nasty goos. By sniff and taste tests, I found three usable gallons, one that I gulped and poured over my throbbing head, and the other two that I brought back to the delirious friends.

"Here we go! Drink drink drink! And bathe! *Yahoooo!*"

We hiked out without speaking another word and survived. I nearly met my maker in Big Bend a few more times, but for many reasons kept coming back for more.

On another wilderness outing there with three guys, I ate one of the fellow's canned chili for dinner, a choice I would normally never make, preferring safer, lighter-to-carry dehydrated foods. It had been compromised and/or insufficiently heated on our backpacking stove, so that was no bueno. We all got sick, but reminiscent of dysentery I had gotten in Istanbul years before, I got so sick I could hardly walk. At that point, we were probably fifteen miles from civilization. Fortunately, using a topographical map and old-fashioned triangulating navigation, the three amigos found a spring barely seeping from the earth and creating a rivulet over rock. Framed in algae, the water snaked out about five feet until it just dried up, capitulating to the desert heat. We spent hours extracting the spring water as it trickled out, sipping, applying it to our baked faces, and storing it, all of which saved our lives. Some of the same characters the year before on a trip in an adjacent area, miles from anywhere, had nearly split up during a delusional argument about routes on the desert floor. Incredibly, sanity amongst the stubborn men prevailed. Angels watched over me and my compadres in the Big Bend that and every year.

The outdoors poses many challenges, especially when you submit yourself to the elements with little room for error. Aside from Big Bend and various other locales on the globe, Colorado's fourteen-thousand-foot mountains provided for summiting misadventures to test one's mettle. Not ever having seen a mountain, let alone climbed one, until I was twenty years old and witnessing the Rockies for the first time in the old Cutlass during that summer job in Montana, I needed to make up for lost time. So, naturally, I wanted to tackle with gusto every summit possible.

A lightning storm on Mount Princeton, near Buena Vista, Colorado, sent me scampering down after summiting late one afternoon, sliding off rocks as if on ice skates in the rain that had started, slipping past memorials where families had erected crosses for members electrocuted in such fury.

Boom boom…Crackle…Boom…whooooosh…Flash….bababa-Boom! The heavens roared all around me.

I yelled out to my friend Mike, a seasoned mountaineer and professional skier, who was quickly moving down.

"Mike, wait up man! I'm having a helluva time."

"Hell no, man! I've got kids—I have to get down fast! I can't afford to get fried! Either haul ass, Jeff, or hide in the rocks. And lose those poles, dude!" he barked before accelerating his pace, broadening the gap between us.

And this was before I had children. His yelp resonates now, as my risk aversion at age sixty-five has grown.

When I finally got down to the car where Mike had been for probably thirty minutes, the storm had passed. Our troubles, however, were not over. We found ourselves blocked in by another vehicle on the short, precarious cliffside road where we'd parked, and had to wait a while 'til the folks returned to their car from wherever they were. It was a narrow dirt road, difficult to turn around on, but we had done it and now waited for them to turn their car around for descent. Unfortunately, the inexperienced driver spun his Subaru wagon around and got it shanghaied in a terrible spot, with the two passenger-side wheels off the side of the cliff, whereupon Mike tapped the horn, prompting them to stop with their car literally teetering on the edge of a thousand-foot fall. We got out and motioned them to roll down the window.

"Don't move, you guys. You are in a crazy spot now, about to fall off the mountain. Just shut the car off, set the parking brake, stay seated, and be still," Mike sternly. "Then let's look at this and figure out what we need to do."

We had the passengers' undivided attention, the four souls in the car beseeching us with their bug-eyed frightened stares. We eventually decided to carefully extract the passengers, two elderly couples—one person at a time—to keep the weight of the total mass uphill and avoid a catastrophe. After having everyone inch up toward the mountain-peak side of the car, we opened the driver's car door and started with him. We had him scootch out to us while his wife worked her way into the driver seat, then repeated the samba in the backseat before removing the final two passengers. No panicking or jiggling yielded success.

"Thank you thank you thank you! We could've died there," they sang out.

"Yes, for sure. Now, we must get back to town so you can arrange to get that car towed off, lest it crash down the hill. Get in our rig."

I'd had my terrifying experience that day and they had theirs. As to my terror, come to think of it, Mike owed me one. A few years before, I'd nearly baked him and his girlfriend in our Big Bend debacle before I found that water cache, leaving us all sunburnt, bloodied up, dehydrated, and exhausted. Turnabout is fair play, especially in the great outdoors.

At another time, an ascent of another fourteener, nearby Mount Harvard, would put me in a tough spot once again. Four guys were in the group, all flying in from a hundred feet above sea level in Dallas, Texas, then foolishly gorging on Mexican food and margaritas before setting up base camp, where we all felt a little altitude sickness setting in. Nevertheless, the next day, we were going to give the summit a go. No pain, no gain. My friend Derik and I would succeed in the quest, taunting the other two by calling them the 13,999ers as they turned back near the summit. I would be penalized for that.

Near the very top, Derik and I took a slightly different route, as we couldn't agree on the final two-hundred-yard scramble, a common theme with all us alpha males. He and I were like true, loving brothers, always wrestling with each other—sometimes literally, believe it or not as grown men.

I took what seemed a direct-route ascent to the top, only to find myself probably fifty feet from the summit on a two-foot-wide ledge looking down some four thousand feet. I couldn't make the move up without tech climbing gear, which I didn't have, and now the move back down from that spot was a little bit beyond my ability. I was beginning to experience vertigo, becoming paralyzed—and barely staved off panic, which I'd experienced a few times before. "Stop looking down," I whispered out loud, eventually gathering myself and making the high-risk, difficult move down, scraping off a good deal of skin, but without falling to my death. Circling around, I then completed the summit.

You would think I would have learned something from my previous mishaps and routing on high peaks. Like many men in their twenties and early thirties, I would try to outsmart others and get there first, willing to risk it all on the perceived shortcut. That is folly, as David Rosell espouses, and I'll quote him once again: "There are no shortcuts to any place worth going." In time, I finally embraced this nugget, as it applies to the outdoors, investing, parenting, relationships, and life in general. Take heed. Amen.

It's one thing to have control of your body and responsibility for your own life at fourteen thousand feet, but quite another to have no control when up at thirty-five thousand feet. I walked into a lot of hair-raising experiences by choice. Others just suddenly happened—often.

I've never had a fear of planes, but having flown millions of miles in my lifetime on many private and commercial flights, I know that you have no input on any outcome once onboard.

Of all the crazy, uncomfortable flight experiences, misadventures in small planes are most noteworthy. Jumping on board a single-engine Cessna with a young lady, and a pilot hired on the spot to go from Nassau to Eleuthera in the Bahamas, proved to be a short, exciting affair. With the windshield duct-taped together, flying in high winds, with an approaching afternoon anvil-shaped storm that would envelop us and have the plane nearly rattling apart, I found myself praying.

On another single-engine Cessna—this time taking off from Canaima, Venezuela, with some friends who knew our pilot—we convinced him to break the rules and get us as close to Angel Falls, the tallest waterfall in the world, as he could. It was another exhilarating, high-wind day, with the pilot on a few occasions nearly losing control of the plane in and around the falls as it blew around like a lottery-machine pinball in the drafts—nearly flipping it on one fly-by, which would've resulted in our deaths. After his aerobatics, it then took two or three approaches to land the thing back on the short dirt airstrip. That was probably the piss-my-pants flight of my life.

During the same Venezuelan trip, I engaged a Dutch pilot, who had been drinking heavily at the airport bar in Punto Fijo, to take me and a young lady on a quick hop over to Aruba in his small Lear. He was flying there anyway, it turned out, so he cut me a deal—and then decided to give us a little extra in unwanted aerial stunts, with me in the copilot seat. On landing, the gal was white as a ghost. I wasn't doing much better.

Back in the States, I would experience more misadventures. On a small twin turboprop flight from Dallas to Austin, Texas, a shiny new pilot—a friend of mine and business partner—was headed for a thrill. On approach to Austin International Airport and gathering his bearings, he was suddenly pressed by the tower to immediately land, as a Southwest Airlines 737 was on our tail. Upon touching down, the tower ordered our craft to rapidly turn off the runway. The 737 swooshed by with a wheels-down blast less than fifty yards from us, its wake nearly blowing our plane over.

Some people don't like flying in small planes, and I can see why. They prefer larger jets. So, the bigger ones are safer, right? Not always.

On a common route for me in the day, a Detroit-Dallas flight at dusk during a Christmas holiday week, an engine on our travel-worn 727 caught fire with a boom just after takeoff out of Detroit. This required immediate evasive action by the crew, as pilots are taught to do a figure- eight pattern while the tower clears the runway to allow for a quick return. The plane sputtered, seemed like it would crash, and then landed. Blaring firetrucks promptly began blasting water on the blown engine, with emergency vehicles standing by, the sum of which made for a 360-degree light show of flashing high intensity—blue, red, and yellow lights eclipsing anything I'd ever seen at a rock concert. With the fire put out, we limped back to the terminal to deplane in normal fashion, then orchestrate ticketing our replacement flight for 5 a.m. the next day. Merry Christmas.

Chicago always provided thrills, apart from the Second City entertainment and the chaos of navigating the patched-together, to-be-avoided-if-possible, giant O'Hare Airport. A couple of stunner commercial jet flights over the years stood out.

On a midsummer flight out of Dallas, I found myself on an ancient DC-9, never a comforting boarding. Things went well on the way to Chi Town, until the pilot announced to the passengers that our plane was running out of fuel on approach, literally hiccupping to the airfield. It just made it, clearing the fence line that secured the airfield by maybe twenty feet as viewed, and then landing prematurely on the grass before catching the asphalt runway. As we deplaned, I waited to be last off and stopped by the cockpit, as I did on these fun flights. The pilot had sweat rings about a foot in diameter around his armpits and was a bit blue.

"Well, that was a new experience for me. Good job," I said.

"Yeah, that was a first for us, too," he garbled.

Another inbound Chicago flight had our 727 hit wind shears, slamming down in thousand-foot drops over ten times without warning, each feeling like the plane was going to break in half. Food trays and belongings went flying everywhere, a stewardess was tossed about and banged up onto the ceiling, people screamed, vomited, and audibly prayed to God to spare their lives. I prayed silently. More sweat. After landing, as the stinking plane emptied with the passenger's nerves frazzled, I took my customary stroll by the cockpit, where I engaged the captain.

"Man, good work—that was one hell of a ride."

"Yes, that was the worst wind-shearing I've experienced flying in my twenty-five years. Nothing I would want to do again. Welcome to the Windy City."

A fourteen-hour Qantas 747 flight from Sydney to LAX was calm and quiet, until we were on approach to land. One hundred feet from the runway after that long haul, then suddenly a radical takeoff, full blast engines pointed skyward, all four engines at maximum thrust with noticeable G-force pinning everyone to the backs of their seats. We had just barely missed another jet that had meandered onto our runway, the captain explained as we circled out over the Pacific to regroup for another try, which succeeded and was met with the passengers' relief and applause.

Thankfully, as time passed, most of these air relics were taken out of service in the US fleets, making way for some less-beat-up models. Still, on occasion, there were still glitches in the routine. During a Dallas to Vegas 757 flight, which took off on a crystal-clear day, I heard some unusual thumps on the climb out. Apparently, we had sucked down some pelicans that smelled like a crispy duck dinner. Nope. No such luck or duck. A fuel burn-off and dumping procedure, executed while circling the DFW airport at thirty thousand feet, would thankfully be followed by an uneventful emergency landing back in Dallas.

Probably the oldest jet I'd ever been on was a Boeing 707 in Zimbabwe. The seats were threadbare, the carpet runners worn through to the bare metal of the plane's frame, half the seatbelts not working, and most of the overhead cargo bins permanently screwed shut, although the in-armrest ashtrays seemed to be functional. Takeoff, albeit creaky, went well, but the landing was another story. After four attempts at the runway in high winds with the old beat-up wings nearly flapping, we finally got onto the ground. Whew. After landing and taxiing with the other noticeably shaken passengers, I began to chat somewhat nervously with a guy across the aisle who was sitting with his family.

"Wow, that was a tough landing," I said.

"Yes. I'm a pilot with American Airlines, and I'll tell you that it was a challenging one."

"So, you're a pilot. I was an engineer in school, and when I hear those wings creaking like they were, I was thinking, My God, we've got some serious metal-stress fatigue going on here after the trillion miles this thing has logged."

"For sure," he said. "It's nuts that we sell these planes to Third World countries so we won't have to fly them or on them, and here we are on safari with our family and we end up on this ancient bus. Something I never anticipated!"

As terrifying as all these experiences were, nothing provided a jolt quite like the supernatural.

I was already exhausted when I landed in Cape Town, South Africa, after a very long trip via Ireland, where I had just entertained my dad, with whom I had finally become close for ten days. In addition to attending a clan meeting in Donegal, we had buzzed around the country. Now I had joined the Capetown group—a wild collection of guys from around the world—on a weeklong party rampage to celebrate the closing of one of our buddy's bachelor years. It was party party party on arrival day and night for these guys, and I was barely hanging in, not imbibing much but rather trying to pick a spot where I could catch up on sleep. A couple nights later at a disco, I found an opportunity to escape without them tackling me, quietly wussing out to get back to the posh hotel they'd organized.

It was one of those beautiful Cape Town evenings. The room's patio doors opened to a full moon shining on Table Mountain in the distance, and the local flowers gave off an incredible scent in the African night. The enchanting setting would prove a paradox for what was about to happen.

I climbed into bed and passed out like a rock and quickly fell into what must have been the deepest sleep of a lifetime. Untold hours later my roommate for the trip, Henry, returned, apparently falling asleep in the second of our two beds, about five feet from mine.

At some ungodly hour, he woke up thrashing about, getting airborne in the bed, and screaming bloody murder. Jolting me awake, I looked his way and saw a huge, powerful, dark figure—akin to a Darth Vader—hovering over his body and choking him. This was the stuff of nightmares, but I was awake, not dreaming. I attempted to yell out and get up to help but was paralyzed. We all have had dreams like that in our lifetime—where we are so terrified that we were immobilized and could not act or speak. Similar nightmares find us on an invisible treadmill where we are chased by something evil we cannot escape. That was me in real time now, plastered to my bed, gasping, unable to help my friend.

Here's how Henry remembers that event:

I had fallen into a three-whiskey sleep when I was suddenly awakened, not by a sound but a feeling. I looked up and saw a dark figure by the window, an abstract shadow moving towards me. I froze. I couldn't do anything but watch this haunting figure come up to me. Without hesitation, he grabbed my neck and began to choke me. Hard. I started fighting him off. Fighting for my life. Then just as quickly, he was gone. Completely vanished.

I woke up. Or did I? For sure I was flailing. All over my bed. I looked over at Jeff who was white as a ghost with the most perplexing look on his face. I could not make sense of what had happened, so I tried to see it through Jeff. He was God-smacked. I knew this was otherworldly.

At that point, I certainly was white as a ghost myself, with my lips quivering, unable to talk or move. I had succumbed to a state of severe shock. Paramedics were called, but I was told it could be a while. We were in Africa. Various members of the staff gravitated toward our room, Henry later told me. Nine in all, but nobody knew how to give CPR. In what seemed like an eternity but was probably an hour, the paramedics finally came. And they were all business. They moved right past Henry's attempted explanation of the situation and went directly to me.

Again, here's Henry's recollection of what ensued:

They needed to lift Jeff up on the gurney. For some reason, this moment vividly stands out to me: Both scared and in great physical pain, he countered, "I'm not getting up there. There's no way."

The paramedics disagreed and were determined to get Jeff on the gurney with or without his consent. And they did. They gave him oxygen and hooked him up with all these tubes. They didn't say anything. These guys had seen the worst of the worst, from township murders in South Africa to horrific accidents on the precarious roadways. They were seasoned.

Off I went to the hospital in downtown Cape Town. If you've never been to an inner-city emergency room in South Africa, you're in for a treat. Patients are lined up in the hallway, getting treated in an overcrowded, hot, blood-spackled, paint-peeling floor of an outdated hospital. I didn't want to go but was left with no choice. Recovering after receiving an IV of something, thankfully untainted, I was released in the morning. HIV negative.

Henry and I talked about it the next day, and he related that he had dreamed that he was being choked by the same exact figure that I saw.

"Yes, Swaindog, it was happening! How totally insane! It was there with us!"

"Well, I hope you have banished it—that scared the living shit out of me, bro! Couldn't do an encore of that!"

I never figured out the meaning of that spirit's visit, but felt that Henry would eventually discover that. Thankfully, that was the only time in my life I've ever encountered that kind of supernatural occurrence.

Still, I've had more than my share of terror. As I inventory bouts, the closest brush with death was not by land, air, mishaps, electrocution, or the maladies of Clubland, nor evil spirits. It was at sea.

I didn't learn to swim until taught around the age of ten, was only adequate, improving in time. I would have never guessed that a near-drowning misadventure during a swim on Papohaku Beach, on the island of Molokai, Hawaii, in the late '80s would rate as the most dangerous episode of my life.

A beautiful ribbon of fine crystalline white sand, with sparkling turquoise waters absent humans, courted a tingling soul. I loved swimming in the open ocean, and felt competent enough to ignore the many international graphic signs of drowning stick figures warning people about the riptides. Those warnings were clearly meant for the tourists.

My girlfriend at the time was sweet and easily frightened.

"Jeff, look at the signs. There's no one out there swimming, and there's no one else around. I don't think you should go out."

"Nonsense, the water is like glass—flat as a board! I've been in water like this and even in five-to-ten-foot waves before. Piece of cake!"

Out I went. Enveloped in the beauty and warmth of the water, losing track of distance from the beach. Eventually, at about a hundred yards out, attempting to start back in, the tow started carrying me farther out in an undesirable western direction parallel to the shoreline. I swam harder and harder to get back but made little progress, and eventually was exhausted. Losing hope of success, a feeling of panic loomed. I couldn't allow that, but was losing control and occasionally dipping below the water line. With water getting into the stomach and lungs, I was beginning to drown. The more I grappled with the thought of drowning, the worse the panic got, threatening to spiral me down to the bottom to meet Neptune.

Summoning inner strength and thought, I began to float on my back and relax, as is taught in these situations, coughing up the little water ingested. Regaining self-control and rhythmic breathing, I began to backstroke a bit toward land, taking advantage of small, heaven-sent, six-inch ripplet waves that started to come in. Continuing to paddle and utilize the waves, timing them out and breathing carefully, everything in perfect form, things started getting closer to the beach. Regaining senses, suddenly realizing that I was coming to the end of the mile-long beach and headed for a rocky point—that was not a good place to land, for sure. I noticed that my girlfriend and some other people were running along the beach, closing in on the point and yelling out. Couldn't make out what they were saying, but knew there was a short window to get to the sand and avoid the rocks closing in. At just the right time I gave it hell, swimming full bore with whatever strength remained, making it to chest-deep water where a couple guys came out to help me to shore in delirium. Onshore, I collapsed at the feet of my girlfriend, who was in tears.

"You stupid ass, I told you not to go out there! You almost killed yourself!"

I couldn't talk.

Then one of the hipster surfer guys barked, "Hey man, you, you don't know how close you were to catching the Molokai Express, dude! Around that rocky point right there you would've been gone, and no one would've ever found your body—shark treat in the open ocean. You are lucky, bro."

"Thank you, Mahalo," I responded and promptly passed out.

Awakening a while later, revived with fluids and giving thanks to everyone, along with a big hug to my girlfriend, time to traipse back to the car and parking lot a mile away. Along the way, and ever since for that matter, brimming with gratitude that my life had been spared.

Before long, I would find that this and all the rest of these life-threatening joys had simply been practice runs for my future challenges. Without them, may not have made it through my ultimate test.

CHAPTER 12

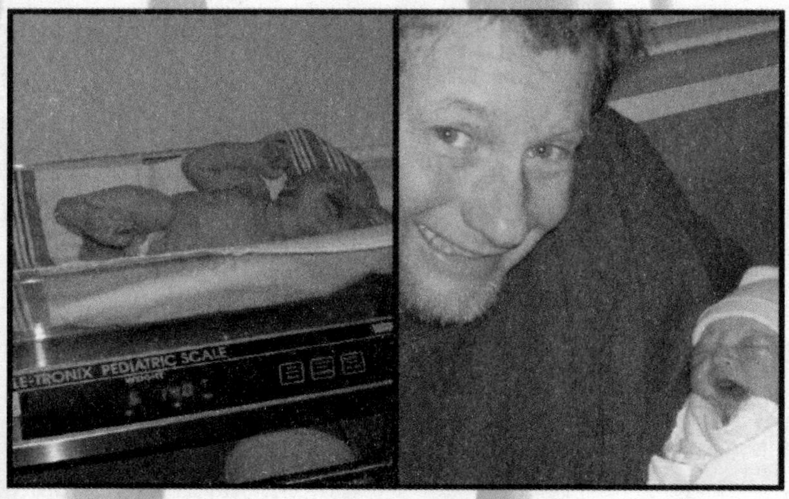

Birth of Cozette

Books from friends

CHAPTER 12

OFF THE EDGE—STRETCHHHHING

Having survived crazy antics, been successful at business with some financial footholds, it was the point in life where maybe I had it all. An amazing run—rising from not knowing where the next meal would come from, to a life where the world just seemed to roll out the red carpet. But something was missing.

Being the good Lutheran boy that I was, I remember entering high school where all the girls and boys were experimenting with a level of intimacy completely unfamiliar. I recall various dates where the girls wanted to get to know me in that certain way, and it would result in just freezing up at the thought. Could not get there. Ingrained in the brain from a Polish Catholic mother was the idea that anything like that should be saved for marriage, as she had done. Needed to find that perfect person; but as it happened, the damn would break in college, launching a raucous bachelor career that spanned thirty years.

I'd find myself fielding serious queries after a few dates, and when cornered, the line of questioning was the same. "What's wrong with you? You've never married—no kids? You seem to be a great guy, handsome and cool, so what's the deal?"

"What's wrong with me?" I would ask with a chuckle. "Do you want a computer printout?" Getting a touch more serious: "Been busy and haven't found the right person or timing. What's wrong with you—or any of us? I'm happy in my own skin. I'm in no rush."

It seemed that women who wanted to get too philosophical, needy, or demanding early on were just not my cup of tea. Let the good times roll; there were always more fish in the pond.

Then there was Sally, a woman I dated for some time but never lived with. After a few months, she invited me to join a session with her psychiatrist, whom she visited with every week and had for years. I liked Sally, and her psychiatrist was married to a local real estate mogul I had dealings with—the invitation was accepted. I arrived at the office separately—a very well-appointed, premium luxe thirtieth-floor space with a sweeping downtown Dallas view. Kind of what to expect from two women with refined tastes.

"Well guys, it's great to have you both here," the doc said. "And Jeff, I appreciate you coming."

"Well, of course."

The conversation went on and it was my turn to speak after listening to the small talk.

"I'm not sure why I am here, other than to be supportive. Don't feel like there are any problems with this budding relationship, so, happy to dive in. I'm aware these meetings have been going on for years, well before I was in the picture, so I'm curious about the reasoning or need. And please pardon me—never done this before."

"We just like to visit every week, that's all," Sally responded. "I like it."

The counselor looked at me, swiveled her chair to Sally, then back at me.

"Well, Jeff, Sally has some issues regarding you. Why don't we let her share what they are?"

She looked back at Sally again. "Go ahead."

Sally paused, collected herself, face twitching a bit, and then blurted out, "Well, Jeff, you are just too much fun. It's fun, fun, fun, eff'in fun, all the time. I just can't stand it. Too much fun. Toooo much!"

I looked at her in amazement, as she was now gritting her teeth, her baby-blue eyes squinting, under the self-inflicted pressure.

"You know, it makes me so angry sometimes…I just wanna… wanna…squash you!" she finally released, almost orgasmically, her facial scrunching now more intensified. "Squash you like a bug!!!"

She made a hand gesture, her thumb sticking down towards the floor, then pressing downward and rotating back and forth in a fictitious bug-smashing display. That bug was dead. The room fell silent.

Compelled to break the ice after that display: "Well, I don't see having fun as a problem, so this is new terrain for me. Perhaps that's something we need to work on?"

Small talk ensued briefly and then the session was over, with pleasantries exchanged as we departed the office. Down the elevator without a word, we walked silently out to the car, holding hands. It was parked in a vast, full lot at this major intersection of town, where thirty-story buildings framed us from every angle. As I got to my car, Sally decided to settle into the passenger seat. I looked at her without speaking, wondering what was next, when unexpectedly, she grabbed me with passion—or maybe it was an attempt at strangulation—and dove in for deep kisses. Nearly choking, with barely time to shift gears, she had climbed her petite frame into the driver's seat and onto my lap. There was love in the air but an issue with venue. To avert a scene in broad daylight, I suggested that we resume the now-private meeting elsewhere. It was an interesting relationship, although short-lived. It was, however, fun.

Dating interesting women with good chemistry was a blast. But without moving the needle forward, the relationships were doomed to fizzle out, resulting in periods of loneliness in between serial dating, girlfriends, live-ins, and breakups. Loneliness. The one emotion humans fear the most. When the holidays approached, there was need for a relationship, a "holiday girl," to use a term one of my partners had coined. It became decision-time every fall, especially with my birthday falling around Thanksgiving, as carrying on without a girl or plans for the holiday season always prompted a feeling of emptiness.

Eventually, succumbing to the rhythms of nature, there was a crossroads at age forty-nine. Having sorted out some of the acronyms and anecdotes of life, when, why, and with whom to procreate, if at all, was a looming question. A key litmus test, whether consciously or not, was the infamous Thanksgiving dinners in Michigan that a few of my girlfriends through the years had attended, meeting my sister and mother, and suffering my mother's extended family. Luckily, there were also entertaining activities to attend, like the downtown Detroit Thanksgiving Day parade with friends Joel, Mike, and others, and often the Detroit Lions football game, and/or the renowned Lafayette Coney Island restaurant nearby, made famous in SNL skits. Lined up downtown on the Woodward Avenue strip, we would consume adult libations passed around the group during Detroit's ofttimes bitterly cold late November days, which was the medication we needed to witness the Lions's consistently crushing football defeats and, for some, the challenging family dinners to be navigated that afternoon.

When I brought up my soon-to-be spouse to the annual party, I was forty-nine—in fact, I turned forty-nine that very week. Years later, my sister confided that they knew this was going to be "the one" even before meeting her. "Mom and I talked about it and with you being forty-nine, that was gonna be the magic number," she said. "That was gonna be the person you were going to end up with. For better or worse."

And so, it was.

She was a beautiful young woman, intelligent, cool with an artsy bent, and seemingly collected. Her family of partiers were fun, melding with my club scene pedigree. She was coming out of a marriage to a Russian husband she spoke poorly of when we first met, and I respected that boundary and didn't want to be a home-wrecker, so backed away, even though she assured me that it was a done deal. Once she became officially single, it was on, with everything going relatively smoothly. Still, there were concerning signs. Friends gently warned me that maybe I was setting myself up for short-term fun and long-term pain. I listened with half an ear.

The word is that men study horses for their temperament, bloodlines, teeth, and hooves before buying in, but with women, they usually jump in blind. I had the blinders on.

We dated for about a year and then I got the ultimatum, one heard before.

"If you want to move forward, get married, and start a family, I'm interested. I don't want to waste my time, so if not, I'm out. Cool either way, but I need to know."

She meant it.

"Well, if we get married, it will be my first and last. I'm only doing that once."

This time seemed reasonable to sign up—but did I want kids?

Babies, infants, kiddos, tots, tykes, yard apes, rug rats, curtain-climbers—those challenging, beautiful, magical, happy, impressionable, unblemished, demanding souls. Children! There were many reasons to endeavor, and yet not to, in this Herculean task. Would there ever be enough money—or, at my age, enough energy—to support children as they would need to be supported?

So many humans on the planet birthing without contemplating any of the associated responsibilities. Repeatedly. You need a license to practice law, real estate, be a doctor, nurse, dentist, or any kind of professional, as well as some credentials to drive a car or get a passport. But you need no training, education, licensing, or oversight to bring children into this world and never mind feeding, clothing, and educating them—nurturing them—one of the hardest, most demanding jobs and biggest decisions in life. And if you fail or bail as a parent, it becomes the children's and/or society's and the world's problem.

In the back of a taxi in Jamaica en route to a destination wedding starring my friend from Clubland, Steve, I was talking to the driver. As per usual, I asked about his family. Always a good opening.

"Yeah mon, I have sixteen children and some grandbabies too. A lot of mouths to feed," he responded, the aroma of ganga wafting out of his pores.

"How do you keep up with them all? Do you even know their names?" I joked, no needling intended, and none taken.

He laughed out loud, contagiously, and had me doing the same. Contact buzz. Then he started reciting the names and attempting to keep count until, by his own admission, couldn't keep the kids all sorted.

"Their mommas take care of them. The truth is, I just must give moms money and it's all cool. Money, money, money, mon. Never enough money."

"Why so many kids, then?" I asked.

"Kids are family—I want a big family. I need just one of the kids to make it. We all need someone to take care of us when we are old, bruuu," he concluded as he dropped me off at the wedding site's hotel.

Another parent once remarked, "I want kids to have something in this world that belongs to me. That's all I will have."

I thought to myself, *Well, then get a dog.*

Although the above rationales may or may not have merit, there are reasons to procreate. The fleeting moments of sheer joy. The prospects of heirs. So, it was time to decide—marriage and kids? Jeff?

It started looking like yes. We shared a Texas-Oregon connection. I had acquired a second home in Bend, Oregon while still living in Dallas, and she had family in Salem. A trip out for a wedding in Salem provided me the opportunity to meet the extended West Coast family, including a grandmother, now deceased, who was a joy, along with aunts and uncles in Salem and Gilroy, California who were just the best. These were some wonderful people—people that I wanted in my life. The family I didn't seem to have.

So, a deal was struck to plan for family life. In the interim, we had time to do some traveling and have some fun. My soon-to-be fiancée had never traveled the world much, so we decided on some bucket-list trips.

"Well, I've been thinking that maybe we could do a month in Argentina, especially the Patagonia region. Love it down there. Or maybe a month in Japan traveling, and a great friend there who I miss; you should meet him. While we are over there, could also pop over to Vietnam and tour the country—that's been on my bucket list for a long while."

"Well, why limit ourselves?" she responded. "How about we just do them all?"

Kind of liked that.

"And heck, if we want to travel when we have kids, I could swing that kid on my back and when they get older, we could even homeschool them on the road," she said.

It was admirable chutzpah. Though homeschooling was perhaps on the menu then for her, that was never to materialize. What would occur years later would be a solo dad orchestrating home-schooling for two years and two kiddos amidst a pandemic—not what was planned.

A storybook engagement during a Thanksgiving holiday on the Oregon coast rather than the traditional Detroit sojourn, followed by an epic wedding and party in Dallas, and a month-long European honeymoon constituted a great start to what looked like an incredible life plan for my second half. The honeymoon program included an initial stop in Istanbul, Turkey, a ten-day private boat excursion on the Turkish turquoise coast and the Greek Islands with friends, sojourns in Athens and Delphi—a place I'd always wanted to see, as it was my company's namesake, and which proved to be sheer greatness—and visits to Paris and the French countryside, to top it off. It was the trip of anyone's lifetime.

Upon returning to the States, we were greeted by a global financial meltdown that I initially chose to ignore, knowing that everything cycled out and that this was just another bump in the road. Summering in Bend, Oregon at a second home, camping, fishing, mushroom-hunting, and doing art classes with my new wife, painting scenes from travels as well as entertaining and continuing a most privileged lifestyle—all that left little time to pay much attention to the bad news.

Sold myself on a partner, starting a family, and moving to that second home in beautiful Bend permanently to have children to raise, enjoy, teach, and travel with. Could not have gotten any luckier.

I always felt that I'd be a great dad, inheriting my mother's nurturing instinct. Many friends agreed:

> "I think you could be great, even at your age. You've got that crazy energy like no one else."
>
> "Jeff, you are just like a kid yourself. I can't imagine anyone else being a more fun dad."
>
> "I don't know anyone as silly as you are at your age. If you can survive it, you're going to have a ball."
>
> "Kids will keep you young."

To become a superdad, like it says nowadays in my bio, my business card, and social-media profiles.

So, with a mix of blessings and trepidation, it was in on the marriage-and-kids wagon, happily ignoring any flashing alert lights. During my adventurous life, I had survived many challenges and near-death experiences—I was bulletproof. Right?

Now Captain Adventure was starting a family. Always a planner, being careful to circumvent becoming a papa by surprise with years of "practice" dodging Daddydom, wondered if I was capable. Then the very first attempt at conception hit the mark. Prego. *Bahhda bing!*

The pregnancy went relatively well as we moved through all the phases. Then the day came for the mystery to be revealed (it had been decided to leave the gender of the kid a surprise).

"Jeff, it's time to go to Baylor," my wife announced early one morning.

I was thrilled to play catcher for my firstborn. I distinctly remember being in position for that reception with the uber-competent Doctor Brodsky and staff at Baylor Hospital Dallas. Brodsky was a rock star in these parts—the top OB there as well as a standup comic. Really! I was fortunate to have him on the team through my contacts with the Baylor Hospital board.

The baby's birthing process was not going smoothly, however, as the umbilical cord had found its way around the unborn child's neck, and preparations were made to move quickly to a C-section birth if needed. Mom had bravely decided to go au naturel—no epidural—but as the time drew near, she changed her mind, too late as it turned out.

In what was becoming a nerve-wracking scene, I assumed the post to assist with the birth despite the still-last-minute curveball possibility of a C-section. The staff was amazed that Doc Brodsky was still going to attempt a vaginal birth with all the complications mounting. Seemed the whole hospital floor was in the room after he decided to forge ahead. From my front-row seat, looking behind me, I saw thirty or more heads craning for position to witness the feat.

Then *bam!* I could see the child's head crowning, and then split seconds later, the whole li'l gooey body was in my hands. The kid, happy with that cord off the neck, thrashed wildly as the nurse handed me the forceps to clamp on the umbilical cord, which were about to be fumbled with the slippery child.

"Mr. Swaney, please apply the forceps to the cord. Now!" she barked nervously.

Stupefied, I froze. That's when the child—born just seconds earlier and eyes still closed—grabbed the forceps from my hand and began whipping them around. Mild panic ensued as the nurse pressed me to the side, retrieved them, and did the job.

"Is everything okay?" Mom then squeaked out. "Is it a boy or a girl?"

I stammered. Couldn't really tell—there was so much excess on the kid and the private parts…couldn't tell if it was a fired-up gal or a shocked boy. Didn't want to screw things up any further.

Doc Brodsky intervened, holding back his impish laughter. "Jeff, if it's not a boy, then…………..?"

"It's a girl………..it's a girrrrrrrrl….. a little baby girl….a GIRL. A GIRL!"

Cozette Swaney had been born. I was in the game.

A dad.

The advent of the parenting era was upon me; it was time to start a new chapter. The missus and I were what you would call partiers—yeah, owned a nightclub for fifteen years, but that was going to be rearview-mirror material. It was time to move away from Dallas, Texas where there was too much temptation for the party-party lifestyle to a place where parenting and the outdoors would be the impetus.

Mom, as I refer to her since she is the children's biological mother, had been abstaining from the party for the entire pregnancy and did so for about a month after. Once she regained that degree of freedom, however, she began getting wild with it. There are stories. I contacted two friends for guidance when these episodes started, being worried sick, especially now caring for an infant daughter. One friend had been in AA for many years as a speaker and sponsor of many; the other became chairman of a rehab center that had saved his life in Seattle, a place Mom would end up for her first attempt at rehab.

The dialogue with both men was similar.

"What do I do? Things are getting out of hand. I'm scared to death!"

"There is not much that you can do. You need to clearly let her know how you feel about it, then let it go. You're protecting your three-month-old daughter and yourself—that's what you need to focus on, Jeff. Period."

"But isn't there some way I can get her into a rehab place now and get her sorted out?" I pleaded. "That's what's needed."

"Not up to you, brother. People must find their own way, and it can get ugly sometimes. When she is ready to ask for help, you will need to move quickly to get the aid she needs. We'll be there for you. But try and help before that, and you will only be blamed for all her behaviors. That's how it is. I know."

She asked for help one morning after a long night out with her friends. Messy. This would be my first experience in dealing with the world of addiction and learning much that now seems common knowledge. With all my school-of-hard-knocks education, wished this had been part of my curriculum long before. Maybe in second grade?

That would be the first of many rehab attempts. As things would play out in our relationship, Mom would eventually become a stranger to me. I relate this all with no remorse, angst, shame, or ill will. It sucked, but it would all just become a sad slice of life that you chew on.

There were many incidents in my marriage related to Mom's rehabs, all terrifying and traumatizing. I found myself akin to juggling flaming bowling pins, doused in napalm, on the back of a one-legged chair in a typhoon. Swoooooosh!

During the resultant divorce much later, the court and children's custody evaluator would deliver a comprehensive fourteen-page report that summarized the challenges faced over this seven-year stretch. It recounted years of Mom's addiction issues.

Her conclusion:

"She is very angry.... Personality test results indicate her to be a competitive, aggressive, and dominating woman.... It is my strong recommendation that primary legal and physical custody of Cozette and Ford be granted to their father, Jeff."

So much fun.

Mom wanted to have five kids, but was not capable of helping to raise any of them if she slipped, and it took me managing work, our daughter, and helpers to keep things together. Still, in between all those attempted rehabilitations, I considered having another child. Things were going smoothly for a while but uncertain they would stay that way, despite all my prayers, and I was getting on in age, and my daughter was very young—wanted her to have a sibling. I felt that later in life, with me gone and if Mom couldn't keep her hands on the wheel, that would be the right move. Friends, a doctor, and my counselor concurred.

The decision seemed the antithesis of sanity—and the definition of dilemma.

Our son Ford was born in 2012. Funny how couples having the most difficult times sometimes think that having a child is a good idea. "It'll fix everything!" I never thought that, but in this case trusted my friends, the pros, and my gut to forge ahead. It was nip and tuck during the pregnancy as Mom was having issues once more, and we didn't want to expose my son, captive in the womb, to excess. The doctors probably breached HIPPA to help us, and dancing in the fire again proved quite nerve-racking. So, it was a relief when there was a buy-in from all parties to have Mom induced, after day-to-day monitoring, to free Ford.

Right after his birth, here was Mr. Mom again for an infant, this time with a two-year-old daughter in tow, as Mom volunteered to return once more to Malibu, the land of many luxe rehab centers, for another stint. Once again, the recovery wrought would be short-lived, as Mom's subsequent acting-out in front of the children in terrifyingly pitiful ways ended up breaking Daddy's back. We could not function in this environment.

I scheduled a call with the counselor.

"I am at the end of my rope here," I said, shaking. "Don't think I can continue like this."

"Well absolutely! You cannot continue, and you need to move forward to separate yourself, especially for the sake of the children," she implored. "If you keep carrying on as you have, you will be destroyed and lose everything. There is no way that you can do this anymore—you are not that strong, and no one is. You must do everything you can to protect yourself and those kids!"

It was time to leave a career in full blossom and millions of dollars on the table to save two children who were witnessing life-altering behaviors at a developmental stage. It was, unfortunately, time for a divorce.

I waited for the result of the divorce filing to be delivered to the rehab center where there would be support for Mom, with high anxiety—anxiety well-merited. We hear the system is broken. I was about to find out how bad it was.

CHAPTER 13

No fun

Family Problems?

FAMILY LAW ATTORNEY
30 Years Experience
Grandparent's Custody & Visitation
Custody • Divorce • Paternity • Child Suppor
Restraining & Stalking Orders

A Real Attorney, For Real People, With Real Problems

CALL NOW –

1 Hour Initial Consultation only $99
$150 Value
WITH OTHER OFFERS. EXP 9-10-16

Opposing lawyer's ad

CHAPTER 13

CATACLYSM—BEATING THE ODDS

Life laces itself with traumatic experiences, but few are as stressful as slogging through a disjointed, heavily biased judicial system. Time to experience debilitating helplessness, desperation, and humiliation in gluttonous portions. With all that, my children's well-being and futures hung in the balance, so it took being committed all-in at the highest stakes, no matter what the cost physically, financially, and psychologically.

I had spent my whole life doing a zillion deals and always sidestepping legal problems not of my design, to acquiesce to extortion and leave money on the table rather than deal with the negative energy and downer of a courtroom and attorneys. Taking the haircut was worth the sacrifice. Time is the premium. Choose wisely. Now, I was about to get stuck in that punishing structure avoided my whole life—to experience the grinding wheels and stench of injustice, reminiscent of that heavy weight felt in my twenties during that summer job in the Detroit factory hellhole.

I finally got the answer on my divorce filing, but not the answer wanted or that anyone had hypothesized.

Unbeknownst to me, Mom had fled rehab and on to the courtroom, first thing, to convince the judge that I was a danger—which triggered a manhunt for me that locked down schools for the day and invoked total chaos. The judge was now on Team Mom and would do everything in the court's power to beat me down, delay, object to my pleas for justice, and generally make my life miserable until finally seeing the truth months later.

Fortunately, I got a call from trusted school personnel warning me of the blitzkrieg and was able to skirt instantaneous disaster, but still had to hand over my kids and vacate my home in a matter of hours. Whew! I was in the Twilight Zone.

Booted from my home, with no place to go on a cold, rainy, miserable evening, I phoned some neighbors with whom I'd become and remain close. They invited me to their home and set me up with a place to stay for a few weeks, a glass of wine and dinner on the table. Gratitude.

This was going to be my first stop in eight months of being spitefully kept out of my home, moving from place to place with no reprieve from Mom, no matter how I offered to placate. It was clear that my pain and suffering were the objective here, along with promoting my financial collapse. These goals were confirmed in voluminous hateful, boasting, foul-mouthed text messages packed with expletives, which would eventually be shared with the court.

After my ejection from home, I had to kneel to The Children's Stop to see my kids. This was the local "safe place" for children's visits—a well-intended cog in the system, serving the purpose of allowing parents to see children while being closely monitored, as well as administering child exchanges if decreed. Typically, there was an awful, abusive father in the mix, but not in this case. Nonetheless, the workers there identify no differences and, in my opinion and in the views of many men, treat dads with barely cloaked disdain. I was now guilty of being a bad dad until proven innocent man, and subject to their yoke.

"They are not your friends—don't talk to them," my attorney warned.

Of course, I did not follow that advice, convinced I could disseminate the truth and turn the tide by foolishly pleading my case with them at every turn—which would only make things worse.

After weeks of waiting, Cindy, one of the honchos there, was my first contact at intake. A short, stubby woman with pursed lips, a Dutch boy's haircut, ill-fitting pseudo-hip eyewear, and the personality of a fence post, she was in my eyes the poster woman for man-hating. She motioned me into her conference room. This did not feel good, as it was clear within the first fifteen seconds that she had not taken a liking to me. It was quickly going to become evident that they had swallowed Mom's wild stories hook, line, sinker, boat, and ocean.

"Well, thanks for getting me in. I know my kids are not safe, and I haven't seen them in two weeks. What can we do to rectify this?"

"We must go through the protocols here, Mr. Swaney. You being pushy does not help," she said sternly.

"Well, this is all wrong! I've brought all these documents. The kid's mom busted out of a behavioral rehab to throw me out of the house and abscond with the kids after I filed for divorce. I have all this to share with you. Let's take a look."

"I'm not interested in your paperwork, Mr. Swaney, just what we need to do here."

I asked her again, and the answer always came back, "Nope, nyet, no no no, uh-uh," reminiscent of an old David Spade Capital One commercial. "We don't need any of that; just this paperwork here," she said, pushing my files aside and giving me some forms to fill out.

I pulled out my money clip where I had my business cards with my credit cards and maybe one hundred dollars total in cash, and gave her my biz card, which she put in her file with the forms. Later in a custody trial, Cindy would testify that I'd pulled out a "wad of cash" in an attempt to bribe her.

"Well, we are done here, Mr. Swaney. I will see you out, now," she snapped.

"When do I get to see my kids?" I pleaded.

"We will contact you. Have a good day."

It would take over three weeks for me to see my children, thanks to purposeful delays by the staff, and Mom and her nasty lawyer playing games.

On my first visit, my daughter Cozette, then six years old, was beyond excited to finally see me. We hugged briefly (you are constantly monitored so as not to whisper to them) and I spent a couple hours with her and young Ford, who was two at the time and didn't quite understand what was going on. We played, and I listened to their stories.

When our time together was up abruptly, Cozi did not want to leave. It took three staffers to drag her off and out, kicking, biting, and screaming, as wild as she had been during her momentous birth. Unable to help her, I was left crying, slobbering, tongue-wagging face down on the dirty asbestos-tiled floor.

One of the workers approached as I lay there in misery. "Mr. Swaney, you need to obey the rules. When the kids must leave, you need to encourage them to do so. If they try to grab on you, you need to hold your hands up and do everything you can to help us get them out to their mom."

I lay there unresponsive. I finally spoke. "I did just that. Is this normal for a child kicking and screaming to have three of you drag her away from her dad, the only rock in her life, where I can hear her wailing in pain all the way out the door and into the parking lot? "

"Oh yes, we see this all the time."

I was speechless.

Over the next twelve weeks, I would be subjected to all that The Children's Stop had to offer. After every visit, they would share with Mom anything they could, triggering a barrage of more taunting and foul-mouthed texts from her within an hour, like clockwork.

Mom went as far as to get the police involved during one of my visits.

I arrived to the customary frisking at intake and was set aside in a room I hadn't seen.

"Please stay here. We have somebody here who wants to visit with you," the staff explained.

I was completely shocked, I'm sure even turned white, when a police officer entered the room, hands on hips, and approached me. A big guy loaded with weaponry.

"Well, hello officer," I stammered.

"Hello, Mr. Swaney. I will keep this simple. I have a couple of options for you. I'd like to review your Miranda rights and if you would like to talk, we can chat here. Otherwise, I will need to take you to the station. Your choice."

I was completely dumbfounded—almost pissed my pants.

"Uh…uh…yes, read me my rights."

After that, he told me I was accused of breaking into my own house and trashing the place earlier that afternoon.

"No officer, in fact, I can detail for you where I was—shopping, the car wash, and other errands. If you'd like, I can go to my car and pull up the receipts on my credit card. My ex has called false 911 calls on me so many times, I document my movements every day. I would never go to the house in violation of court orders, as I have court dates coming up to resolve all of this in my favor."

He believed me, and after forty-five minutes bid me a good day—the most cordiality I'd ever experienced in that building. I was then escorted to a man-rodent staffer who sat me down in another holding tank on the premises. "I'm sure you're a bit shook up and probably don't wanna go through with meeting your kids, so it's okay. You don't have to do that now."

"What are you talking about? I've already lost an hour. That's ridiculous! Let's get on with it. All cool, I'm ready to go."

And so, I got my abbreviated visit with the kids.

After that episode, I made a point of going down to the police station to try to quell the number of false 911 calls and explain my dilemma. The female officer I met with confidentially showed me a fragment of a report where they had answered ninety-two 911 calls from another spouse. She also spoke to me about having to personally move a woman from her own home because a guy she'd met on Match.com and had been dating for two months moved in with a backpack, filed a restraining order, and had her thrown out of her own place.

"How can all this be?" I asked. "It doesn't make any sense!"

"I know. It is what it is," she said. "Unfortunately, we bear the brunt of all this and the courts seem to do little about it."

I gained a new respect for the police force for their unenviable role in these messes. They seemed the only sane cog in the system. Not a group to be defunded.

Over the next three months, I suffered through The Children's Stop one Friday every two weeks for three hours. It was akin to a prison, bringing back memories of visiting my friend in the pen years before, and the checking and shakedowns that occurred when entering the facility. I felt like a prisoner, with buzzing doors, double locks, and stringent rules greeting every time. Loved seeing my kids, but I was treated so poorly that it led to an inexplicable mix of emotions. Longing for something so badly yet loathing it at the same time was draining. As friends followed my odyssey, several spoke candidly. "Honestly Jeff, I don't think I could handle this," said one. "I think I would just give up. I don't know how you do it."

"Well, I don't know, either," I replied. "It is hell! But it's something you just have to do. I'll never give up on the kids, that's just the way I'm wired—couldn't live with myself otherwise."

As if all that wasn't enough during this period, I was living a couch-surfing lifestyle under high stress brought by the relentlessness, lengthiness, uncertainty, and high stakes of my plight, while waiting for a long-delayed parenting-time hearing to improve the children's situation. Things would become even more unmanageable after a debilitating accident.

On a dusty, seldom-used, lava-rock hiking-and-running canyon trail, perched on a ledge high above the Deschutes River, I sought decompression in the fresh scent of pines, enveloped by the views and sound of the river tumbling below. It was near sunset and visibility was poor, with a thermal-induced breeze as I walked westward, deep in thought. Traversing the gritty lava path and struggling with a haze, I felt a lightning brush on my right side and the flash of a runner blasting by me. Knocked off balance and blinded by the blaring sun, stumbling forward, the Vibram soles gripping the lava rock with each exaggerated step, things accelerated as I tried to get my footing. Covering about fifteen yards before finally falling onto the rock at full speed, hands and arms locked in full extension. I lay flattened, screwed to the earth, unable to even twitch for what seemed a cosmic eternity but was actually a few minutes.

Once my brain assessed the damage, it instantaneously caused my body to release its full course of magic, lifesaving chemistry to get me up and going, while bleeding everywhere. Being somewhat versed in lifesaving from my wilderness experiences—and knowing that I had a finite amount of blood, and that chemicals would mask problems only for a short time—I bushwhacked down to the river and packed cold river sand on the a deeply sliced knee wound to congeal it. By then, beginning to feel pain in hands and arms, I had to beeline to my car over a mile away on pure adrenaline.

"Are you okay? Can I help you?" several hikers and runners asked along the way. It was a solid mess.

"No, no. I got it, thanks," I replied, pushing ahead without looking at them.

One of the ladies seen peripherally actually did follow me to the car. "Are you okay to drive?"

"Yeah, yeah, I'm good. Just heading to a condo down the street."

It's amazing what your body can do with broken bones when it releases its chemical power to get you over the hump for that hour or two before the storehouse empties. While in transit, I called my friend, Karen, who had been graciously letting me use a spare room in her condo while homeless.

"Hi. How are you? I've had a trail accident. I'm heading to the condo. Be there in five." I grimaced.

"Well…what? Are you okay to drive? Where are you?"

Pulling up to the place, I stepped out of the car a tad wobbly as she pulled up alongside.

"Oh my God, what happened to you? You look terrible. We need to get you to the ER right away!" she exclaimed.

"Oh no, I'm fine—a little bloody, but I'll be all right. I just need to get cleaned up a bit."

"Oh no, no, I don't think so! You need to get checked out. Get in my car. We're going now."

"No, no, I don't want to go…Well…Okay, I will if you let me get a quick shower first."

I thought if I got cleaned up, I could get out of this trip; but in the shower, I noticed I had difficulty moving about and getting dressed.

I presented myself.

"You are a mess, all right. Let's get your butt to the hospital."

We were about halfway there when the endorphins started wearing off, pain intensifying. Both elbows were now on fire.

"I'm going to the ER. I'm going to the ER. Thank you for taking me! *Woohoo!*" I babbled, like a delirious little kid.

The prognosis there was not good—two broken elbows. Bilateral damage. Ouch!

At this point, homeless, post-surgery to get pieced together, and unable to drive or do much for myself, I hired a Visiting Angel, a sweet elderly Romanian woman, to help me shower, floss, brush my teeth, dress, and more. An invalid in a pickle.

None of my friends could believe this. Responses ranged from "You can't possibly deserve this" to "How do we chase that black cloud off you?" and ultimately to references comparing my travails to that of the biblical character, Job.

Didn't know much about Job except that the Devil made a deal with God, and Job got stuck in the middle with a world-class ass-whipping as his reward. Screwed. The third or fourth time someone drew that comparison, I responded. "Yeah, I think that's me! I think I'm ready to just fling open the front door and let the locusts come and eat my eyeballs out and be done and over with this shit once and for all."

Being unsure about the locusts, and with all the hubbub about Job, I figured I'd pick up my Bible and re-read the story studied in Lutheran school years before, discovering that his name is, of course, synonymous with suffering but, more importantly, with faith. The faith that pulls us through our torments. Faith that would sure get tested.

After missing an important court date due to the surgery, I had to show up at The Children's Stop two days later—still beaten and bruised, a sling around my neck, rungling along without the forbidden pain meds I needed—to see the kids. Of course, the staff at The Children's Stop inquired about this condition but did not believe the story. Perhaps they imagined a loser in a barroom brawl. Looked the part. Not a Job thing. The kids found my scab-covered knee and sling novel. As my boy brushed my leg, the scab cracked and blood trickled, and as they were just three and six at the time, they endeavored to finger-paint my legs with the blood, which entertained them to no end. Mom would be told of the injuries and send me a berating text in gleeful celebration.

By then she had assembled quite a team I would have to battle to save kids and sanity. The lineup included my mother-in-law, a twice-board-suspended lawyer, The Children's Stop staff with Cindy leading the charge to the bitter end, and a buffaloed judge. The deck was stacked.

The days began with serious, painful dry heaves for the first thirty minutes. Many were worried about me, including myself.

How did I get here? On the verge of financial ruin, being hog-tied, and not able to help my kids, knowing yet not knowing how much they were suffering. People thought I would become a victim of depression—and probably was, since there were more than a few days of being slow to get out of bed. Warding it off somehow, objecting to medications, like Job, I needed relief; but pills were not it. Had witnessed the damage they did.

A critical court date came up regarding parenting time and a chance to parent outside of The Children's Stop. Due to the court's rotational format, there was to be a different judge, thank God—a wise magistrate, now deservedly presiding in that courthouse.

Prepared for that court date, we had a nanny helper who calmly testified the truth about what she had witnessed during her five years of experience with us. Team Mom labeled me a monster who should never see the kids again and offered Cindy from The Children's Stop as a star witness. I'll never forget Cindy testifying that I had somehow put tracking devices in the sealed apple slices in a Wendy's kid's meal, which they had then somehow smuggled out. The judge craned his neck at the witness in disbelief, holding back his laughter. That fable iced the cake. He was the man who would get me out of that Children's Stop hellhole.

"That place is not designed for everybody," he ruled, giving me parenting time outside The Children's Stop while waving his finger at Mom, warning her to be compliant with the details of his ruling. This long-awaited reprieve bolstered hope.

Even after a small victory, the constant pounding of Team Mom led me to shamelessly reach out for help in all directions.

My self-esteem and life were in the toilet now and needed support—from friends, organizations, counselors. Any and many sources were required. Pride had waited too long to ask. A mistake.

One of my friends in a similar predicament turned me onto an Al-Anon handbook. I had heard of Al-Anon group meetings, but hadn't the faintest clue of what they were and wasn't very motivated to find out. After a few chats, during which he deflected my pissing and moaning, he finally sorted me out.

"Stop trying to figure everything out," he directed. "Your smartest thinking is what got you here in life. Now you know you don't know shit. Go to the meetings ASAP, or lose my number!"

He was serious.

I wound up attending many an Al-Anon meeting, modeled after the well-known AA meetings, listening to people's mind-numbing stories and anecdotes. You take what you want and leave the rest, all in strict confidence. Loudmouth that I was, I didn't speak there for over a year. I was still so traumatized; couldn't bring myself to do it. A regular, and the only one who didn't talk. Folks who caught my gaze at meetings were clearly curious about my story.

Finally, just barely and on the edge of tears, belting out the *Reader's Digest* version of my travails was a relieeeeeeef! Even in a room like this with all the stories, everyone was floored by mine—an unwanted trophy. After the meeting, two teary-eyed women followed me out and asked how they could help, which was contrary to the Al-Anon way. Politely declining, I never spoke at another Al-Anon meeting, but attended often.

In addition to Al-Anon, attending church with an elderly neighbor, now passed, afforded meeting Father Jim there, who comforted. Being in the church services was emotional, leading to fighting back tears and weeping on Sundays.

Friends asked what I was doing wrong. Wrong attorney? Overthinking? Too emotional? Wrong color suit in the courtroom? Need to file more motions? What is going on in those Oregon courts? I hear Portland and Oregon have gone crazy! This would never happen in Dallas! Why did you move from Texas?

One friend lamented, “I’m sorry I seemed I bailed on you. I couldn’t help you and I’m a very caring person and it was just killing me seeing what you and the kids were going through. I couldn’t sleep pondering that.”

Didn’t know all of the answers, just knew to do my best to help myself and the kiddos.

Wanting to be strong, found myself crying in the office of the custody evaluator, as she explained to me, “Jeff, you are trying to rationalize incredibly irrational behavior here. You can’t do that; you’ve got to stop. There is nothing to be gained in that quest.”

My attorney was pressed to get something done. “How can this go on? And why? This is ridiculous, insane! We need to do something!”

“Well, it just isn’t that easy,” she explained. “It’s a process. We’ve got a difficult buffoon of an attorney across the aisle, and you’ve got a newly hatched judge who bought their story and now does not like you. Of course, the topper is your wife, who is unreal. You’re the one who married her, and this is where we are now.”

“What? What?” I grieved.

"We must prepare for the long game now—talk with kids' teachers and caregivers, set up a mediation to get your house back and stabilize your finances. At the end, the custody trial will determine where kids' home will be, and you'll finally be granted your divorce. We got this. Keep your eye on the prize, Jeff. Hang in there."

It took five months to get to the financial mediation and allow myself to be extorted, of course, despite signing off that I wasn't, and another three months to get the house back. It had been abandoned, the thermostat set on max ninety degrees mid-winter, all lights left on, in terrible disrepair, full of trash, insects, feces, and mice, with significant water damage throughout. I won't even endeavor to explain what was found in a bathtub with my childhood pictures, which added to the stench in the house that would have to air out for a full week. Three months of repairs, working with crews seven days a week, would eventually get the place habitable.

I would experience newfound freedoms after that mediation was completed and the ridiculous restraining order against me dropped. During Mom's temporary custody over a period of eighteen months, reports from Child Protective Services would document that the children had been neglected and abused in the home, as well as in a daycare closed by the Oregon State Police and DA there. And yet they had done nothing. Cigarette burns and broken bones were the minimum standard required for CPS action, my attorney related. Later, my kids would volunteer stories, which I believed, of near drownings of my son in swimming pools and the Columbia River, domestic violence they had witnessed, NATs (Non-Accidental Traumas) they had suffered, including being left to wander the streets after bus drops—lost and scared and at risk of being picked up by total strangers. My daughter fell to the bottom of the barrel academically, sporting the worst attendance record of over five hundred children at the elementary school she went to. The kids had gone feral.

I was livid, but had to stay cool. This was my children's life as mandated by the court. Any misstep and I would be toast.

Years later, after the kids did not have to see Mom anymore, they became comfortable with sharing many more stories of that time without the fear of consequences. Sitting at dinner one night, Cozi suddenly said, "Dad, I remember all of these mice that were in the house. They were everywhere, but mostly in this pantry. We had a couple favorites. One was named Alex, a boy mouse, and he was kind of the ugliest of the bunch. The other was a girl we named Poppy. She was so cute!"

I choked down my food and grinned.

Usually, the stories were shocking and maddening, but kept my cool even while being blindsided. I listened and validated their feelings while underscoring that they were now safe and could move on in their lives. Things for them had been worse than imagined, and there was thanks they survived.

I, too, had survived the low point of life and was going to pull off the bottom now, belly-crawling out of the mire. There would be more challenges, but we were on the long road back.

With my home now intact, but prior to the final custody ruling, the kids could enjoy much-better-quality time with me when they visited every other weekend, and on some holidays and summer breaks. Although Mom was still the temporary custodial parent, with all the associated heartburn, my elbows had healed, and financial ruin had been deftly averted, with things on all fronts on the mend. Of course, we still had a way to go with the children's health and education, both of which had taken a beating, and had to endure long drives from central Oregon to Mom's home in Hillsboro, Oregon, west of Portland, at minimum a four-hour drive, subject to traffic, snowstorms and ice storms in the winter, and wildfire firestorms in the summer. With no options to reschedule, as Mom had the screws tightened, some drives took over twelve hours depending on the situation. We all suffered.

Everything now was building up to the custody trial. Getting sole custody would mean having the children get back to their home full-time, avoiding the nonstop smoking and vaping at Mom's place that made them feel sick. And less of the domestic violence they witnessed between Mom and her boyfriend, now hubby, evidenced in restraining orders they filed against each other, together with bloody mugshots on public record. It would mean getting long-neglected, in-depth healthcare and counseling, as well as tutoring and that complete school reboot, socializing with friends and engaging in inspiring activities—all that had been lacking for over a year. The clock was ticking.

Children's custody has historically always been granted to mothers, irrespective of any facts that would make that disastrous for the children. Even up until recent years, it was rare for the courts to ever grant sole custody to a father. You'd have to have overwhelming evidence to substantiate your argument—way over the top. I'd always had all the information but had found few listeners in the system, since most were cemented in their biases. Even though the deck had been stacked, the pendulum was about to swing.

The Family Abuse Protection Act (FAPA), established in 1996 and updated in 2012, essentially created a guilty-until-proven-innocent mandate, intended to protect women and children from the wrongs they might suffer at the hands of men who'd previously had impunity for their misdeeds. That's what had been falsely served on me, rubber-stamped after my divorce filing. I would discover that I was far from the only one, and that it was now used as commonplace leverage. According to one online article, the perversion of the tool equated a dad's starting point in a divorce and custody battle with being "hogtied with an apple in their mouths set on a readymade bonfire awaiting a match." Wow! Could I ever relate to that. There were a zillion stories complaining of this injustice locally and nationally, but no political will to fix it. It was a hot potato—no one wanted to touch it—and most of the lawyers and players in the system that made a living thereby liked things as they were, victims stuck with the playbook.

The backdrop on everyone's mind as my custody trial date came into view wasn't about North Korea, COVID, or the Russian-Ukraine invasions. The front-page news was polarized politics, male bad actors and their horrid personas, characterized by the Me-Too movement. I could feel the reverberations of this societal earthquake on every trip to the sprawling concrete courthouse complex. Right or wrong, the buzz wasn't favorable for my case, as I could see Mom's attorney characterizing me with all the twisting jargon then in vogue, as a wild, crazed, rich, hateful, and controlling bully. I was the one being bullied, but the confluence of the weekly news of many Hollywoodies' alleged misdeeds that had captured the public's attention, did not improve chances of success.

These transgressions in Hollywood shone spotlights on Cosby, Spacey, Weinstein, Epstein, and others, resulting in blasting media blowout made even more nuclear by the tense political fireworks of Donald Trump and Hillary Clinton battling in partisan DC, and the whole country seemingly angry and on edge. It was nerve-racking.

"Jeez, this current media situation is just not feeling helpful. Is it just me, or are we facing some headwinds exacerbated by all the craziness out there? Every day there's some new insane shit flying that's uglier than the last fling!"

"I think you're right. You just need to keep your head down and stay the course," she responded.

As the trial date arrived, cortisol levels reached a crazy high. I had periods during the day being perfectly fine, and others extremely shaky, as the stress continued to build. This terribly long torture, unjust and uncertain in outcome, with two innocent children's lives in the balance, was taking a toll. Gearing up for this July trial, fifteen months after filing for divorce, friends reorganized their entire summer family vacations and travel schedules to help me with the kids, testify, and/or keep me from falling apart. Lo and behold, the judge rescheduled the trial just days before the weeklong event and reset it for October. This would mean that my daughter would start in school in Hillsboro, where she'd just had a pitiful year, and allow for an argument of keeping her there rather than changing schools midyear. God forbid that the judge who had issued the restraining order, which was finally beaten back with help from other judge's rulings, and who seemed bent on my demise, would allow another judge to hear the case. She had drunk the Kool-Aid. It was a mind melt.

I told my seriously inconvenienced friends, "Dammit, I am so sorry. I just cannot believe this. They are doing everything they can to make it impossible for justice."

"It's okay, Jeff, we will be there for you," they all replied in so many words. "We've got to do this. And just so you know we wouldn't be doing this just for you, we are doing this for your kids." They knew the stakes.

A recurring dream crept into my nights, a premonition of a beautiful little girl dancing in a field of flowers, picking them and tossing them about under a crystal blue sky with sweet wisps of clouds above. And then the appearance of a giant toilet bowl, white and gleaming in the sun, twenty times the size of the girl, its handle about to flush and suck everything down in it, the entire scene, including the small child. *No!*

October arrived, and the long-delayed trial finally began. First off, the judge offered to disqualify herself, something I'd motioned for and been denied over a year before. This, after all the witnesses had to be reorganized again for this weeklong shit show. Really? What's the thought process there, knowing what was going on? I wondered. Screw our lives all up and then, knowing the truth, bail out? It was a little late for that. My jaw dropped.

My attorney responded, "Your Honor, I need a few minutes to discuss this with my client."

"What the hell good would this do?" I seethed. "We are going to lose all my witnesses finally, and my kids will continue to be screwed in Hillsboro!"

"Well, it's a gamble. It's your call," she answered. "I'm happy to forge on."

"Let's do that. We have to!"

A week of insanity ensued—a lopsided program in the courtroom in Dad's favor, sickening and sad. It should have never had to come to that. On one side, Mom with her mother, her newfound Romanian boyfriend, The Children's Stop dweeb, and a worker from the soon-to-be-shuttered-by-the-Hillsboro-DA-and-Oregon-State-Police children's daycare facility, where the kids had spent ungodly amounts of time in misery. An army of teachers, doctors, psychologists, school counselors, nurses, nannies, neighbors, lifelong family friends, and even the custody evaluator were enlisted—over twenty witnesses culled from a list of over forty volunteers, with even more who had heard of what was going on and wanted to come to our aid.

Truthfully, the trial should have been stopped mid-week since the evidence was so overwhelming. This can happen ofttimes to ease the backed-up court schedules, and save countless wasted hours and taxpayer dollars; but the trial was allowed to drag on. Even at the end of the five-day drudgery, coming home completely exhausted every night, the judge could not reach a decision and had to create a laundry list of more homework for us. With that information, she would decide three weeks later. Preposterous.

The day finally came when the judge, after receiving all the requested reporting, rendered a decision in the case. Watching in trepidation and witnessing the judge literally wringing her hands, ala a Pontius Pilate, looking down at her papers, then holding her head in her hands, it was somehow a difficult call for her, as she had to do an about-face after eighteen months of beating me down. Finally, however, the facts and testimony of the case took precedence, and the court exited Team Mom. She noted that neither parent should have custody, but that Mom had "sunk her own ship"—the ship the court built for her—and custody was finally granted to Dad. In addition, the kids needed to be surrendered without delay. It was bittersweet.

The next day I received a text message from Mom.

"You are in for the worst f---ing nightmare of your pathetic life dealing with me for the next thirteen years. I'll make sure I'm the death of you. Don't worry. F--- '——' (she named the judge)—she took my children away…I'll tell her that in person."

Yes, and she made good on that promise.

The judge, even after seeing the light and begrudgingly granting me sole custody, maintained an elbow in my neck by ordering Mom's mandated visitation time rules. Mom still lived three to five hours away over the Cascade Mountains, and her lawyer asked that exchanges occur in Mill City, Oregon, the least desirable of any possible options. Despite objection, I would have to deliver the kids to the west side of the range for visitation every other weekend and at other prescribed times, with me, rather than Mom, having to navigate the oft-dangerous and impassable mountain pass between us.

Mill City was a logging town that had fallen on tough times in an industry in turmoil in the state. As I had to drop the kids off on Fridays after school and pick them up on Sundays, rather than driving back and forth through the mountains, it made sense to find lodging there and sort out workable options. Like everything in my life, made the best of it—part of my way—lemons into lemonade. So, every other weekend, I struck out to see some beautiful country on the outskirts of Mill City, including the stunning Opal Creek Wilderness, before much was destroyed in wildfires a few years later.

Prior to that, however, since the kid exchanges could be contentious at times with Mom and her boyfriend, I decided to contact the Mill City police and get acquainted in case things blew up. Searching for a police station there led me to the tiny City Hall on a late Friday afternoon, right before closing. I was greeted by a kind, happy clerk.

"Well, hi there," I said. "I was hoping you could direct me to the police station. I have parenting pick-ups and drop-offs here in town, and I wanted to introduce myself. I plan on staying here some weekends."

"Well, you are one of those fortunate souls. There are no police stations here or anywhere near—if you're on one side of the road, your police station would be in Salem, and if you're on the other side of the road, your station would be Albany, each about a forty-five-minute drive. So, we handle a lot of things ourselves in the community. It'll be great to have you around. If you come by next week, I can introduce you to the mayor and some other people."

At this point, it was understood exactly why Mom's attorney had recommended this location. It was terribly inconvenient, and it was lawless. In one of the early exchanges, I detected pungent aromas bellowing out of Mom's car at the pick-up. I was reticent to let the kids go, so I called my attorney and explained the situation, as well as the lack of police in Mill City.

"What am I to do about this? I feel it's a dangerous situation for the kids."

"Well Jeff, are those two obviously intoxicated, like stumbling around?"

"Well, not really stumbling."

"Then you do nothing. It must be ironclad. You must be cool. I know it's hard and I know it seems wrong, but it's the only way to go. You are not out of the woods yet."

I couldn't believe I'd have to turn the kids over in these circumstances. There was never a consideration that in making things harder and even more dangerous for me—the only capable parent—which the court had consistently done, all these decisions would impact the children, as well. Blind injustice.

So, with these parameters, we continued driving to Mill City, often through snowstorms and occasionally through firestorms, even after being granted sole custody and with all the court had learned. My opinion was that any parenting time Mom had should be monitored and be near the children's home, but that made too much sense. We endured drives where trees were literally on fire all around us, flaming black bark and the AQI exceeding 800 as we choked our way through. On one occasion, going through Detroit, Oregon—which unbeknownst to me had been evacuated—I thought we were all going to suffocate and die.

Another time, we went through an ice storm over the Cascades with cars flipped upside down—people bleeding, screaming, and trying to get out. I nervously crawled by in our car at five miles per hour on the ice, unable to stop for fear that we'd lose traction and slide off into the ditch with them.

"Daddy, are we gonna die?" one of the kids asked.

It was a microcosm of what we'd been through; I kept resolute and calm. "We are good, we just must be careful. There will be people coming to help them."

Even with all this challenge, I had gotten the kids back, which was a huge step. However, a lot of damage had been done, and getting us on track was going to be a Herculean task. At times, I'd bemoan my situation. And then one day it finally struck me. I was so fortunate and happy with these kids, and it was all meant to be. I had a purpose in my life, and an opportunity to help others in similar situations, going forward. There were to be no sour grapes.

I can see why my dad did not want to talk about some of his wartime stuff, now. PTSD. The experience I had in the Oregon courts had been traumatizing. My counselor told me I had suffered Post Traumatic Stress, but, thankfully, without the "D" for Disorder. My dad had run the same route, but his childhood had made him stronger. I inherited that ultra-resiliency gene. Reliving traumatic experiences and recounting them generally serves little purpose; however, it might be cathartic if you can handle it, and coping skills developed might be used to help others.

In the meantime, the kids and I bonded as three. We worked hard for stability and practiced hugs and love. A lot of lessons were learned in these days.

If you ask the kids, "What can you tell me about a Swaney?" they will say, "A Swaney will never give up!"

CHAPTER 14

Waimea Canyon Kauai

Mount Rainier

CHAPTER 14
HUMANIMAL

Thankfully, that patience and perseverance paid off, and life's rhythm became a million times better than the construct that existed for over five years following my divorce filing, which provided enough crazy stories for ten unprintable books and a Netflix miniseries. It would take another three years more to feel nearly relieved of the madness. Despite the tenacity to make the best of it all, many magical years had been stolen from us. Now we forged on with new directives, joy, and a special appreciation for all we had and could be.

All of us must take stock of our strengths and weaknesses, as this will direct us to know who we are and how we can live our lives to the fullest, and benefit ourselves and others. Looking back, I've definitely been a seeker and never wanted to get overly tied down in the material minutiae machinery. So, I've tried to limit that as much as possible, delegating, outsourcing, and deflecting, albeit at great cost, to make time for myself.

With the court chaos subsided, to fulfill a long-burning desire, it was time to simplify life. To work in earnest on downsizing, minimizing, shrinking footprints, and getting back to the basics that brought joy. It was going to take some doing, with a basket of complicated finances and partnerships and, thankfully, just one single giant house, though loaded with stuff I never needed.

Without giving it any thought, had gone from owning one set of clothes freshman year of college and world travel—and zero dollars—to being a collector of sorts through the prosperous thirties, forties, and fifties, just following the herd.

Seeing the writing on the wall just before a painful choice to divorce—and being able to sell two of three homes, as well as an office loft, and shrink to one home in Bend, Oregon—kept me from getting sunk. I'll never forget the moving van pulling up from Dallas to an already-full house in Bend, with 514 items and boxes, all numbered and tagged, many still here and unopened.

Beginning the process of full-scale purging, it was focus on the mantra "Working with what we have." If all the retail stores out there had to count on people like me for business, they would all close. Performing eradications over time—as my focus was on the kids, the outdoors, friends, and some travel to enjoy life—blended these worlds, while remaining engaged in minimalism.

Being self-taught minimalism, thanks to backpacking the wilds, as well as the world, with nothing but rudimentary items on hand for survival, was an asset. Survival. As a single dad, integrating these skills, together with inherent training in logic and utilizing systems engineering from college, brought about a metamorphosis. Smoothly, almost subconsciously organizing life's basics, streamlining with efficiency, aided me in raising two young children.

Recycling, reusing, and repurposing became our family way before it came in vogue. We did it and do it. We became the "Enemy of Waste," as a dear friend's desk placard reads. In the reboot of our home, we found immense pleasure in discovering some things we never knew we owned, jumbled in with useless items, and creatively put much to use. These skills were utilized in the kitchen as well—practicing zero waste.

Along the way, my daughter Cozi, now fifteen years old, had become adept at both food management and gourmet cooking. One of our favorite traditions became the biannual creation of a special "Jeff Mix," our version of a multipurpose dry-herb-and-spice blend. It was always a little different, but we had to get the approximately one to two pounds of blended garlic, onion powder, cumin, chili, oregano, basil, and other ingredients just right, which was a process of mixing, tasting, dashing, and remixing to get to the perfect blend. Recipes be damned, as always.

"What do you think it needs now?" I'd ask Cozi as we began our first machination.

"Well, Dad, we don't want it too spicy, so let's try more basil, onion, and garlic. I'll add it in; I think we're close," she would declare.

"You have the gift, Cozi. I'm just the sous chef now."

Adding and mixing again a few more times, we neared the goal line.

"Okay, Cozi, now what's the verdict?"

"Dad, this might be the best one ever. I love it! Thank you, this will make people happy."

It did.

Interweaving magic moments with the kids during ongoing cleanup at the house, along the way we found several of Mom's books on the topic of, among other things, shopaholics, including *Confessions of a Shopaholic*. I was half-aware of the shopping malaise issue due to rapid-fire, married, work, and travel lifestyle, going a thousand miles per hour with myriad responsibilities. A five-thousand-square-foot house was groaning, with every square inch cluttered, and the entire underbelly packed with boxes and totes full of knickknacks and useless items I hadn't bought. There were cheap placards, vases, statues, pillows, mirrors, picture frames galore, plastic flowers, and bath products, all by the dozens. Also, miscellaneous gadgets, some indescribable, and every conceivable kitchen, household, and gardening tool, many in triplicate. Pre-divorce, to avoid conflict, I had dutifully organized it all in between my business trips, family trips, scheduling help, and time with the kids. Now—just wanted to dump it all.

I know I'm not the only one to have engaged in—or accepted—the automatic acquisition of stuff, although perhaps not to this extreme. A dear friend of mine, now passed, shared that in his moves from Dallas to New York to LA and then Austin, he had collected unconsciously to the point where he finally did a blind purge. "Jeff, I had all these boxes I kept moving across the country," he recalled. "I didn't even know what was in them, and I had about ten to fifteen that I hadn't unpacked. I finally, without opening them for fear I'd keep the shit, took them to Goodwill and dropped them off. Never have missed them."

"You didn't, bro! Seriously? That's crazy," I exclaimed.

"Yep, I did."

Conversations with clients and friends as we've gotten on in age have revealed that many are drowning in their bounty. "I am really working to simplify things in every way I can, getting rid of more and more stuff, consolidating in every direction, and getting everything screwed down," I shared again and again.

"Well, why would you do this?" some responded in disbelief. "Wouldn't you wanna keep all your stuff for your kids? That's what I plan to do."

"Nope. I've seen too many friends pass away in recent years—seen their kids come to their home after they die, maybe grab a few things, then have the estate salespeople take over and sell whatever is left, with the remainder either going to Goodwill or a forty-yard dump can in the driveway. No thanks, I don't wanna burden anybody with that. I have some pieces of art that they love, and have penned a discourse on the back of each that explains the connection to them, signed and dated. They're so young, I'm sure they wouldn't want most of these possessions or have any place to keep them if they did."

"Hmmmm, well maybe you're right."

"Yes, seen this play out many times in my career. Kid essentials are the three M's: memories, mementos, and money. And unfortunately, heirs often fight about the money. Hence, having liquidity and order in your estate at any age is a gift to your family and trustees."

Simplify, simplify, simplify. After years of not noticing things getting complicated as possible in life, this was a huge task to unravel, and in the technology maze that has become the order of the day, simplification was even more necessary. In the resulting "The World's Gone Mad," let us have less stuff, fewer forms, fewer passwords, less security, fewer portals, less complexity, fewer agencies, less government, fewer rulebooks, fewer manuals, fewer laws, less regulation, less insanity, and overall, less bullshit. Less is more.

Having accumulated, like so many, so much in the land of plenty, purging solved both immediate and long-term needs. But there was more to purge on other levels that required going deep. Needed an oxygen tank for that.

Certainly, the most challenging purges would become the mental and spiritual ones. Between Mom, her attorney, the mother-in-law, the judge, and the various agency personnel blindly putting my kids in life-or-death jeopardy, there was a list of bad actors to forgive if not forget. The group, some perhaps unknowingly at first, had created situations that made daily lives almost impossible to grapple with. I had to take stock of all of that.

Mom was the easiest to forgive, even though she had been pushing the buttons. There was compassion to a point, even with her scorched-earth tactics and complete irresponsibility. Where does one draw the line? I had no feelings of love, hate, or otherwise for her, thank God, because that would have surely destroyed me. The person Mom had become, I simply no longer knew.

Forgiveness, however, would take a while. The court's mandatory trips to visit Mom had come to an end when an emergency order was granted to halt them, due to restraining orders filed by Mom and her husband on each other. Then there was more wildness that led to Mom being sentenced to lengthy probation for crimes in the Portland area, none to do with us. All the while she continued to file crazy motions in the courtroom against me in Bend, which eventually petered out as they were rejected at hearings, granting me relief and attorney's fees. If that wasn't enough of a grind, her filing board complaints on the kids' counselor, dentist, and attorneys made life more challenging. I share just the tip of the iceberg on these truths as I see them, not to disparage, but rather to convey my version of how difficult it all was to manage, and what a feat to get to a place of sanity and forgiveness. It was sad to see a person who'd had an enviable life years before falling to these depths.

With all that mess, Mom would still attempt to reach out to the kids again, utilizing the system and an agency galvanized to support her. After all we had been through, however, the kids understandably had no appetite for any kind of connection. And that meant that there was an agency to forgive for a second time, the very one that had given me the most grief of my life and worked with the court to doom me and the kids. The Children's Stop actions remained inexplicable. After almost three years of Mom not seeing us, we were contacted to schedule virtual meetings, due to COVID, for the kids to Zoom in at Mom's request.

The awkwardness of the meetings, and the idea that we would be thrown back into the fire after finding our sweet rhythms, initially freaked me out; but after talking it through with friends, thought it might be therapeutic for them to meet with her online, and even encouraged them to do so. I didn't want the perception to surface in later years that I had denied them access. Even so, the kids never wanted to meet with Mom, even virtually. Of course, since the court had sanctioned it, they seemingly had no choice. "You might even like it," I told them.

So, after all the paperwork and hassle with the agency again, the kids got set up at my home office, as required, where they could privately talk to the staff who, with Mom on hold, worked to convince the kiddos to chat with her. By then, Cozi and Ford had been through so much that, despite my requests, they refused to engage with Mom each time they were scheduled to do so.

I had sent The Children's Stop numerous documents via third parties, police, courts, and others that explained Mom's egregious behaviors so they would finally accept the truth about what they were dealing with. Still, over a three-month period of biweekly repeated attempts, the people there ratcheted up the pressure on Cozi and Ford to the point of ganging up, three-on-one, on each individually in what then would be the last session. The kids ended up crying and screaming, as I teared up, shaking in anger. Still, I held my tongue.

At the onset of this last Zoom attempt, they proceeded to explain their reasoning to me. "Mr. Swaney, this could be healing for you and the children; we have helped many families through these things. Let us help you."

"Well, thank you," I replied politely. "We are already healing here. If you've read what I sent you, you must know we've been through too much; this is just pulling off scabs and upsetting us all to no good end. This is not a one-size-fits-all situation."

things in the direction that it wants to. In the meantime, you and other beings pluck the cords of its web to a confluence of the now, with the Higher Power reveling in this creation. Everything has its time and season, and being aware and centered allows you to get to where you need to go. That journey always takes longer than you want. Go with the flow and stay the course.

Most importantly, the ability to cope and provide worthwhile advice in life requires lessons in patience. While recalling and counting blessings long ago, I realized that patience was not one of my virtues. "I have many gifts and good fortune, and we don't get everything, so that's just one of the things that's not me," I rationalized. However, the importance of this skill would become evident many times, and most poignantly when forced to bite my tongue while internally kicking and screaming, in the years forcibly subjected to the waywardness and molasses of a broken court system. To save my kids and my sanity—had to be patient. That is where that mega-grueling lesson was mastered.

What is patience? The capacity to accept or tolerate delay, trouble, or suffering without getting angry or upset.

Bingo! I became obsessed with what I had so little of! Patience, patience. Needed it and yearned for it!

So, I polled fifty friends and asked them for their take on patience. I got these top results:

> One vote for "Be Buddha."
>
> Two mentions for "Be present, centered, and open to the possibilities of the moment." (Rings with *Be Here Now*—my favorite book of all

time—thanks Ram Dass, co-conspirator of my friend Tim Leary.)

Two for "Patience is a virtue."

And finally, some scripture—James 1:19-20:

Know this, my beloved brothers: let every person be quick to hear, slow to speak, slow to anger; for the anger of man does not produce the righteousness of God.

Inexplicably, I rarely felt anger even when impatient, even when merited in extreme cases, but rather feelings of frustration or dismay.

Now, in addition to acquiring patience—along with refining other symbiotic tools, such as empathy, compassion, better listening, abstinence from judging, and sharpening my overall mindfulness—the toolbox was rocking.

With bandwidth adjusted, I am blessed to live the fourth quarter of life through the eyes of children, which is an anomaly of sorts at this age. It also generates new challenges. Contemplating mortality, while striving to raise children in the best way possible so they'll succeed for themselves and humanity, has led me to ponder the kind of advice this out-of-the-box guy can offer.

Modern man lives in the dichotomy of a race against time, with short lives and inspired plans destined to be changed, instead of living one day, or even one minute or one second at a time. Excess ambition can create that feeling of "running out of time," as it did with Alexander Hamilton. He certainly did.

There is no telling how long any of us have to live, and with the heart disease I inherited from my dad who died at sixty-two, there's no telling how long I'll get. I've used every gadget in the modern medicine kit and all the experts' input to foster the best possible outcome, for my own and my kids' sake. Folks might say they do not care about mortality, but when it gets down to it, they do. Most, if thinking clearly, would give anything for one more day.

Certainly, without being completely aware of it, I've led a balls-out, full-steam-all-the-time-and-all-the-way life, resulting in all those nonstop wild experiences. Surviving them, and more importantly learning from—and sharing—them, is growth. Those life events, observations, and resulting counsel originates from a different orbit than most. Advice comes in all different shapes and sizes. Unsolicited advice is seldom wanted, rarely heeded, and even loathed. Living by good example provides advice without fanfare. Free advice is exactly that—worth what you paid for it. The perfect advice, divine, wherever it comes from the situation at hand, is priceless.

That all being said, I am not here to suggest to anyone what to do, what to believe, how to act, or how to plan their life—made too many mistakes. But always happy to opine if asked, which may be helpful grist. So, I would suggest that you not let ambition or mishaps steal you away from smelling the roses and enjoying the fruits of your labors if you tilled, planted, and watered in season. "Be Here Now" is more important than ever. Live in the moment first, then unfold your plans to ride on this spinning ball of mud. Look up at the stars at night and realize that as amazing as you are, you are a pissant in this universe. Of course, only you can make your choices, and all of us have an innate knowledge of what is right and wrong, and gut instinct to rely on, if we trust it.

There are already so many self-help, philosophy, investment, and parenting books and blogs, many emanating from a self-righteous soapbox, with the authors of these watered-down publications and series wanting you to keep buying. Few are good, and most are hash and rehash. If anybody had all the answers in any of these books, there wouldn't be a need to write anymore. Right?

But people out there want to give you—or sell you—advice. Financial planners want to tell you what to buy, and no matter what happens, to stay their course. Others hold fast to their religion, or subset of a religion, or political views they espouse, and often ask you to fund their causes. Despite some of my opinions, I expressly avoid in-depth religious or political discussions, as I prefer to coexist and focus on what we have in common rather than stumble into conflict. As I've learned from Tim Leary who, as I've noted, felt religion should be disorganized, this ideal can help defuse divisiveness. The advice is to take what you like from all of these and leave the rest. Read and explore some. Then maybe write your own book, or just live as if you were going to. In short, be advised to do whatever you must to solve the riddle of life for yourself. That's what it's all about.

In my search for the naming of my real estate company The Delphi Group, I encountered ancillary nuggets. While digging into all that Greek thought, venturing in depth on readings of those philosophers, Socrates stood out. He declared the unexamined life is not worth living, hence our explorations. When he asked his friends about visiting the Oracle at Delphi, they replied, "The Oracle related that you—Socrates—are the wisest man in all of Athens." To which he humbly responded, "And yet I know nothing." That epitomized wisdom.

Kinda what they told me on arrival at my first Al-Anon meeting, and echoed by my friend who sponsored me there. Welcome to the metaverse of humility, truth, never-ending learning, and self-discovery.

I do know this. Even with all the knowledge you may consume, analysis is paralysis, and there is nothing like just living your life. You've got one to live, so don't overthink it. As Socrates knew, you will never know it all or have all the answers. Those who attempt to study life without books sail an uncharted sea, but those who only study books never set to sea at all.

Read a book, then get out to sea. Chronicle your journey and life. Live free with full throttle, nuanced with a brake pedal to avoid crashing, and interludes to take stock and adjust, especially later in life. Keep it rockin' but don't burn out—thank you, Neil Young, and God bless you, Jimmy Hendrix and Janis Joplin. Just make sure to carve out a life that aligns with your prerequisites and passions, and you will be rewarded.

That's what I did.

My first and only gig in corporate enterprise was as a computer salesman after a backpacking world adventure, which both afforded the freedom and space a seeking soul requires. That's one reason I could empathize with "homeless" stragglers. My true love in life was that personal freedom and communing with nature which—just as for Oliver Sacks, Zane Grey, Henry Thoreau, Edward Abbey, and John Muir, all in their own quirky ways—was religion. Muir, my biggest hero, found his Higher Power in the natural world, which he referred to as his "church." That is why I never had a quest for more and more money, workload, or fame, like many of my friends and contemporaries—just wanted enough to generate time and space for limbic explorations. Looking for love and finding it—in nature and friends—has been my respite.

I personally couldn't survive without regular trips to the natural world. I've always felt that getting homeless people I'd met in my Deep Ellum days, or anyone for that matter, out to breathe in a more natural setting could be a big part of a potential solution to their issues.

We all are a little bit crazy, aren't we? But some folks are more than others, and that's just the luck of the genetic draw and childhood environment, I imagine. Yes, admit it or not, thankfully, you are a little crazy.

Nature and connection to a Higher Power, rather than too much of humankind, can assist us in avoiding any potential path that does not bode well. The natural world and faith are not optional—they are necessary for recovery and recharging. So, TFYQA, as Dr. Tim said: "Think for yourself and question authority." Or as expanded and reconstituted here, question humanity and trust your gut.

As you rock along in your amazing gift of life, consider reviewing all that, along with these tidbits that could supplement your toolbox:

- Awareness, acceptance, and action.
- Less is more.
- Simplify simplify simplify.

- Know your stuff.
- Take a chance.
- Patience, perseverance, and persistence bring resilience.
- Listen and learn.
- Trust your gut.
- Follow your heart.
- Immerse in humor.
- Coexist.
- Have faith and gratitude.
- Live with grace and love.

And most importantly, don't forget to enjoy your trip and bring the love.

Let go and laugh!

With that, the best free advice that could ever be given has to be:

Be mindful of the causal loops in your journey and your actions, and the benefit to yourself and the cosmos. And, like I ask of my kids and myself regularly, "Just do your best." The world is counting on us.

ACKNOWLEDGMENTS

As always, there are too many people to thank in this odyssey. It would not have happened without the early encouragement of Dr. John Corso, and his and my first writing coach Vicki Grant (RIP).

I'm grateful for the support of my family and friends, and all the folks who endorsed this labor of love. Special kudos to Linden Gross, my writing coach and editor, and lifetime friend and fellow author Craig A. Williamson for pushing me.

Artist Tim Karpinski blew me away and captured the essence of this book—and my life—with his website work, book cover, and other designs. Boom!

The infamous Ron Hall blessed me with an outrageous forward to the book as well as other efforts. Special thanks to brothers Brian and Mark Cuban for their help and to the whole team at Post Hill.

But most importantly, thanks to my resilient kids, Cozi and Ford, for reminding me daily about the patience, persistence, and purpose I profess.

Enjoy the book and share it. Go out there and live large.

ABOUT THE AUTHOR

Jeff Swaney is an American entrepreneur, super dad, outdoorsman, and friend. Licensed through the school of life and never-ending learning, he leverages his experience in entertainment, finance, small business management, investments, family matters, spirituality, and silliness. This breadth of knowledge, all in a simplified and conscious capitalism vein, is availed to high-net-worth clients, family offices, and others through both formal and informal engagement. Jeff is a Michigan native, proudly born in Detroit during the city's final heydays of the late '50s and early '60s.

He grew up in neighboring Royal Oak, and is a Michigan State University Engineering grad ('80), Hewlett-Packard alum, and world traveler.

Stay in touch with author for events at jeffswaney.com and follow at @jeffswaneyauthor.